WHY I DON'T CALL MYSELF GAY

DANIEL C. MATTSON

WHY I DON'T CALL MYSELF GAY

How I Reclaimed My Sexual Reality and Found Peace

IGNATIUS PRESS   SAN FRANCISCO

Cover design by John Herreid

© 2017 by Ignatius Press, San Francisco
All rights reserved
ISBN 978-1-62164-072-1
Library of Congress Control Number 2016956073
Printed in the United States of America ∞

To my godparents, Robert and Susan Cavera,
whose prayers helped bring me home.

We owe a definite homage to the reality around us, and we are obliged, at certain times, to say what things are and to give them their right names and to lay open our thought about them to the men we live with.

—Thomas Merton, *No Man Is an Island*

About sex especially men are born unbalanced; we might almost say men are born mad. They scarcely reach sanity till they reach sanctity.

—G. K. Chesterton, *The Everlasting Man*

The Lord Jesus promised, "You shall know the truth and the truth shall set you free."

—Congregation for the Doctrine
of the Faith, *Letter to the Bishops
of the Catholic Church on the Pastoral
Care of Homosexual Persons*

CONTENTS

Foreword by Robert Cardinal Sarah ix

Preface xiii

Acknowledgments xvii

Introduction by Father Paul N. Check xxiii

Part One
The Prodigal and His Return

In the Beginning 3

Christopher Street 7

Immaculate Heart of Mary School 11

The Barn 17

Barnes Elementary 21

The Curse of Phys Ed 27

Rock Hudson, Rambo, and AIDS 32

Porn: A Dysfunctional Love Affair 35

It Is Me, Isn't It? 41

Flint, Michigan 46

Kelly 52

The Ring 57

Unrequited Me 63

The Wound of Living 68

Courage 75

The Return of the Prodigal Son 82

Part Two
Reclaiming Reality

Reclaiming Sexual Reality   89
Reclaiming the Dignity of the Word   106
Why I Don't Call Myself Gay   127
The Empty Promises of Coming Out   141

Part Three
How to Run the Race: Living Out
the Daily Battle for Chastity

Jesus Is Our Holiness   163
The Wisdom and Example of the Saints   174
How to Run the Race   192

Part Four
A Miscellany: Reflections on the *Catechism*,
Friendship, and Loneliness

What Does the Word "Disordered" Mean Anyway?   209
Disinterested Friendship   233
The Temptations of Friendship   242
The Gift of Loneliness   263

Part Five
The Most Important Things

Humility and Magnanimity   281
Claiming Our Belovedness   289
Coda   297

FOREWORD

Sanctified in the Truth

In October 2015, two days before the Synod on the Family began, I participated in a conference at the Pontifical University of St. Thomas in Rome, sponsored by Courage International, Ignatius Press, and the Napa Institute. The conference was entitled "Living the Truth in Love", which considered pastoral approaches to men and women who experience homosexual tendencies. I gave a presentation and afterward listened to lectures about Christian anthropology and the Church's norms for pastoral care.

Then I heard talks unlike any I had ever heard before, from three men and one woman who experience same-sex attractions (SSA). Their testimonials moved me deeply. In each case, they recounted how they lived a homosexual life, but then had a change of heart. Their stories were not sentimental. They did not gloss over their struggles with superficial or insincere expressions of piety. On the contrary, with evident humility and courage, they opened their hearts to the audience in a sincere and compelling way.

I came to learn how these four souls suffered, sometimes because of circumstances beyond their control, and sometimes because of their own choices. I sensed the loneliness, pain, and unhappiness they endured as a result of pursuing a life contrary to their true identity as God's children. In time, however, their suffering became an occasion for

grace, for they came to know the Lord and the beauty
of the teachings of his Church. Only when they lived in
keeping with Christ's teaching were they able to find the
peace and joy for which they had been searching. They
still encounter the Cross. Their lives are not easy or without sadness. But now, with the help of the Church, they
are living the truth of the Gospel and the peace it brings—
in the Sacraments and in prayer, in chaste Christian friendship, and in the hope of the Crucified and Risen Savior.

We are frequently reminded by bishops and priests that
the *Catechism* states that men and women who experience
SSA "must be accepted with respect, compassion and sensitivity", and that the homosexual tendency "constitutes
for most of them a trial" (*CCC* 2358). For me, the four
speakers put a face on the topic of homosexuality, so I can
better testify to the Church's wisdom in providing these
valuable words in the *Catechism*.

Yet in her maternal charity and wisdom, the Church
indicates several other things in the *Catechism* about homosexuality that some members of the clergy choose not to
quote, including the clear warning: "under no circumstances can [homosexual acts] be approved" (*CCC* 2357).
The respect and sensitivity to which the *Catechism* rightly
calls us does not give us permission to deprive men and
women who experience SSA of the fullness of the Gospel.
To omit the "hard sayings" of Christ and his Church is
not charity. Indeed, it is a disservice to the Lord and to
those created in his image and likeness and redeemed by
his Precious Blood. We cannot be more compassionate
or merciful than Jesus, who told the woman caught in
adultery two equally important messages: "Neither do I
condemn you; go, and do not sin again" (Jn 8:11).

People who have homosexual tendencies "are called to
fulfill God's will in their lives and, if they are Christians,

to unite to the sacrifice of the Lord's Cross the difficulties they may encounter from their condition" (*CCC* 2358).
They "are called to chastity", and we demean them if
we think they cannot attain this virtue, which is a virtue
for all disciples. Like all members of the Church, "they
can and should gradually and resolutely approach Christian
perfection", the vocation of all the baptized (*CCC* 2359).
These words of the *Catechism* are equally valuable, because
they express authentic pastoral charity. They invite us, as
members of Christ's body, to accompany our brothers and
sisters who experience SSA, as they seek to achieve the
Christian perfection to which the Lord calls all of his children. Jesus does not ask anything from us that is impossible
or for which he does not supply the grace. It is the Church
that is the source of this grace.

The Church faces many challenges and threats today.
For that reason, the unity for which our Lord so urgently
prayed (cf. Jn 17:21) is imperative, especially among the
clergy. Jesus prayed that his priests would be sanctified "in
the truth" (Jn 17:17). We can only be holy, and lead others to holiness, to the degree that we allow ourselves to be
"consecrated in truth" (Jn 17:19).

I encourage many to read the following testimonial,
which, like the four that edified me, bears witness to the
mercy and goodness of God, to the efficacy of his grace,
and to the veracity of the teachings of his Church. Voices
like these are seldom heard in the discussion surrounding
pastoral care for those with SSA. I especially encourage
my brother bishops and priests to read this book, which I
trust will deepen their conviction that the wisdom of the
Church in this difficult and sensitive area expresses genuine love and compassion.

"You are my friends if you do what I command you",
Jesus said. (Jn 15:14). Only Christ can heal the wounds

of sin and division. Only the Church has the answers to man's deepest questions and his deepest needs for love and friendship. Only the fullness of the Gospel fulfills the human heart. Only the commandments mark the path to friendship with Christ, and with one another, for God's "commandments are not burdensome" (I Jn 5:3).

Robert Cardinal Sarah
May 13, 2017
Memorial of Our Lady of Fatima

PREFACE

I first began writing publicly about faith and homosexuality in an article for *First Things* called "Why I Don't Call Myself a Gay Christian".[1]

In the comments to my essay, a young man by the name of Gerardo wrote the following:

> First of all, I want to say thank you for sharing this. I am 19 years old, and I feel that my same sex attractions have been a curse ever since I was a little boy. I never would have thought that this cross I bear can actually be a way for God to show His majestic works to the world and enter the Holy Spirit through me and help me overcome this. Thankfully, I have never acted upon my desires and I never will. These testimonies that I have seen just inspire me that it is possible to be one step closer to God. At the same time I feel a hollow space and kind of lonely sometimes because I have not told anyone about my struggle. I have not told my parents or any priest about this because I feel ashamed and conflicted in telling them so. I love God so much and I want to be in the right path. If being celibate for life is what it takes, then so be it. I cannot force myself to marry a woman if I am not ready for that. I want to serve the Lord and know Him more. If anyone could give me some advice, that would be greatly appreciated. Thank you and God bless!

[1]Daniel Mattson, "Why I Don't Call Myself a Gay Christian", *First Things*, July 27, 2012, http://www.firstthings.com/web-exclusives/2012/07/why-i-dont-call-myself-a-gay-christian.

Church's teaching. I do address certain aspects of Church teaching, but this is a story about a man who wrestled with the Church's teaching, and then accepted it and wanted to learn how best to live out the call of chastity in his life. The veracity of the Church's teaching is taken as a given, and most of the second half of the book is concerned with helping other Catholics who live with same-sex attractions to live out the Church's teaching and there find peace, joy, and happiness. That being said, the advice I give can be of help to any Christians who are committed to following the path of chastity in their own lives, or who struggle at times with loneliness or the question of suffering, or who desire to understand the inherent logical problems and consequences of the societal push for acceptance of gender ideology in our schools and in the public square.

By God's grace, I hope and pray my reflections here may be of help to someone.

Daniel C. Mattson
Divine Mercy Sunday
April 23, 2017
Grand Rapids, Michigan

ACKNOWLEDGMENTS

John Donne's poetic line "No Man Is an Island" best describes my experience of writing this book, for I could not have written it on my own. Though it is impossible to thank the many people who have somehow shaped what you hold in your hands, a few stand out, whom I need to praise and thank publicly for their help and assistance.

After hearing me share my conversion story, Dr. Janet E. Smith urged me to start writing and speaking about the good news of the Church's teaching on same-sex attractions and chastity. She has helped me in countless ways along the way, helping me find clarity in my thinking, challenging me on some things she disagreed with, encouraging me in my pursuit of chastity, and more than anything else, being a great friend. Dr. Dawn Eden Goldstein, whose book *The Thrill of the Chaste*[1] was in my library long before I met her, has been a voice of encouragement and wisdom to me, and an inspiring example for me to follow in her pursuit of chastity. Dr. Jennifer Roback Morse, head of the Ruth Institute, has become a good and dear friend, both of me and of the Courage Apostolate, and has been an inspiration to me in her own mission in helping rescue victims of the sexual revolution. The fruit of many conversations we have had over the years can be seen in much that I have written. On the issue of the natural law and the meaning of sex, I am greatly indebted to

[1] Dawn Eden-Goldstein, *The Thrill of the Chaste* (Notre Dame, Ind.: Ave Maria Press, 2007).

Dr. J. Budziszewski, whose book *On the Meaning of Sex*[2] is essential reading for anyone who wants to understand the beauty and dignity of human sexuality. He has been a teacher to me, through personal conversations and emails, as well as in his writings and his lectures, and for that, I am forever grateful. Emails and conversations with Anthony Esolen have helped clarify my thinking on the nature of reality and the importance of words. His courageous witness to the truth in his own writing and speaking have inspired me to be bold in sharing my own thoughts and convictions. Finally, I must thank Dr. David Schindler of the Pontifical John Paul II Institute at Catholic University of America. I am always enriched by conversations we've had, either over the phone, or in person, or through email. I must thank him as well for inviting me to excerpt part of this book in *Communio*. His thoughts helped clarify my writing, particularly in the chapter that explains the *Catechism*'s thinking on the word "disorder".

I am grateful to Rusty Reno, editor of *First Things*, for publishing my first essay on the subject of chastity and same-sex attractions. "Why I Don't Call Myself a Gay Christian" at *First Things* contained the seeds of my thoughts that resulted in this book.[3] I must thank John Vella at *Crisis Magazine* for believing in my writing and message, as well as the editors at *National Catholic Register* who have given me a voice to share my writing with a wide audience too.

I am grateful for several radio hosts who have supported my work and the ministry of the Courage Apostolate. Thanks go to Al Kresta, Teresa Tomeo, Patrick Coffin,

[2] J. Budziszewski, *On the Meaning of Sex* (Wilmington, Del.: ISI Books, 2014).

[3] Daniel Mattson, "Why I Don't Call Myself a Gay Christian", *First Things*, July 27, 2012, https://www.firstthings.com/web-exclusives/2012/07/why-i-dont-call-myself-a-gay-christian.

and the good people at *Catholic Answers Live* for believing in the Courage Apostolate enough to share the good work of Courage on air. I, and all of the other members of Courage, thank them. It's been an honor to be on the air with them all.

The brothers and sisters of the Community of St. John in Peoria, Illinois, have been hosts to many retreats I have taken since I came back to the Church. Their wisdom, spiritual direction, prayers, and gentle and loving guidance have been a balm to my soul. I love them all dearly. Many of the thoughts in this book were watered by their prayers, by their prayerful witness to the truth, by their love of Jesus, and by their words of wisdom to me. I thank them all.

I also thank the Companions of Christ the Lamb from Paradise, Michigan. There, on a four-day retreat deep in the woods, I discovered the beauty of the poustinia, and the writings of Catherine Doherty, which transformed my understanding of loneliness and changed my life.

There are too many priests to thank for their investment in my life to mention them all, but a few I must thank specifically. Father James Chelich, pastor of St. Thomas the Apostle Church in Grand Rapids, Michigan, was the priest who welcomed me home to the Catholic Church in 2009. He has been the Courage chaplain for the Grand Rapids Diocese for over twenty-five years. His kindness, compassion, wisdom, and humor have been a shining light for me during my own journey in chastity. He is a wise counselor and confessor. I would not be where I am today without him.

To Father Robert Sirico, my spiritual director, I owe special thanks. He has been an encouragement along the arduous path of finishing this book and helped shape its direction. I'm especially grateful to him for introducing me to the thinking of William H. DuBay through the book *The*

Gay Identity: The Self Under Ban.[4] I'm thankful for our many conversations and for his suggestions, prayers, and help.

Father Philip Bochanski, executive director of Courage, has generously provided feedback on important theological issues and philosophical considerations in my book. Most importantly, he has asked the right questions and posed the right counterarguments, which have clarified my thinking and writing, and helped me find the right words when they were hard to find.

Father Paul Check, the former executive director of the Courage Apostolate, has become a spiritual father to me, a wise mentor, and a good friend. He has been my greatest teacher in the faith. His love, guidance, and gentle correction when I needed it has helped me to be a better man. I thank him for all that he has given to me and for his tireless service to the Courage Apostolate. He is one of the best men I know, and if I become half the man he is, I will consider my life well lived.

I am grateful to Fr. Paul Murray for his permission to share his poem "A Note on Human Passion", from his collection *The Absent Fountain*, written during a time when he was ministering to men and women suffering from drug addictions. I am deeply humbled and honored that Robert Cardinal Sarah has written the foreword to my book. Words fall short of expressing my gratitude to him for taking the time to read these meager words of mine, and sharing his own wisdom to the readers of my book. He is a hero in the faith for me, whose example and faithfulness inspire me to run the race that is set before me.

I owe a special debt of gratitude to the co-subjects of the documentary *Desire of the Everlasting Hills*, Rilene Simpson

---

[4] William H. DuBay, *The Gay Identity: The Self Under Ban* (Jefferson, N.C.: McFarland, 1987).

and Paul Darrow. Their love for the faith, for the virtue of chastity, for Jesus, and for the Eucharist have helped and encouraged me more than they can ever know. Thanks goes as well to the wonderful men who made the film. Only they could have made such a beautiful film. I'm thankful for the love and respect they gave to our stories and to those who shared our lives.

I could not have written this book without my superb and tireless editor, Diane Eriksen. For helpful feedback and initial editing of my book, I have to thank Dianne Check and my godparents, Robert and Susan Cavera, who were with me every step of the way, reading every draft and giving me helpful feedback; but more than anything, they supported me with their prayers and encouragement. I also thank Angelo and Jonah for reading my manuscript, and Sam Granger and David Phelps for their invaluable feedback during many conversations we had during the course of the writing of this book.

I could not have written this book—or kept my sanity—without my Wednesday night beer-drinking friends whom I regularly joined for Mug Club nights at Founders Brewery in Grand Rapids, Michigan. They know who they are. I know not all of them agree with my thinking, or will like this book, but I know they love me anyway, and for that, I love them all right back. I'm thankful for their friendship. And excellent taste in beer.

Most of all, however, I owe a debt of gratitude to my family. Their love, prayers, and encouragement along the journey of life have brought me to where I am today, and helped make me into the man I am. I love them all dearly, especially my parents who lived out the call of Proverbs 22:6 in raising their sons: "Train up a child in the way he should go, and when he is old he will not depart from it."

INTRODUCTION

Father Paul N. Check

"Our best ambassadors are our members," said Father John Harvey, O.S.F.S., as he helped me prepare to succeed him as the executive director of Courage International in 2008. Having served as a diocesan chaplain for the apostolate since 2003, I had learned to trust Father Harvey's insights and to respect his decades of faithful service in one of the most demanding fields of pastoral care in the Church today. I also knew from my familiarity with Courage members the unique challenge they face. Within themselves, they can feel the "collision", as one of our chaplain says, of the Church's teaching on homosexuality, the cultural forces that fight resolutely against that teaching, the occasional counsel of family and friends and even of some clergy to "find a partner", and their own erotic attractions to members of the same sex.

The often painful effects of this collision notwithstanding, Courage members persevere in their trust that the voice of the Church on the topic of homosexuality is the voice of Christ. They remain steadfast in their pursuit of chastity—and more than that, of holiness of life—because of their belief in the power, wisdom, goodness, and mercy of the Crucified and Risen Savior. In that, they are remarkable examples of authentic discipleship. The members of Courage—and of its allied ministry, EnCourage, for family members of those who experience same-sex attractions (SSA)—have greatly enriched and blessed my priesthood. They offer the world a faithful, sharp, and much-needed "sign of contradiction" (cf. Lk 2:34), at a time when we are easily confused and misled about something so foundational to the human person as sexual identity.

My nine years of service in the central office of Courage validated Father Harvey's statement. I have participated in many conferences and study days for clergy, religious, and lay faithful serving in ministry, here in the United States and overseas. While the various audiences were attentive to what I wished to convey about Christian anthropology and the Church's norms for pastoral care, they were always eager—and rightly so—to hear from Courage members about their personal experience of SSA and to learn about the Church's response, and particularly about what was and was not helpful to them. While the strongest arguments for the Church's teaching come from human nature and divine revelation, these arguments are not always persuasive in a world where empiricism and individual experience trump metaphysics, the natural moral law, and Sacred Scripture—even among some within the "household of faith" (Gal 6:10).

The "dictatorship of relativism", as then–Cardinal Ratzinger characterized the moral methodology of today,[1] has roots that reach far back in human history. Since the Fall of Adam, man has felt within himself a double movement with regard to truth, so well captured by Saint Mark in his description of what was happening inside Herod's soul when he listened to Saint John the Baptist: "For Herod

[1] Capella Papale Mass "Pro Eligendo Romano Pontifice", Homily of His Eminence Cardinal Joseph Ratzinger, Dean of the College of Cardinals (April 18, 2005), http://www.vatican.va/gpII/documents/homily-pro-eligendo-pontifice _20050418_en.html.

feared John, knowing that he was a righteous and holy man, and kept him safe. When he heard him, he was much perplexed; and yet he heard him gladly" (6:20).

Why did Herod hear John "gladly"? Because Herod was made for the truth, and he could recognize that John preached the truth to him with an evident charity. So Herod was drawn to that truth. Yet at the same time, Herod was "perplexed" because John was calling him to step away from something—adultery—and from someone—his brother's wife, Herodias—who was harming Herod's soul and whom Herod was likewise harming, through an unchaste relationship. Both men fall victim, if in a different way, to the dangers posed by sexual immorality. Herod, because his will is weak, beheads John and he remains a prisoner to his passions. John becomes a martyr for the chastity that Jesus will soon proclaim as a human virtue necessary for everyone's freedom, peace, and salvation.

"Heaven and earth will pass away, but my words will not pass away," Jesus said (Lk 21:33). Sacred Scripture retains a prophetic value for Christians because we believe that it tells us our story, the story of the children of God whose hearts are often a mixture of virtue and vice. We profit from reflecting about Herod because we know, in humility and honesty, that we experience that same double movement, toward and away from truth, as he did. Not everyone is an adulterer, certainly, but we all confront our human weakness in one form and measure or another. Even the great Saint Paul humbly admitted, "For I do not do the good I want, but the evil I do not want is what I do" (Rom 7:19).

I take Herod as a figure of our culture, even if I prefer that it were Saint Paul. In so many circumstances, our relationship with the truth is both yes and no. We are "glad" but we are "perplexed" at the same time. We admire and would often like to imitate those who keep their promises when it is difficult to do so. Indeed, we expect that people will keep their promises to us. But we also want to be free to be released from ours. We esteem humble and grateful people, and we would like to have these traits ourselves. But we excuse ourselves for our pride and selfishness. We hold in high regard those who make the greatest of sacrifices, and we hope we would be so noble if and when the time comes. But we avoid giving even from our surplus. We demand truth from others, and each of us wants to be known as a person of integrity. But we dissemble.

Perhaps one hope we have, however, is that, even in a climate of moral relativism, no one wants to think of himself as a hypocrite, or to be called one. Embedded in everyone's heart is the desire "to do the right thing", and so only with partial success, thank God, can we escape from the realization that our words, actions, and truest desires do not always align. The question then becomes, do we choose the path of Herod or of Paul?

Herod's story instructs us, but of course, he is not a hero for Christians to admire. We need Saint Paul and Saint John the Baptist, and other voices that speak "the truth in love" (Eph 4:15), to rescue us from self-imposed contradictions and from coming into conflict with ourselves. It seems to me that this self-harm, which in turn harms others and offends our Creator, is nowhere more evident than in matters related to sex. Here, especially, we are the cause of our own unhappiness, because we tend to "call evil good" (Is 5:20). To be sure, we can also call "good evil" (ibid.). In a former time, what would have been considered sexual "promiscuity"—sex outside of marriage—has now become the acceptable norm. On the other hand, virginity, chastity, fidelity, purity of heart, and modesty in attire and in speech are increasingly regarded as peculiar and even abnormal.

There are many indexes of misery and suffering when it comes to the misuse of sex. Having dedicated much of my priesthood to teaching sexual ethics and to trying to help heal the wounds of sexual sin, I will just mention a few: loneliness, broken hearts, and unfulfilled hearts. We could look for empirical data to verify those indexes. But I am guessing that the stories of people we know, or perhaps our own stories, will suffice to validate them, and, I hope, move us to do something.

John could call Herod away from a sinful and destructive relationship precisely because there was—and is—a standard to which he could point, a standard that was imbued deeply in Herod's own being, because he was created in the image and likeness of God (cf. Gen 1:26). Jesus did the same thing himself with the woman caught in adultery, as recorded in chapter 8 of Saint John the Evangelist's Gospel. We are relieved and grateful to hear Jesus say to her, "Neither do I condemn you" (v. 11). On the other hand, Christ's remaining words in the same verse, "Go, and do not sin again," pose a challenge for us, even with the grace we are sure to receive for a transformation of life. Will I choose my birthright, or a mess of pottage? (cf. Gen 25:29–34).

Those words of Christ do not make sense unless there is something—indeed, a virtue—recognizable and achievable in human nature. That virtue is chastity, a standard that lies within every human heart, to include Herod's, the woman's in John 8, and yours and mine. The Lord knows we can be especially vulnerable to sexual sin, because we are made for love and for relationships. But a legitimate desire can easily "miss the mark" when chastity is lacking.

Jesus' example with the woman caught in unchastity is, to my mind, the model for catechesis on sexual sin. Christ came to win hearts, not arguments, and we can learn much from his method here. Verse 11 from John 8 has been called the "Gospel in miniature": the simultaneous call to *compassion* and to *conversion*. Jesus lovingly, but clearly and firmly, places a soul on the right road to purity and to freedom. He knows the tangle of the human heart, but he also knows the nobility of the human heart (cf. Jer 17:9 and Mt 5:48). In fidelity to the Lord, our own "catechesis has to reveal in all clarity the *joy* and the *demands* of the way of Christ".[2]

The Church's teaching on chastity forms a consistent and coherent tapestry because that tapestry already exists in the mind of the Lord. In his commentary on the Decalogue during the Sermon on the Mount, Jesus gave us a proper understanding of the Sixth Commandment: "You have heard that it was said, 'You shall not commit adultery.' But I say to you that everyone who looks at a woman lustfully has already committed adultery with her in his heart" (Mt 5:27–28). Christ goes right to the heart of things, as he always does. The root problem of all sexual sin is lust, and therefore he does not need to provide a specific list of the ways we can break the commandment. They are all included in his teaching against lust.

A proper explanation of that teaching will help prevent the not uncommon misunderstanding that the Church focuses severely on one group of people—those who experience same-sex attractions—and arbitrarily tells them, "No!" While the Sixth Commandment forbids adultery, a sin against marriage, it also forbids sins against chastity and the *nature of marriage*, which, sadly, are many: lust, masturbation, fornication, pornography, prostitution, rape, homosexual acts,[3] contraception and sterilization,[4] and divorce.[5]

---

[2] *Catechism of the Catholic Church* (*CCC*) 1697 (italics added).
[3] See *CCC* 2351–59, 2396.
[4] See *CCC* 2370, 2399.
[5] See *CCC* 2382–86, 2400.

The widespread use of contraception, including among Mass-going Catholics, has paved the way for the acceptance of same-sex unions. If we allow that *deliberately* separating sex from babies will "improve" marriages (it does not), then soon we will find ourselves separating sex from marriage, and then separating sex from the design proposed to us by reason and confirmed by divine revelation: husband and wife becoming "one flesh" (Gen 2:24), always open to life. Another case can be made that no-fault divorce (widely accepted as another improvement for the real challenges of married life; again, it is not) contributes to the acceptance of same-sex unions. If husband and wife can, on their own, determine when their marriage is "over"—and thus, redefine marriage apart from indissolubility—then why can't marriage be "redefined" in other ways by other people?

In twenty years of priestly ministry, what I have learned about the good of chastity and the damage done by its converse, I would happily communicate with anyone who would listen. But to many, I am not a credible witness. I am a celibate man, a priest, who represents the very institution that tries to impede the happiness of many, according to the prevailing cultural narrative. In all fairness, we should also note, sexual misconduct among priests has gravely undermined the clergy's credibility on this topic.

Given the opportunity, however, I would like to protect people, no matter their sexual attractions, from the harm that inevitably follows from unchaste behavior of any kind. With a mother's heart, the Church wants to warn us away from danger and point us to the path to joy. She knows, from the words of her Founder, that joy and fulfillment can only be achieved, with God's grace, by respecting the design of the heart (cf. Jn 15:9–11). The question for those of us with responsibility to shepherd and teach Jesus' flock is this: Have we lost confidence that chastity, though challenging, is part of the *Good News of Jesus Christ*? Chastity leads to freedom and peace. Among other things, it ensures that people are loved and desired first for *who they are*, and not for *what they can do*. Isn't that something we all want?

So, I return to the wisdom of Father Harvey. The best witnesses today to the veracity of the Church's teaching on homosexuality are those who experience SSA and who believe, sometimes through a painful personal history, that the teaching is true—and that the teaching applies not only to them. Dan Mattson is one of these witnesses, and I am grateful for his testimony, one I have listened to, learned from, and promoted for many years now. I hope that a world that so values personal experience will give Dan—and several of his brothers and sisters in Courage who also graciously share their stories—a hearing.

Still, we must know some metaphysics, the most pastoral of the philosophical sciences, because "action follows being": we will know how to live well only if we know who we are, both in nature and in grace. Thus, we must also still learn our Christian anthropology, grounded in Jesus, the New Adam, who "fully reveals man to man himself".[6] We profit by knowing the story of our origin, as given to us in Genesis, chapters 1–3, since it is there that we discover what may be the most controversial of all verses in Scripture at the moment: "So God created man in his own image, in the image of God he created him; male and female he created them" (1:27). Whether the controversy begins with the Bible's assertion that man has a creator, or with its teaching that the twofold expression

[6] Second Vatican Council, Pastoral Constitution on the Church in the Modern World *Gaudium et Spes* (December 7, 1965), no. 22, http://www.vatican.va /archive/hist_councils/ii_vatican_council/documents/vat-ii_cons_19651207 _gaudium-et-spes_en.html.

of human nature is male and female (not heterosexual and homosexual), the "glorious liberty of the children of God" (Rom 8:21) depends on natural and revealed truth, not on the good will of civil society.

The greatest teaching tools ever devised are the parables of Jesus Christ. Their simplicity and richness capture the imagination, such that most quickly grasp the meaning of the phrase "prodigal son" or "good Samaritan", for instance.[7] Wrapped in human clothing, we find truths in these stories whose appeal and power are universal, because they transcend time and culture. They attractively introduce complex realities. The parables reveal to us our story, a story taken up into God's story: the Incarnation. The parables tell us about ourselves, yes, about human nature, but they also unveil the workings of the grace, mercy, and peace of God our Father, who sent his Beloved Son to free us from the false narratives to which we are prey from the world, the flesh, and the devil (cf. 1 Jn 2:16).

A well-done and useful testimonial is like a parable. Its value lies in the way in which the human attire, the personal story, does not distract us, but rather provides enough frame for the universal truth to edify, enlighten, and encourage us. The human elements engage the imagination, so that intellect and will might apprehend the true and the good. The experience of one person invites our attention to the *human experience*—for example, of our need for humility, for healing, for conversion of heart, and especially for grace. To hear a good witness talk "gladly" is a fine start. To be "perplexed" may also be a good reaction, if things do not rest there. A good testimonial points us to the One who can help us make sense of our experiences,

---

[7] For the Parable of the Prodigal Son, see Lk 15:11–32; the Parable of the Good Samaritan, Lk 10:25–37.

by clarifying which ones are counterfeit, and which ones lead to human flourishing and to the fulfillment of the heart, now and in eternity. A good testimonial, like a parable, will stretch my heart—if I will allow it to do so.

Dan Mattson offers us such a testimonial. I first met him as he was returning to the Church, a story you will read about in the following pages. Later, he generously responded to my invitation to join the "Courage speakers bureau", if you like, and to be one of three people whose stories are recounted in the 2014 documentary film *Desire of the Everlasting Hills*,[8] produced by Courage International.

What I admire about Dan is that he continues to deepen his understanding of the human condition, as taught to us by great writers and saints. He is still perfecting his art, by sitting at the feet of others, so that he can be a more faithful and fruitful instrument in God's providence for the benefit of many. In no way does he present himself as a member of the Church of the saved, but as a member of the Church of the *striving*—which is the same Church founded by the Lord (cf. Mt 24:13). In the way he lives, Dan testifies to the wisdom of Pope Benedict XVI: "To be sure, we do not possess the truth, the truth possesses us: Christ, who is the truth, has taken us by the hand, and we know that his hand is holding us securely on the path of our quest for knowledge."[9]

Before he became Pope, Cardinal Ratzinger said that one of the few credible arguments for the faith today is the communion of saints. The *Catechism* is indispensable,

---

[8] *Desire of the Everlasting Hills* (Norwalk, Ct.: Courage International, 2015), https://everlastinghills.org/movie/.

[9] Address of His Holiness Benedict XVI on the Occasion of Christmas Greetings to the Roman Curia (December 21, 2012), http://w2.vatican.va /content/benedict-xvi/en/speeches/2012/december/documents/hf_ben-xvi _spe_20121221_auguri-curia.html.

to be sure. But the saints, and those striving to be so, put a human face on the teachings of the *Catechism*, making them more appealing and accessible. Blessed Paul VI said it this way: "Modern man listens more willingly to witnesses than to teachers."[10] Dan wants to be a saint; he wants to be a faithful witness to Jesus Christ—but he also knows that he needs much grace, as we all do, to achieve this most noble of goals. That's what makes him a good witness and his testimonial a good "parable" for our consideration.

As the priest who asked Dan and several others to "go public" with their stories, I do have, as an expression of spiritual fatherhood and Christian solicitude, some concerns. It takes a special kind of courage and humility to stand up, even in a friendly audience, and disclose one's struggles and failures with chastity. But not everyone will appreciate that courage and humility. Some will say that Dan and others like him are filled with shame and self-loathing; that they are not being true to themselves; that they never were really "gay" to begin with; that they are only acting from a kind of "Catholic guilt".

None of these things describe my experience of Dan and others, but it troubles me that his talks and writings, and those of his confreres and friends, can become the occasion for such character attacks. I imagine such attacks will only increase in the wake of the publication of this book. Of course, any story deserves respectful critique and even spirited exchange. It is the derision, contempt, and condescension that Dan will receive—and again, in some cases from within the fold—that troubles me. Indeed, we

---

[10] Paul VI, apostolic exhortation *Evangelii Nuntiandi* (December 8, 1975), no. 41, quoting Paul VI, *Address to the Members of the Consilium de Laicis* (2 October 1974): AAS 66 (1974), p. 568, http://w2.vatican.va/content/paul-vi/en/apost_exhortations/documents/hf_p-vi_exh_19751208_evangelii-nuntiandi.html.

seem to be moving in the direction where some ideas, and therefore, some speech, may no longer be protected. May God bless and reward Dan and others for their willingness to tell their stories, knowing how they may be treated in some quarters.

I have another concern, based on almost fifteen years of working in this field. In giving talks, especially to my brother priests, I would often say that I was less an advocate for a specific apostolate than I was an advocate for an *underserved population*: men and women who experience SSA and look to the Church—with various levels of conviction or uncertainty about her teaching—for help, for understanding, and for guidance. My concern is whether we, as the Mystical Body of Christ, respond to them with a *charity* and *clarity* worthy of the Master, who protects bruised reeds and smoldering wicks (cf. Mt 12:20). Our standard should be the example of Jesus in the passage from John 8 on which we have already reflected: equal measures of compassion and of encouragement for a change of mind and heart.

A further point is also needed, lest we fail in charity by binding up heavy loads for people to carry, without assisting them (cf. Mt 23:4). The Church has a teaching about homosexuality, which can be difficult for some to accept and to live. Simply as a matter of natural justice, let alone supernatural charity, when the Church has a particularly challenging teaching, for a given time in salvation history, she must also provide the *practical means* to live it. In my opinion, we are failing here, terribly, but this is something in our power to address.

We all acknowledge the weight of the societal resistance to or rejection of the Church's teaching on marriage and sex. The opposing forces are formidable. Out of fear of being called a "hater" or "homophobe", or worse consequences, we can remain silent and unwilling to raise the banner of truth in a compassionate and thoughtful way. We are "perplexed". And so there is another and perhaps even greater problem today that hinders the offer of compassion and the call to conversion we observe in Jesus' encounter with the woman in John 8. Dan's voice will also be considered unhelpful or inconvenient in this case as well, because it will be received as an unwelcome judgment by many Christians.

That problem is *sentimentality*. Sentimentality looks like compassion—there is a pleasing gentleness about it—but it lacks the truth that gives compassion its substance and strength. Try to imagine Jesus saying only, "Neither do I condemn you," without the rest of his message to the unchaste woman, "Go, and do not sin again", and you have a definition. Sentimentality grants permission for people to continue in sinful and self-destructive behavior because they feel it is "right" for them. It gives primacy to passions over reason and to emotions over the teaching of Christ and his Church, because we give *too* much weight to personal experience.

We can become sentimental because of our bonds with people whom we know and love and who experience SSA (or those who don't have SSA and live in other unchaste relationships), and who are living out those attractions and who assume our approval and support. Sentimentality begins with a strength—the respect and affection we rightly have for people close to us—but that strength is turned against us, because we lose confidence in the existence of a universal truth about human sexuality, as taught by Jesus and his Church. To the degree we exchange sentimentality for compassion, Jesus' words when he said, "You will know the truth and the truth will make you free," have lost their power (Jn 8:32). Sentimentality is both a cause and effect of the "dictatorship of relativism", the phrase that Cardinal Ratzinger used in the sermon at the Mass that opened the conclave that led to his election as the Vicar of Christ. And just two weeks prior, he said something also of interest to us: "Very soon it will not be possible to state that homosexuality, as the Catholic Church teaches, is an objective disorder in the structuring of human existence."[11] The prophetic voice of Christ in his Church, like that of Saint John the Baptist to Herod, has always encountered a mixed result in human hearts.

Those hearts may hear the Gospel "gladly" but may also be "perplexed", a response that can give way to stronger and even more violent emotions as we know from the story of the Baptist, emotions stirred because of his message about chastity. As civil society appears to make the "narrow path" (cf. Mt 7:13; Lk 13:24) even more demanding, may we recall that John's teaching arose from his pastoral and fraternal charity for Herod and that John was prepared to accept the consequences of his charity out of fidelity to the Lord.

Saint Paul was also a man of great charity who likewise faced resistance to his preaching of the Gospel. In his Letter to the Romans, he prudently writes, "If possible, so far as it depends upon you, live peaceably with all" (12:18). And in Second Corinthians, he warns us not to let our ministry give offense (6:3). But he also says, "Woe to me if I do not preach the gospel!" (1 Cor 9:16), and, "If the bugle gives an indistinct sound, who will get ready for battle?" (1 Cor 14:8).

So how do we—clergy, religious, and lay faithful—overcome the understandable tendency to avoid our

---

[11] "Cardinal Ratzinger on Europe's Crisis of Culture" (lecture, Convent of St. Scholastica, Subiaco, Italy, April 1, 2005), http://insidethevatican.com/news/newsflash/letter-24-2016-synod-document-t-minus-1.

prophetic role because we lack the resolve or the words, or both, to explain or defend the truth? For starters, the example of Dan Mattson and other witnesses like him should fortify us and inspire us to *stand alongside them*, in testifying to the truth. Their willingness to tell their stories of conversion of heart and of life deserve more than just a grateful hearing from faithful disciples. These generous souls *call us* to a greater level of generosity, trust, and sacrifice for the One who gave his all for us. We must admit, however, that our hesitancy and unsteadiness will likely grow as hostility to the teaching of the Church about homosexuality intensifies.

For myself, I also look to my patron saint, Saint Paul, who wrote about the "power" of the Cross of Christ (cf. 1 Cor 1:17–18) and who experienced that power in himself and was transformed by it. "For when I am weak," he said, "then I am strong" (2 Cor 12:10). The Cross is the meeting point, the intersection, of heaven and earth, of human freedom and God's will. From it, Christians derive not only meaning for suffering, but also strength— the strength of the Crucified and Risen Savior. I quote Cardinal Ratzinger one last time, from his meditation on the Twelfth Station of the Cross, when Jesus dies on the Cross, where Jesus "makes God present in the very place where he seems definitively vanquished and absent."[12] Christianity is a religion of paradoxes, but it is also a religion where God's promises to us are always kept. Jesus promised never to leave us orphans, especially in trial and suffering (cf. Jn 14:18).

---

[12] Office for the Liturgical Celebrations of the Supreme Pontiff, Way of the Cross at the Colosseum, Good Friday 2005, Meditations and Prayers by Cardinal Joseph Ratzinger, Twelfth Station, "Jesus Dies on the Cross", Meditation, http://www.vatican.va/news_services/liturgy/2005/via_crucis/en/station_12 .html.

In the seminary where I currently serve and teach, we have a splendid chapel dedicated to the Holy Cross, which reminds the faculty and seminarians of the centrality of the Cross of Christ to the Paschal Mystery, to the Church, and to the life of the priest. In this chapel are several handsome stained glass windows, one of which depicts the scene from John 8 we have been considering. In it, our Lord has bent down to write "with his finger on the ground" (Jn 8:6, 8). The Gospel account suggests that Christ was still in that position when he finally spoke to the woman who, like us, was in need of compassion and conversion; for verse 10 states that "Jesus looked up" at her when he said, "Woman, where are they? Has no one condemned you?" And this is why I am grateful that this scene is in our chapel: to remind us that God has not only come down from heaven to save us, but that he has also *bent down* to save us—in humility, and in service and sacrifice, and in love.

Now, if we are to imitate Jesus the Good Samaritan, we must go and do the same.

> Father Paul N. Check
> Rector, St. John Fisher Seminary Residence
> Diocese of Bridgeport
> Board Member, Courage International
> Solemnity of the Annunciation
> March 25, 2017

PART ONE

THE PRODIGAL AND
HIS RETURN

In the Beginning

"Lift off! We have lift off at forty-two minutes past the hour. Lift off on Apollo 11!"[1]

It was 10:32 on the morning of July 16, 1969, and the whole world was watching as Neil Armstrong, Michael Collins, and Buzz Aldrin left the earth on a mission that would change the world forever.

Walter Cronkite, America's most trusted newsman, announced the countdown. "Good morning. It's T minus one hour, twenty-nine minutes, and fifty-three seconds, and counting. Just an hour and a half—if all goes well—Apollo 11 astronauts Armstrong, Aldrin, and Collins are to lift off from Pad 39A out there, on the voyage man always has dreamed about. Next stop for them: the moon."

My family at the time—my dad, mom, and three older brothers—watched along with the rest of America. History was being made, but little did my family know how much their lives would be changed forever the week Apollo 11 launched for the moon.

"Building's shaking," Cronkite said as kerosene mixed with liquid oxygen, thrusting the 36 story, 6.5 million pound Saturn rocket into the air. Cronkite rattled off the raw power contained in the belly of a Saturn V rocket. "The engines that generate that thrust have a combined

[1] All Apollo 11 launch quotations are from "Apollo 11 Launch", CBS News Live Coverage, July 16, 1969, accessed March 22, 2017, https://www.youtube.com/watch?v=ykRmdXzO9EI.

horsepower equal to 543 jet fighter planes; they burn 5 million, 662,000 pounds of fuel, the equivalent of 98 railroad tank cars, and the capacity of a small town's water tank. At lift off, the noise reaches 120 decibels. It's been compared to 8 million hi-fi sets playing at once."

The sound rumbled and shook the building. "Getting that buffeting we've become used to . . . ," he said, as the rocket broke free from the grip of gravity and sped toward space.

"What a moment! Man . . . on the way . . . to the *moon!*"

As the rocket propelled its way into the deep blue of the upper atmosphere, Cronkite said, "So, we've seen another *beautiful* Saturn launch, but this one will never be known in history—or by those of us who watched it—as 'just another Saturn 5 launch.' Not if all goes well."

He took his glasses off, midsentence. "Because this is the flight from which man will first set foot on the moon." He paused, stunned by what he had just said. "We almost glibly toss that line away now, 'man on the moon'. But by golly, just think it over!"

My dad had always been interested in space exploration. He had studied astronomy at Cornell University and taught astronomy at Lansing Community College, in the heart of Michigan's capital, as well as managing the school's planetarium. He had followed the space program from the very beginning and passed on his zeal to his young family.

Dad was thirty; my mom was twenty-nine; married for just over ten years. My two oldest brothers, Dave and Steve, were as excited as Dad was about the moon landing coming up in a few days. My four-year-old brother, Jim, was excited because everyone else was. But the launch was just the preamble—the real show was four days later, when man was about to set foot on the moon for the first time in history.

The family huddled around the TV again as Cronkite said, "Apollo 11: Everything going well for a landing on the moon, three hours, twenty-one minutes, fourteen seconds from now."[2]

But it wasn't guaranteed to happen until the words came from astronaut Charles Duke, stationed on the ground at Mission Control in Houston: "Eagle, Houston. You're go for landing. Over."

"Roger. Understand. Go for landing," Buzz Aldrin replied.

At 4:17 P.M., Buzz Aldrin reported, "Contact light": one of three probes at the bottom of the lunar module had just touched the surface.

Armstrong issued a command to Aldrin: "Shutdown."

"Okay. Engine stop," said Aldrin. "Descent Engine Command Override: Off. Engine Arm: Off."

"Man on the moon!" exclaimed Cronkite.

Command Control in Houston said, "We copy you down, Eagle."

"Houston, Tranquility Base here," said Armstrong. "The Eagle has landed."

Six hours later they were ready to set foot on the moon. Armstrong opened the hatch of the Eagle.

A foot going down a ladder was seen by millions around the globe. "There he is—there's a foot, coming down the steps. Armstrong is on the move!" Cronkite says. "Neil Armstrong, thirty-eight-year-old American, standing on the surface of the moon, on this July 20th, nineteen-hundred-and-sixty-nine."

---

[2] All Apollo 11 landing quotations are from "Man on the Moon: The Epic Journey of Apollo 11", CBS News Live Broadast, July 20, 1969, accessed March 22, 2017, http://www.cbsnews.com/videos/man-on-the-moon-the-epic-journey-of-apollo-11/.

It was 10:56 P.M. when Armstrong said those words forever ensconced in the history of man: "One small step for mankind, one giant leap for mankind."

The young Mattson family watched as Armstrong and Aldrin roamed along the lunar surface. But it was late, and soon my dad put the boys to bed.

He tucked them in, shut out their lights, and hurried to my parents' bedroom. He locked the door behind him, and slipped into bed next to Mom.

"What better way to celebrate the giant leap for mankind than to make a *baby*?" he whispered in her ear, as his hands moved across her body.

At the tail end of April 1970—nine months later—I was born.

Christopher Street

It was the tail end of June 1969, in the early morning hours of June 28. A different kind of labor pain began on Christopher Street, five hundred miles to the east from the house where I was conceived. In the heart of Greenwich Village, in New York City—at a bar called the Stonewall Inn—the gay rights movement was born.

Cops raided the Stonewall Inn, a mob-owned bar that catered to the homosexual community. It was one of the few places they could gather in relative peace. At least until the police came. Vice squads formed during the 1960s in New York City to enforce anti-sodomy laws that were still on the books. Some of their frequent targets were bars like the Stonewall Inn. By 1966, over a hundred men were arrested each week in stings that often employed decoys and entrapment. In a documentary about the Stonewall riots, as they came to be known, Yale Law School professor William Eskridge said, "It was a nightmare for the lesbian or gay man who was arrested and caught up in the juggernaut but it was also a nightmare for the lesbians or gay men who lived in the closet. This produced an enormous amount of anger within the lesbian and gay community in New York City. Eventually something was bound to blow."[1] The pressure cooker burst that night in late June of 1969, when for the first time the fed-up

---

[1] *Stonewall Uprising*, directed by Kate Davis and David Heilbroner, written by David Carter (original story) and David Heilbrone (New York: First Run Features, June 16, 2010).

patrons resisted arrest and turned the tables; the police became trapped inside the Stonewall Inn with angry protesters outside.

News of the pushback spread quickly, and over the next few nights violence and resistance escalated. The men and women on Christopher Street were angry—and they demanded more than just acceptance. They demanded a revolution.

Writing three years after the riots, John Murphy wrote in his book *Homosexual Liberation,*

> Many people are unhappy with this kind of oppression. They want something new, and they are determined to get it. They constitute a potentially enormous revolutionary force. For we—I now include myself among these men and women—are not merely interested in being accepted. We don't need new bureaucracies to make a government more responsive to our "needs." Nor will we be content with new political entities created in the name of social revolution if they embody the same old repressive attitudes. We intend to restructure the most basic attitudes toward sexuality, the importance of the individual, the function of the family. We are going to try and make a *total* revolution.[2]

Walter Cronkite, reminiscing about Apollo 11, said, "Everything else that has happened in our time was going to be an asterisk, really, in the history books."[3] But Cronkite was wrong. The Stonewall riots and the birth of the gay rights movement will be what's remembered

[2] John Murphy, *Homosexual Liberation: A Personal View* (New York: Praeger Publishers, 1971), p. 41 (italics in original).

[3] *Man on the Moon: With Walter Cronkite*, hosted by Dan Rather, featuring Walter Cronkite; produced and written by Robert Northshield; edited by Jorge J. Garcia (New York: CBS/Fox Video, 1989).

of the summer of 1969. All else will be an asterisk in the history books, for that's the year man began to forget who he was. The Stonewall riots dramatically accelerated the trajectory of the revolution "to restructure the most basic attitudes toward sexuality, the importance of the individual, the function of the family".

On June 26, 2015, the day after the United States Supreme Court decision *Obergefell v. Hodges* made same-sex "marriage" legal in all fifty states, gay activist and blogger Andrew Sullivan would write of the revolution simply, "It is accomplished."[4]

The *total* revolution that the gay liberation movement demanded had finally been achieved. The world didn't change all that much because Neil Armstrong landed on the moon. Neil Armstrong's "one small step for man, one giant leap for mankind" is merely a footnote compared with what Stonewall brought into the world. The gay rights movement accomplished its goal: two men can get "married" now—the Supreme Court has spoken; homosexuality is supposedly as natural to mankind as husband and wife. The revolution was achieved. A man like me who is attracted to other men is supposed to celebrate. Yet I don't.

My life has been lived, pulled between two poles—two views of mankind, two visions of happiness and freedom—between two competing worldviews. One side believes that there are moral absolutes in the world, that there is a God, that he loves us, and that human sexuality is a great gift to mankind that brings joy and fulfillment and pleasure. It insists, though, that this fulfillment comes when one accepts the reality that our sole sexual identity is male

[4] Andrew Sullivan, "It Is Accomplished", *The Dish* (blog), June 26, 2015, http://dish.andrewsullivan.com/2015/06/26/it-is-accomplished/.

and female, and that to be truly satisfying and fulfilling, sex must be used rationally, according to its inherent design, and be open to the precious gift of new human life. The other side produced the sexual revolution, promoting contraception, free love, and the gay rights movement and creating the ideology of gender that supposedly proclaims a message of liberation from what it viewed as outdated notions of "male and female". It claims that feelings and whom we're attracted to are more reliable indicators of truth about our sexual identity than the design of the human body. It is an ideology that rejects moral absolutes. It is a morality based on mutual consent, which views sex primarily as a means toward pleasure. It is an ideology that views pregnancy as an inconvenient side effect of sexuality, usually to be avoided. Children are commodities that enhance a couple's life and are only an incidental aspect of human sexuality—and usually perceived as an obstacle to human happiness, unless in the mind of the parents the child will somehow add something of value to the life of the parents and their idea of happiness.

I have traveled in both camps throughout my life, always in search of happiness. My life has been lived between these two visions of fulfillment and happiness—one, represented by the love of my parents, who came together in one flesh and produced my life; the other, the ideology of the gay liberation movement.

But I didn't know anything about that when I was born, crying, longing to be made happy—a desire that has shaped every choice I've ever made.

Immaculate Heart of Mary School

All I knew was that I wanted to touch his chest.

From the beginning of the day I couldn't keep my eyes off him. He was wearing a Pittsburgh Steelers football jersey, a jersey with perforated holes, the sort of shirt worn over another one as part of a uniform. But he didn't have a shirt on—just the jersey. I had never seen a shirt that you could see through before. I became mesmerized watching him, and that day, I became obsessed with finding a way to touch his chest.

I was six and so was he. We were in the first grade at Immaculate Heart of Mary School on South Cedar Street in Lansing, Michigan, not far from the forges that supplied the nearby Oldsmobile plants with steel for their automobiles. Our playground felt as industrial and car centric as the community around us. We played on asphalt, making up games as we dashed between lines on the parking lot.

The boy in the jersey was the star athlete of our first-grade class. He dominated the kickball "field" in the southeast corner of the parking lot. Most of the class would join in these kickball games, and he was usually one of the captains. I remember him as brusque, exhibiting an easy confidence about the game with the rest of the boys, but their banter was a mystery to me. I felt like an outsider then, a feeling that lasted most of my life anytime I was forced to play sports.

When we picked teams, I was picked after some of the girls. It was mortifying, but it was a regular occurrence. I was known as an unreliable asset. At the young age of six, I knew that I didn't hold much worth in the eyes of whatever boy was choosing the strongest and fastest kids for his team. I was being weighed and measured on an unseen scale, evaluated for the worth of what my body could do for the team. In the balance, I came up short. I wasn't strong enough, or fast enough, or coordinated enough to be wanted. I envied the boy in the Steelers jersey because he was what I wasn't. He was strong, fast, and confident, the opposite of how I felt.

When I could, I'd play with the girls. We would jump rope together, making up silly nonsense songs to accompany our jumps. We giggled a lot, and I liked that.

I wasn't very good at jump rope either, but the girls didn't seem to mind. I could make them laugh when I didn't jump quite fast enough. I wasn't very coordinated, but it wasn't a liability with the girls. The girls were safe, unlike the boys.

I remember a sixth-grade boy on my bus who teased me often. He once looked at me and said, "You know, you must use mascara. Are you a girl or something?"

"No!" I said. "I don't even know what that is."

"Well, you have such long eyelashes. They're like a girl's; they're so long. I bet your mom puts mascara on your eyelashes, doesn't she? Look in the mirror when you get home. You really could be a girl with eyelashes as long as that!" It was horrible. He would often say such things to me.

I was teased by the boys in my class too. The first day back to school after my dad's mother's funeral is seared in my memory. The whole class gathered around our teacher, Sister Johnson, for story time. She knew why I had been away from school, and so she told the other boys and girls about my grandmother's death. To comfort me, she offered to let me sit on a chair instead of on the floor, cross-legged, as we usually did.

But as I went to sit down, one of the other boys pulled the chair out from underneath me, and I tumbled to the ground, bursting into tears.

Some boys snickered, while Sister Johnson's angry eyes blazed at them behind the blue-tinted glasses she always wore. She scolded them and consoled me, while the other girls gave me their pity too—yet one more reason to distrust the boys, and stick with the girls.

In that moment, I felt trapped—suffocating feelings of confusion hit me. "Why did they do that?" I asked myself. But in situations like that, wondering why things happened didn't matter. The key was to navigate life so things like that didn't happen again. I learned quickly that I could survive, just so long as I made people laugh.

When I went for the ball at kickball and would miss it, I would feign an exaggerated disappointment. Eventually, I joked even before I went to kick it. "Well, here I am again! It's probably not going to go anywhere this time either, so you guys out there, in the outfield, well, just keep talking." And when it didn't, everyone would laugh, and I laughed along with them. I learned that they wouldn't laugh at me if I laughed at myself first. Laughter became a mask that I put on for survival. And joking around became the way I got my way.

Joking around is how I found a way to touch his chest. That's all I could think about that day. It wasn't just his chest either. I could see his biceps clearly through the mesh of his jersey too. When no one was looking, I flexed my own muscles, then looked back at him. I fell short. His arms, his chest, were so different from my pudgy body. He was lean. He was strong. I must have wanted to feel what that felt like.

So I joked with him, somehow teasing him about why he didn't have a shirt on. Maybe I tried to do a "titty-twister" or something that the other boys did with each other, but finally I was able to put my two hands on his chest. Feeling the skin of his chest on my hands thrilled me. I lingered a bit too long, but I quickly made him laugh. No damage was done.

"He won't think I'm weird, will he?" I worried. His laughter assured me I had covered my tracks.

I knew it was wrong and not normal to want to touch his chest—I wouldn't have schemed and worried otherwise about how to try and find a way to do it without him thinking I was odd.

That day is the first moment I recall ever being drawn to another guy. I wouldn't say it was sexual, but it's clear to me that the seeds that would lead to my sexual attractions to men were already present in my life in 1976.

Looking back on that boy in the first grade through the lens of the twenty-first century, a lot of people would tell me this is proof that I was born gay.

But I see it very differently. We live in a world guided by cause and effect. Everything always comes from something. Even things that are hard to explain ultimately have an explanation.

My whole life I've wanted to know where my attractions to men came from. In my case, the "hard to explain" hasn't been so hard to explain.

* * * * *

My mom always wanted four daughters. After three sons, both my mom and dad thought it would be nice to try for a daughter. I was the one baby that they planned for, and as the pregnancy went on, my parents made plans for a girl.

It was a scary delivery. After three births by Caesarean section, the walls of my mother's uterus were paper thin, and she required another Caesarean with my birth. She bled a great deal, but soon I was delivered and the doctor declared, "It's a boy!"

My parents embraced the son God had given them. But because of medical complications, she couldn't have any more children; I was their last child. My parent's dream of having a daughter ended.

But thoughts of what could have been weren't absent from my mom's mind. On a Saturday afternoon in the summer when I was three or four years old, my parents had my aunt Ann and uncle Jim over for a cookout. Their two sons, Jimmy and Robby, came along too. Jimmy was a year older than me, Rob a year younger.

My mom and aunt Annie pulled me toward them. I had a headband on, keeping my hair out of my eyes.

"You've let his hair grow so long, Janny!" my aunt said. "Are you turning him into a hippie?"

"Oh, of course not! But he does have such nice hair, doesn't he?" my mom said, as she brushed my hair with her fingers. "You know, that hair would look so pretty in ponytails, don't you think? Let's just do it. 'Just to see' what he'd look like, if he had been a girl, after all."

They oohed and aahed over me, as they found some rubber bands and pulled my hair into ponytails. I looked just like a little girl, and then I pranced around in front of them.

My brothers saw what was going on and didn't like it. "Mom! What are you doing? He's a *boy*, not a girl!"

My cousins looked on the scene with some confusion—they were too young to really know what was going on. I remember that day, one of few that I remember distinctly from my childhood. I remember I didn't like the negative attention I was getting from my brothers. It felt wrong to me somehow, though I couldn't have known why, being so young. My uncle Jim even remembers that day from so long ago. At a recent family gathering, I recalled that moment to him, and he recalled that he told my aunt Ann never to do such a thing to either of their boys. He understood that it was wrong for a mother to do that to her son.

We live in a world where we are told that "being gay is just a normal variation of human sexuality." Contrary to what we're told we need to believe about homosexuality, I see a clear continuum of events within my life that ultimately led me toward attractions to the same sex. I am convinced this sort of gender-bending moment, teasing and bullying, and feeling weaker and less athletic than other boys, along with a myriad of other events that happened in the course of my life, became the seedbed in which my attractions to men were planted and flourished.

A mom randomly putting a boy in pigtails doesn't make that boy desire men more than women, by itself. A boy feeling inadequate playing kickball won't make him want to have sex with another man, by itself. But, of course, those aren't the only things that happened to me when I was young. There's that bit about what happened in the barn.

The Barn

My dad was a country boy at heart, even though we lived in the city. As a boy he spent his summers with his uncles and aunts on the Stonington Peninsula of the Upper Peninsula of Michigan, on a finger of land that juts into Lake Michigan forming the eastern edge of Little Bay de Noc. He helped them work the land, making hay and cutting timber in the family woodlots. Farming had gotten into his blood. So he built a barn in his backyard.

"Mort's barn" was the talk of the neighborhood. All of the kids watched with wonder as the concrete trucks poured out sloshing rocks, like molten lava for the foundations and floor. A week later, the newly poured floor of the barn served as a roller-skating rink for everyone in the neighborhood and a canvas for massive chalk art too.

Slowly, the frame began to take shape. The neighborhood fathers got in on the action. "We're having our own barn raising!" they'd joke with each other as they hammered the framing together.

The children followed close behind. With each new element, a new game was created. We weaved in and out of the two-by-four framing as if it was an obstacle course.

The roof took shape, and then the peak was built, and soon the roof was complete. Then the last shingle was in place. The barn was finished, and then the fun really began.

Our imaginations soared. With the extendable stairs pulled tight to the second level, we pretended we were flying in a zeppelin in World War II. Sometimes we dove deep below the sea, on a daring mission for the navy. Sometimes we were on the Starship Enterprise, catapulting through space at warp speed.

"I'm heading out to the barn" was a phrase we'd often say to our parents.

The front of the barn was our playground, but the back quickly became filled with antiques my parents collected. No one really went back there, but for a seven- or eight-year-old boy, the tiny crawl space between the angling slope of the roof and the beams that created the boundaries of the room became tunnels in which to imagine great adventures. They were too small for someone of twelve or so, but for the youngest kids in the neighborhood, the "tunnel" became a great place to play. Or to be hidden from view.

I don't know when it began, or how it began, but a neighbor boy and I often went into the tunnel, took off all our clothes, and explored each other's bodies. I don't have any specific recollection of what we did, thankfully, but I remember it being fun and exciting. Nothing really was as fun for me as what we did together. We did it for years. How it began is fuzzy. Did I initiate it? Did he? I suppose such questions don't matter.

It stopped at some point a few years later. I have often contemplated what impact this must have had on our developing psyches, on our understanding of ourselves and our sexuality. Is it mere coincidence that he came out as a gay man as an adult, and that I too live with deeply held sexual attractions for men? I don't think so.

I believe our sexuality is like a river, designed to flow along a certain path. But when things like what I did with Joey enter our lives, it's as if a boulder crashes into the stream, blocking in some measure the path of a healthy and normal sexual development. Sometimes it can overflow

the bounds of the boulder and find the path it would naturally have taken; surely there are boys who experimented
with other boys, and grew up without attractions to the
same sex.

In his book *Love and Responsibility*, Pope Saint John
Paul II writes,

> The orientation given to a person's existence by mem-
> bership of one of the sexes does not only make itself felt
> internally, but at the same time turns outwards, and in
> the normal course of things ... manifests itself in a certain
> natural predilection for, a tendency to seek, the other sex.[1]

Yet I am convinced that for some men and women,
these moments in youth can sometimes divert their sexual
development from its original course. When I think back
on those moments with Joey, I often reflect on a passage
from the Song of Songs. It's a refrain that repeats several
times throughout the book:

> I adjure you, O daughters of Jerusalem,
> that you stir not up nor awaken love
> until it please. (8:4)

This is a plea to maintain a person's innocence, to refrain
from immodest speech or actions that would awaken sexual desire outside of the context for which sexual intimacy
is created, the holy union of husband and wife. I believe
those secret rendezvous with Joey did great damage to
my sexual development, and to his. We stirred up desire
before it was ready, and in the wrong way; by doing so, we
placed an obstacle in the path in some measure that steered

---

[1] Karol Wojtyła, *Love and Responsibility* (San Francisco: Ignatius Press, 1993),
pp. 47–48.

us away from the "normal course of things". In the stories I hear from other men and women who live with same-sex attractions, early sexual experiences very often feature prominently, often stemming from abuse. Certainly it's not everyone's story, but it happens too much for it to be a coincidence. Attractions to the same sex never just happen, all on their own.

Barnes Elementary

In the third grade, my family moved us to a nondenominational Christian school. My older brothers were in the public school, and my parents were fed up with some of the educational shenanigans that were taking place—especially about sex education.

The move was good for me. Thankfully, the teasing from my old school didn't carry over to this one. The teachers were on top of any nonsense like that, and the kids were friendly.

I made friends quickly and soon was happy. I was popular at my new school—enough to be voted class president of my fifth-grade class. The lessons I had learned back in the first grade held me in good stead: I'd survive if I made them laugh. I was the class clown, but without being a rabble rouser. I was viewed as the perfect kid—well-behaved, always doing and saying the right thing. Miss Wright beaned me with a chalk eraser for gabbing too much in class a couple of times, but beyond these little infractions I was a compliant kid. The other boys knew it too. I was Mr. Goody Two Shoes in most of their eyes. They never invited me to join in on anything questionable.

So it's no surprise what happened in the bathroom that February of 1981. That moment left an indelible mark on my memory. I went into the bathroom and found four of my classmates huddled together, looking at something just under the window. They looked up sheepishly as I came in and hid whatever it was from my view.

"Hey, what are you guys looking at?" I asked.

"Nothing," one of them said, as they gathered even closer together, hiding what they had.

"Come on, let me see," I pleaded.

"No—it's nothing. We're not doing anything."

I walked toward them, but stopped when they moved closer together. It was clear I wasn't welcome.

"What's that?" I asked again. "It looks like some sort of magazine."

"It is, but you can't see it," one of them replied.

"And you'd better not tell Mr. Murphy that we have it!" another said quickly.

"Why would I? What is it?"

"It's the *Sports Illustrated* Swimsuit Issue."

I had heard about this before, and I wanted to see it too. I wanted to see the models—I had seen my fair share of the swimsuit and lingerie sections of J. C. Penney catalogs, as well as the cover of Herb Alpert's *Whipped Cream and Other Delights* in my parents' record collection. And I liked what I saw. Even though I had messed around in the barn with my neighbor, and admired my classmate in the Steelers jersey, I still thought girls were cute. But that moment in the bathroom wasn't about seeing women in swimsuits anyway. I just wanted to be doing whatever it was they were doing—*with them*.

I felt this way often around boys. I was popular and had friends who were both girls and boys, because I had learned to be a chameleon. But around most boys—and the stuff boys did together—I felt like an outsider. That day with the swimsuit issue, I wanted to be in that circle—with them. I wanted to talk about how good-looking the models were, because we would be doing it, together.

But they wouldn't let me see it. I felt rejected, so I played the part they expected me to play: Mr. Goody Two

Shoes: "You really shouldn't be looking at that, and you certainly shouldn't have brought it to school."

And with that, I left the bathroom with puritanical dismissiveness, wishing with all my heart that I had been let into their little band.

That longing was the same ache I had felt when I was younger on the kickball field. I wanted to be one of the guys, but I never felt like I was. Everyone at least liked me at the new school—but there always seemed to be a distance between most of the boys and me.

Boys want to be welcomed by other boys—and to do risky and dangerous things with them. At least I did. Naturally, looking at the *Sports Illustrated* Swimsuit Issue wasn't a good channel for that desire, but at that moment what I wanted was to be *with them* in what they were doing. Pushing the bounds, pushing the envelope—that's what I wanted to do. I was always playing it safe. And I hated it.

* * * * *

Despite moments like this, however, I did have some friends who were boys. This was an improvement over the old school too.

In the fourth grade my friend Kevin invited me over for a weekend birthday party to his home, on a small private lake. The other invited boys were all into sports, so of course we played basketball. Just like on the kickball field back in the first grade, I made jokes about how bad a shooter I was. I played a little bit, watching and modeling what they did, but I was uncomfortable the whole time. I hovered on the edge of the driveway and played with my friend's dog instead. It was something I could be doing—no one would think it weird if I played with the dog, instead of playing basketball.

As I look back on those moments, what I remember most isn't any fun we had—it's memories of how I navigated the weekend. When we played basketball, all I could think about was how to get *through* that moment. There was no enjoyment in it. "Getting through moments" was what most of my life felt like to me.

The invitation to the party had mentioned swimming in the lake. That was something else I would need to navigate. I purposely didn't bring my swimsuit, because I was afraid of the water. But my plans to avoid swimming were dashed. Kevin's mom found a pair of his shorts I could wear, so I had no choice but to get in the lake.

I waded in the water, watching the boys off in the distance, wishing I had the guts they had—feeling like a runt. My friend's mom figured things out quickly and looked with compassion on me and said, "You know, you could go out to the dock, where the diving board is, if you want to. Let me go get you a life preserver." So she did and placed it on me.

I felt like a helpless little boy.

As I type this, nearly thirty-five years later, my chest constricts as I think back on that day. I made my way out to the diving board, bobbing safely in my life vest. I see my friends, swimming recklessly around the dock, splashing each other, fearlessly jumping off the diving board—while I float next to them, pretending to have fun, all the while wishing I had their fearless courage. I wanted to be like them, if there was any way I could, but fear gripped me.

Yet another boulder had been dropped into the path of my developing sexuality. I wasn't *like* the other boys—at least that's what I believed. I wanted to be like them, but didn't know how to be. The "hard to explain"—not so hard to explain, after all.

That was the last time I ever swam in front of any of my classmates. By that time, I was convinced I was pudgy and fat, which was the other reason I had left my swim trunks at home. I didn't want anyone to see my body. (And yet, the irony of all of this is that I could fit into Kevin's shorts. He was skinny—so why did I think I was so chunky?)

I never went swimming with friends from school ever again. It took me more than thirty years to feel comfortable enough in my own skin to swim in public again because I was embarrassed of my body.

That year, in the fourth grade, was the year I became dreadfully focused on *me*. It wasn't just swimming. That was the year I realized I wished I had a different jaw.

There was a kid in my class who had an angular jaw. For some reason, this seemed more desirable to me than the shorter jaw I had. I'm not sure how I discovered that my jaw was somehow different from his or the other boys around me, but I did.

Kids notice things though. Maybe we were sticking our jaws in and out and noticed this difference about ourselves. I remember my mom had silhouettes made out of black cut paper of my brothers and me around this time. Maybe I noticed it then, examining my silhouette, wondering why my jaw didn't look like the jaws of some of my classmates. I sometimes stared in the mirror and stuck my jaw out, and wished there was a way to change the contours of my face.

This thought consumed me for years. I obsessed about this so much that in college I researched chin implants. Apparently I'm not the only man with a fixation on the cut of his jaw. I'm still self-conscious about it. It's one reason I've had a goatee for over twenty years.

Every man who I've ever found attractive has a jaw like I wish I had. I don't find that coincidental. Envy—yet another boulder that sent my sexual development coursing toward men. But the biggest boulders were yet to come. Adolescence hadn't hit yet. And with that, all hell broke loose.

The Curse of Phys Ed

Gym class was hell. It wasn't just having to play sports, though that was agonizing: a stint in Little League had been a major-league nightmare back in the third grade. The bluster and swagger of braying fathers, howling at us boys to stop swinging the bat like a girl, made me hate organized sports, and the brand of masculinity that went with it.

It wasn't my hatred of sports that made me hate phys ed, however. The real terror of gym class was the nakedness.

I suppose I was just as nervous as the rest of the guys that first day of gym class in junior high. We'd never seen our classmates naked, and no one really knew how to handle it. The only naked bodies I had seen were my own and Joey's in the back of the barn, but we had stopped doing that a few years before junior high, before we hit puberty. Now, my classmates and I were on the verge of becoming men. But as soon as we stripped down, it became clear that some of the boys were men already, and that I wasn't one of them.

Shame. All I felt in the locker room was shame. Every single day. And dread—because I had to do it all again the next day. We were forced to take showers. I hid my body as best I could in my towel, slunk to the shower, hoping to get one on the wall, instead of being forced to circle around the pillar of showerheads in the center of the room. There you were forced to stand in a circle, opposite the other boys. I didn't want them to see me.

The men among us knew they were men. One of my classmates sometimes stood on top of the bench to towel off, as if on a pedestal to show off his body—chiseled pecs, rounded shoulders intersecting with his biceps. I would steal glances when I could, longing with all my heart to be like him. When he walked, the muscles in his thighs and calves looked like iron cables beneath his skin. When he toweled off, his body roared masculinity. I was a mere cub around him and many others. I didn't belong with them. I wasn't worthy to be counted among them.

Shame. That's all I felt. The burgeoning men who had sprouted chest hair had bragging rights—some of the boys in junior high even had started shaving. I was traumatized being naked with my classmates. I felt like a pathetic excuse for a man. I didn't have any chest hair, no hope for a mustache, and below the belt, well, I was still very much a boy. I was a late bloomer, in every way. Each day I ran a gauntlet of shame for the two years I was forced to take gym class. All I thought about was how to survive the showers. "They'll all see me, and laugh at me." So I thought.

Whoever thought throwing adolescents together, naked, in the midst of the turbulent angst and perpetual navel-gazing of pubescence should be required to pay for a lifetime of therapy for everyone forced to take showers after gym class. My life would have been a lot better with a little bit of B.O. if not the noses of my neighbors.

Shame of my body was how I learned how to masturbate. I discovered it on my own, in the privacy of my bathroom. In adolescent angst, I tugged, wishing what I had could be bigger, like some of the other boys who had already turned into men. Then suddenly it felt good.

Shame, envy, self-loathing, doubts—all present in the first moment of my sexual awakening. My first experience of full-blown sexual pleasure came because I was ashamed of my body. The "hard to explain" isn't all that hard to explain.

This self-doubt, this shame of my body—this was no boulder dropped into the stream of my sexual development. The nakedness of gym class mangled my psyche, like an earthquake ripping a crevasse through my soul.

Reminiscing about these feelings of shame many years later, in a letter I wrote to my therapist at the time, I wrote:

> As a young man, I so desired to be able to shave, but I was so far behind my classmates. I didn't have any chest hair to speak of, and I was embarrassed. I didn't feel like a man, and was envious of those fellow students who needed to shave every day. They had bragging rights. I remember being at my Uncle John's house in Florida, when I was in high school ... and a student of his came over during break, and he had a full beard. Uncle John laughed, and told us that the students were having a beard growing contest over break, and I ached inside, knowing that I hardly needed to shave at all. In the presence of that boy, or to me, a man, I felt only as a boy. I was a musician, and was still a child, and here was this burgeoning man, the same age as me, an athlete, and a good one. He was a football player, handsome, built like a man, with strong features. I certainly found him attractive. It's a memory distinctly imbedded in my brain. And I suppose I wished I were him, or like him at least.

I felt like a bull without horns, and I became consumed with figuring out how to feel more like a man. When I went to college, I dug into the research stacks of the library at Michigan State University. There I thought I had found the answer to my worries: get a diagnosis of "delayed pubescence", and receive injections of testosterone.

I went to the health center and had a physical. It was agonizing and shameful to share my concerns with the doctor, but I was desperate to feel like a man. I clung to injections of testosterone as the answer to all of my doubts and worries, so though he told me I was fine and normal and healthy, I cajoled him into giving me a referral to an endocrinologist.

A few weeks later I was with the endocrinologist. She agreed that I was on the slow end of pubescent maturity, and so she did a thorough blood screening. We set up an appointment the following week to determine what treatment I might need, if any.

A week later, the doctor told me that testosterone is measured on a thousand-point scale. The normal range for men was between 300 and 1000. If I was below 300, I'd receive injections. I crossed my fingers, hoping beyond hope that I fell below normal levels.

My levels were 333. *333*. I was normal. But I was a mere 33 points away from abnormal, and nearly 700 points away from the peak of masculinity. This brought me no consolation. It was a direct blow. It just confirmed everything I had always felt about myself. If I was a man, I was one just barely. A mere 33 points away. The "hard to explain" isn't so hard to explain.

I envied other men and had sexual fantasies about the men I wished I could be, which is a common experience for men with same-sex attractions. I wanted to be what they were, to have what they had, to be anything other than myself. In college, I always sized myself up with the other men who walked by me. In my mind I usually fell woefully short. "If I looked like that guy, or had his body, or his muscles, I'd be happy," I thought. Nothing about me was desirable. I resented God for making me the way I had been made.

I now know that hidden deep within my pain was pride and rebellion against God and how he made me. But I must be gentle with myself. I was a hurting, confused young man who didn't know where to turn for help.

All I knew then was that I hated myself and the way I was made by God. The way I salved the pain was through pornography. I lusted after the men I wished I could be. None of them looked like me—all of them were men whom I wished I could be.

It was then, in college, when I first thought perhaps that I was gay. But back in adolescence, at the beginning of my attractions to men, I didn't even know what "gay" meant.

Rock Hudson, Rambo, and AIDS

In adolescence, at the beginning of my attractions to men, I hadn't even known what "gay" meant; I just knew that men were sexually attractive to me. I didn't really know what I might have done with them if I was actually ever with one, except to touch them.

I had lived a very sheltered life. I don't even know when I first heard the words "gay" or "fag" or "queer", or even the word "homosexual". In the seventies and early eighties homosexuality just wasn't talked about much, at least in my sheltered surroundings. I do know, however, when I first learned what men who liked men liked to do with each other. I found that out in Mr. Potter's algebra class, my sophomore year of high school.

It was 1985, and news of AIDS was all over TV. I was starting to learn more about gay people, but sadly it was often associated with rumors of people dying from this new and horrible disease. It was also the year Rock Hudson died from AIDS.

That was the year the second Rambo film was released, and through the convergence of the two—in the crudest of ways—I learned what gay sex was about.

As we gathered for class, one of the boys said he had a joke to tell us. "Did you hear that Sylvester Stallone and Rock Hudson made a movie together?" he said.

"What was it called?" someone asked.

"Ram-butt!"

Everyone laughed. Including me. But I didn't get it. Ever the chameleon, I laughed, only pretending that I got it.

I leaned over to one of my classmates to get the scoop. " 'Ram-butt.' I don't get it. Why's that funny?" I asked.

"Seriously?" he said.

"No, I don't get it. Really, I don't. What's so funny about it?"

"Well, uh, you do know what gay guys *do*, right?" he said.

"What are you talking about? No, I don't know," I said, now a little embarrassed.

"Um, well, they don't have someplace to *put* it, you know?" he said, seeing if what he was saying sunk in. "I mean, come on, where else do you think they put it than *in there*?"

The idea sickened me, and I was overcome with nausea.

I think back on that moment now and see it through the eyes of G. K. Chesterton, who wrote in his 1925 book *The Everlasting Man* of love between men in ancient Greece. He writes of a young person first hearing of the mythical story of Zeus and Ganymede,[1] the young man kidnapped by Zeus who became his cup-bearer and lover. Chesterton writes,

> Let any lad who has had the luck to grow up sane and simple in his day-dreams of love hear for the first time of the cult of Ganymede; he will not be merely shocked but

[1] "Ganymede ... clearly functioned as a code, perhaps almost 'slang', either for a male youth desired by men or, more generally, men involved in homosexual activities." Ralph J. Hexter, "The Kisses of Juventius, and Policing the Boundaries of Masculinity: The Case of Catullus", in *Ancient Rome and the Construction of Modern Homosexual Identities*, ed. Jennifer Ingleheart (New York: Oxford University Press, 2015), p. 275.

sickened. And that first impression, as has been said here so often about first impressions, will be right. Our cynical indifference is an illusion; it is the greatest of all illusions; the illusion of familiarity.[2]

In 1985, I was that lad who had grown up sane and simple in my daydreams of love. I may have found guys attractive, but the thought of joining my body with another man in anal sex had never entered my mind. It was a revolting idea to me. Nor could I understand how two men who loved each other could pretend to themselves that it was the same love that existed between a husband and wife. How could it be? It made no sense to me.

That moment, in the tenth grade, was a pivotal moment in my life. The revulsion I felt toward the idea of anal sex was the correct response. I believe if I had heeded my first impression, I would have been saved from a world of heartbreak and pain later on in life. There were seeds within me, no doubt, of attractions to men. I didn't choose to be attracted to men, nor does any man.

But we do have choices. We choose what we do with them. For that, I am culpable, and my life and the growth of my attractions for men weren't completely out of my control. All it took to help them take root was a whole lot of porn.

[2] G. K. Chesterton, *The Everlasting Man* (San Francisco: Ignatius Press, 2008), p. 154.

Porn: A Dysfunctional Love Affair

I've heard it said that once you try heroin, you're instantly addicted.

My "heroin" was pornography, and my addiction to it began on a Boy Scout camping trip. One of the guys in my tent had pilfered a bunch of hard-core magazines from his dad's stash. I devoured them as if I had discovered the mysteries of the universe. Long after my fellow scouts were asleep and snoring, I turned page after page, absorbing everything. It was one of the most electrifying moments of my life.

I felt awful the next day. I knew it was wrong and resolved never to do such a thing again. But I couldn't stop thinking about what I had seen. I wanted—and seemed to need—more.

During my teen years, it was hard for teenagers to get porn—the only way was to get it from a friend, or to buy it somehow. There were no smartphones back then. But that didn't stop me. No one is as conniving as a teenager who wants to find pornography.

On my way to work one day, I saw a rundown store. I had never noticed it before, but somehow I knew that was where I would find what I was looking for. And I did. I steeled my resolve, grabbed one of the magazines I had seen on my camping trip, and hoped the fellow behind the counter would sell it to me.

He did. I nervously paid, then walked through the door and slid the magazine between my shirt and my coat. My heart pounded with excitement as I opened my car door, fumbled for my keys, and sped off to work.

I didn't know that I had just opened the door to a prison cell.

* * * * *

I've often wondered what my life would have been like without pornography in it. I'll never know. I was enslaved to it for decades.

Pornography woos and whispers, camouflaging itself with a veneer of beauty. It hides behind a soothing mask of intoxicating perfumes, always whispering, always cajoling—always enchanting, always promising more and better pleasures, slowly hypnotizing its victims deeper and deeper into a languid stupor of unquestioning obedience. Porn is a parasite, slowly sucking joy, laughter, and life. All that is left in its wake is dust, ashes, and pain.

Such was my existence. Such pain, such turmoil, such guilt, such agony. I was a prisoner for so, so long. Nothing was enough to sate me. Porn is unquenchable. It's always hungry. It always needs to be fed with something more.

That's one reason I turned to gay porn. Occasionally I would feel the need for a bigger "hit" than the usual hard-core fare I bought, and so I'd buy gay porn, until gradually, the tide of my attractions turned in the other direction. The balance swung toward men, with occasional moments of thinking about women. I certainly didn't choose to be attracted to men—that's a given. Yet I nourished and helped my attractions grow with a thousand choices I made. Porn—and my fantasies—were my fertilizer.

Saint Gregory of Nyssa writes, "We are in some manner our own parents, giving birth to ourselves by our own free choice in accordance with whatever we wish to be."[1] He writes in another place,

> For whenever a man drags down his mental energy to these affections, and forces his reason to become the servant of his passions, there takes place a sort of conversion of the good stamp [of the Divine] in him into the irrational image, his whole nature being traced anew after that design, as his reason, so to say, cultivates the beginnings of his passions, and gradually multiplies them; for once it lends its co-operation to passion, it produces a plenteous and abundant crop of evils.[2]

Saint Gregory could have been writing about me and my lust for men. I was not merely subjected to the desires, though they came unbidden and unlooked for. My childhood desires for the boy in my first-grade class show me that. But across a thousand steps, and a thousand moments of decision, I cooperated with my passions because it was exciting and taboo to do so. The plenteous and abundant crop it helped produce was an intractable attraction to men.

I don't believe my attractions toward men are a case of "nature" or even merely of "nurture" from my environment. In part, they are there because I watered them, and I harvested them. I helped them take root in my psyche, fertilizing them by my lust, a lust driven by my envious desires to be someone other than me. Porn became for me a catalog of men who had features and traits I wished for

---

[1] Gregory of Nyssa, *The Life of Moses*, trans. Abraham J. Malherbe and Everett Ferguson (New York: Paulist Press, 1978), pp. 55–56.

[2] *Gregory of Nyssa: Dogmatic Treatises, etc.*, vol. 5 of *A Select Library of Nicene and Post-Nicene Fathers of the Christian Church*, 2nd series, ed. Philip Schaff and Henry Wace (New York: Christian Literature, 1893), p. 48.

myself. I lusted after the men I wanted to be. This became an uncontrollable desire, which I realize now stemmed from deep wounds in my psyche.

In her book, *Crisis in Masculinity*, Leanne Payne, who counseled men and women with same-sex attractions for many years, wrote about a young man named Richard who came to her for counseling. His story is much like mine.

> In his fantasies, Richard was seeing in its idealized form the part of himself from which he was estranged. For him that part lay in what he perceived as the sexual virility of the athletic type. He was looking at others and loving a lost part of himself, a grievously unaffirmed masculinity that he therefore could not recognize and accept. Homosexual activity is often merely the twisted way a person tries to take into himself—in the mistaken way of the cannibal—those attributes of his own personality from which he is estranged. It is actually a form of self-love or narcissism.
>
> Richard had no problem seeing this to be the case in his own life.[3]

Payne calls this a "cannibal compulsion" because of the curious fact that primitive societies don't cannibalize their enemies merely as an act of power—rather, as conquerors, they only cannibalize those enemies whose strength or power they desire to have *literally* in themselves. This is an uncomfortable comparison, to be sure, but like Richard, I see this "cannibal compulsion" very clearly in my own life. Every man who has ever been attractive to me has features or traits about him that I wish were mine. My attractions haven't changed over time: I've never been attracted to a man who looks like me.

[3] Leanne Payne, *Crisis in Masculinity* (Grand Rapids, Mich.: Hamewith Books, 1995), p. 25.

The gay rights movement seems to have convinced society that homosexuality is a normal variation of human sexuality, rather than a symptom of deep, unresolved wounds in the psyche. Those therapists who desire to identify and help heal these wounds are portrayed as un-scientific and backwards, urging people to "go against their nature". This is a grave injustice, for as much as the gay rights movement wants to say otherwise, and say that "being gay" is as natural a part of human sexuality as father, mother, and child, our bodies show us that homosexuality cuts against the grain of human sexuality. We all play a game of pretend when we think otherwise, and we do injury to the free will of people to choose their own destiny by preventing people, especially teenagers, from finding help in resolving their unwanted same-sex attractions.

In my life, the seeds of my same-sex attractions are all clear to me: seeds sown with my neighbor when I was a boy, seeds of teasing and alienation from other boys, seeds of envy stemming from doubts about my body, seeds from gruff men and a father who sometimes intimidated and scared me, and seeds from rejection from women, as well as a mother who had an unhealthy and controlling attach-ment to me because of her own wounds. It's all there, in my life—all that the experts once were still free to say—it's all there. Now, all these theories of causation have been stifled as "homophobic" or pejoratively labeled and dis-missed as archaic psychobabble. But it's all there, in my life, tracing a line as clear and as inexorable as the course of the earth through the heavens. We live in a cause-and-effect world. Everything comes from something; every-thing has its starting point; every fruit must first be planted. It's not hard to trace the contours in my life that led to my attractions to men. At times, I helped them along their way. When I turned to gay porn, I put my hand to the plow that would sow desires for men deep into the fertile soil of my adolescent imagination. The path is as clear to me as if I was looking back on my life through the ridges and furrows of a plowed field in the countryside in a Michigan spring.

It Is Me, Isn't It?

My whole life I expected and assumed I would be married. Even though my attractions for men grew exponentially through high school, I still found some girls cute enough to believe I could find someone to date and marry, at least if they would have me. I had a girlfriend named Katy in the fifth grade. This lasted about two days, and the rest of my time in school, I was relegated to the "let's just be friends" category.

The pressure to find someone to date always doubled down when the prom came around. As senior prom approached, I decided to ask Katy out again. She was in the band with me, where I played trombone. I wasn't any good at sports, but my senior year I had been named by the *Detroit News* as the "Outstanding Graduate in the State of Michigan in Music". Out of a field of thirty-three thousand students in the state's music program, I was top dog and, since she was going to be a music major in college like me, I naively thought maybe my prowess at the trombone would somehow make me more alluring to another girl in the band.

I steeled my resolve and asked her out. She said she was flattered, but wondered if I could wait until she found out if Chad would ask her out. Chad did—and she went with him, not me. It made perfect sense: Chad was captain of the football team, strong, athletic. A man. I was just a boy.

I tried romance with a girl again when I was twenty-one. I was working the summer at Epcot Center, performing in the All-American College Orchestra at the American pavilion. It was a highly competitive summer gig, and I was thrilled to be invited. And there, I fell in love.

I dated the first trombone player, a girl from a prestigious music school out east. She was my first real love. We were together for six weeks, and in that time I believed she was the answer to all of my prayers. I just wanted one woman I was attracted to—I didn't need to be attracted to all women, just a woman who could be my wife.

Raised in a Christian home, I memorized Jeremiah 29:11 in my Protestant high school and clung to its promises as a life buoy of hope, so much so that I successfully convinced my fellow classmates to make it our class verse: " 'For I know the plans I have for you,' declares the Lord, 'plans to prosper you and not to harm you, plans to give you hope and a future' " (NIV).

The only hope and future I believed that would prosper me and not harm me was to find just one woman I could love and with whom I could build a family. I thought the woman at Epcot Center was the woman I had been hoping for, so that summer I mapped out a vision of our life together. But it all came crashing down on a manicured lawn in the heart of Epcot Center.

"We have to talk," she said, saying those words so many people have heard before. "It's not you—it's me."

When I found out she broke up with me to date a girl, I didn't believe her—it *was* me. I was so unworthy as a man that she preferred a woman over me—or so I told myself, in my pain and insecurities.

The news devastated me. It confirmed everything I had ever believed about how worthless I was as a man. Women became unsafe to me, and unattainable. My desires for men grew.

Several years later when I was twenty-eight, I tried to put in words how worthless I had always felt around women, and how psychologically impotent I felt around other men. I wrote a poem and called it simply "Ram Poem":

No part play I in this ritual of rams
The rut is called, and I turn to run away.
Others may I meet whose feet are hurried
To the battle grounds:
They bow their heads to test my mettle,
But I, no ram—mere outcast lamb—hug the
    ground in fear,
Cowering in the presence of their towering
    power.

On they bound to find a worthy foe,
While I, merely child, clamber to cliffs far away.
Yet still I hear the crack of their horns, each
    distant echo
Cleaving my soul, crying aloud to me in
    accusation:
"Eunuch! Though art unworthy! Oh ramless
    ram: You are ewe!"
Listening, I lie down alone, licking the wounds
    of my soul,
Where none may mind my mournful bleating.

The scribbles of my draft show how I felt about myself:

A ram am I,
Though some might think me ewe.
A eunuch or lamb am I,
What ewe would call me "mine"?

I wrote, "These horns adorning this brow / Seem a worth-less crown to bear. / I wear them shamefully." It didn't matter that I had the body of a man—I still felt like a boy.

My scribbles showed how much I longed to be "one of the guys", just like the other men I always compared myself to. Even men younger than me seemed more like men than me. "I scurry from mere juveniles / Who jubilantly test their ramhood / Grappled, locked horn to horn / In their breathless struggle to be fully ram."

I remember as I grew older, I started looking with envy at men younger than me who seemed to have a natural and easy confidence about them that I felt I lacked. How did they grow up to be men like they had become? I felt like a boy among men, and now the younger guys who were kids when I was in high school had become men, while I just stayed a boy.

I wrote, envying the confidence I saw in them:

Their aggressiveness—it chills me,
Though I long to play their game.
To eye the other down,
Lowered horns, snorting defiantly.

Oh! Then to run, like a whip!
Full-force, head on to meet them!
"CRACK!" crash the echoes from cliff to cliff,
Proclaiming, "We are fully ram!"

I couldn't compete with men for women. I knew that now.

But I could lock horns in one area and come out on top. After the devastation of my romantic endeavors at the Epcot Center, I decided to close the door on dating. Instead of getting into the game of finding a spouse, I put all of my energies into music. I might not be able to compete in the realm of romance, but trombone playing was something where I could lock horns with anyone.

Six years later I was done with school and had fulfilled my dream: I was a professional member of an orchestra, making my living playing trombone.

And then I realized how miserable and lonely I was.

Flint, Michigan

Though I had a job, I wasn't happy, and my drugs of choice, my source of comfort, were pornography, phone sex, and webcamming. But eventually I grew tired of fantasizing. I wanted the real thing. I'd saved myself for my future wife—I had assumed that a God who loved me, and had plans to prosper me, could at least bring me a wife whom I could love and be loved by. Surely he would honor my thirty-two years of holding back and refraining from having sex? But it just wasn't happening.

All of this made me angry at God. I took to flying the middle finger at the Basilica of St. Adalbert in my hometown. Though I no longer considered myself Catholic (my family had left the Church when I was young), those three copper domes began symbolizing God for me. It became a regular habit for me to flip it off as I drove by, saying, "F—— you, God," in defiance.

I had stopped going to church quite some time ago. I was tired of trying to follow God and his promise of "plans to prosper you and not to harm you." "Bunk! All of it bunk! God's a cruel liar!" I said to myself.

I couldn't deny that God existed. That would have done too much injury to my brain; the New Atheists and their logic made no sense to me. Nor I could I buy what I had read of revisionist gay theology, that God somehow blesses sex between men. No, I believed there was a God and that God didn't bless the way I wanted to live my life.

Instead I consciously rebelled against him, and with a flip of the bird at the basilica, I drove to Flint, Michigan. Flint, Michigan—the former automobile capital for Buick, and now a decimated rust belt city and occasional murder capital of the world per capita—that's where I chose to take my stand against the absurdity of God's commandments, lose my virginity, and claim my freedom, all with a man whom I had only ever met online.

We'd been webcamming for a while. I told him beforehand that I wanted to "get to know him" a bit before we settled down to do the deed. It seemed there needed to be some concord of familiarity before diving right into bed for the first time in my life.

I took him to breakfast. He ordered an omelet. It had raw onions. They were astringent to my nose.

We engaged in small talk, the sort of small talk I suppose that only ever happens between two people who've never met, yet have already seen each other naked.

We went back to his house. He lived in a large home with several other guys. It was a Saturday. Two of them were sitting on the couch, watching a game. I waved awkwardly at them as we climbed the stairs to his room. "Do they know what's going on?" I wondered.

We sat in his room with the door closed. We talked some more.

"How does something like this begin?" I wondered.

Finally we started. The clothes came off, fingers probed, skin touched skin. We kissed. He tasted of onions.

We used a condom. We were being "safe", but I still wondered if I'd get AIDS. All I could think about was venereal diseases, the guys down stairs. And onions.

We cleaned up. I put my clothes back on, said good-bye.

He walked me downstairs. The roommates watched with knowing eyes.

Then I drove home, wondering what I had done.

* * * * *

"That was it?" was all I could think. "I waited thirty-two years, for *that*?"

It was supposed to be amazing.

As I drove home across Michigan I was filled with disgust for myself. The sex was unmemorable. I wouldn't be fantasizing about or reliving that moment over and over again in my mind.

Where was my personal dignity? Was I going to give up my thirty-two-year-old virginity to just turn into a slut?

The reality of what I had done came crashing down on me and, for a time, caused me to consider repentance. But I wasn't ready for that just yet. If I was going to turn my back on God and his silly commandments, I wasn't going to turn my back on a sense of basic morality. I didn't want to become a whore. Random sex with a stranger wasn't what I really wanted. It made me feel undignified and horribly trashy. What I wanted was a boyfriend. So I went looking for him.

I set up an account on Yahoo dating sites for men. It took about a year, but I found a good man. I didn't do anything with any guys in that time. I wanted to be as traditional—and moral—as I could be, even though I was looking now for a life partner who was a man. What I wanted was what everyone else had available: someone to love and be loved by, with whom I could share my life. I didn't want to be alone, and I wanted to be able to have a sexual life. Jason and I started chatting one night, and our friendship flourished. I told him my entire story, my hopes and dreams, my religious background, as well as how I didn't feel any connection at all with the out and proud gay community. He felt much the same—we were just two regular guys who weren't interested in political activism or shock, or going to gay bars, or any of the more wild aspects of gay life. We just wanted a best friend and lover.

We finally decided to meet. It was as much like a date as I had ever had with a woman before, but far more exciting for me. We had dinner, then saw a movie. Our first physical contact was holding hands in the darkness of the theater. It *felt* right, and it filled me with great warmth and happiness.

We went on a few more dates and often chatted late into the night online. He learned of my career as a musician; I learned of his life and dreams. Soon we were in a relationship. Jason accepted me, and I loved him for it. I finally had someone whom I could share my life with—I could call him when I had a bad day, or share with him something interesting that happened at work. I was the same for him. And of course we had sex. Not often—certainly not as often as I would have liked—but when we had it, I enjoyed it. Our relationship wasn't about sex though.

What we both really wanted, I'm convinced, was a deep and abiding friendship. I really think that at the bottom of any male gay relationship, what motivates men more than anything else is a deep void that stems from a lack of communion and relationship with other men. Sex with another man is a powerful and intoxicating attempt at deep and abiding intimacy, but sex will never be the answer to the true intimacy those men are really looking for. It's hard to see this truth, though, while you're in a relationship.

Jason's love was what I thought would bring me happiness. We were together for a year, and it was, honestly, in my experience, a happy year. It's absurd to believe that men who are in a relationship together don't feel happy, just because it's opposed to God's commandments, or to argue, as I've seen some Christians do, that men and women in gay relationships must *feel* miserable because they're living outside of God's plan for humanity. Such arguments will never convince anyone who is *in* a relationship to end it. Because when they look at their relationship, they usually believe that they're better off now than they were before. Such was the case with me.

But there's an important distinction here that one of my good friends has said of his own past life, when he was active in a gay relationship. He was happy then—*but only as happy as he knew how to be.*

I was happy with Jason, but only as happy as I knew how to be. What should have been, and could have been, a deep and intimate friendship between two men who longed for closeness with another became tainted with romance and sex, a situation that will never be appropriate between two people of the same sex. And our sexual relationship blinded us both to the truth of our situation.

Here I think of what Saint John Chrysostom said in a homily about Romans 1:26–27, where Saint Paul states that "God gave them up to dishonorable passions. Their women exchanged natural relations for unnatural, and the men likewise gave up natural relations with women and were consumed with passion for one another, men committing shameless acts with men and receiving in their own persons the due penalty for their error." Saint Paul, Chrysostom says, "shows that the punishment was in [the] pleasure itself." Chrysostom could have been writing of me when I was in the throes of enjoying my sexual life with Jason: "If they perceive it not, but are still pleased, be not amazed." I didn't know what was sane in the realm of human sexuality. I was driven mad by my passions and lusts. "For even they that are mad," says Chrysostom, "and are afflicted with phrenzy, while doing themselves much injury and making themselves such objects of compassion, that others weep over them themselves smile and revel over what has happened."[1] How true this was of me! G. K. Chesterton once wrote, "About sex especially men are born unbalanced; we might almost say men are born mad. They scarcely reach sanity till they reach sanctity."[2]

I couldn't see clearly then what I see clearly now. I thought I would be sharing my life with Jason for the rest of my life. I was certain that this was the way I was. I was preparing to tell my friends and family and find a way to finally "come out".

I had come to terms with my faith too. I didn't care if God was angry with me—I was angry with him, so we were even.

I was trying to figure out how best to come out, and when to do it. I was determined to live my life openly, as a gay man, but I just didn't know when or how to do it. And then I went to a party for work. What happened shattered all of my plans—and just made me drive around the basilica an extra time, flipping off God, more angry than ever with him.

[1] St. Chrysostom: Homilies on the Acts of the Apostles and the Epistle to the Romans, vol. 11 of A Select Library of the Nicene and Post-Nicene Fathers of the Christian Church, 1st series, ed. Philip Schaff (New York: Charles Scribner's Sons, 1899), p. 357.

[2] G. K. Chesterton, The Everlasting Man, in The Collected Works of G. K. Chesterton (San Francisco: Ignatius Press, 1986), 2:248.

Kelly

Meeting Kelly at that party changed my life. A friend had been trying to introduce me to her for a while. Not knowing about Jason, he assumed I was interested in dating women. She worked in his office with him, and he thought we had a lot in common. To appease him I agreed to meet her. It was just a bother to put him off any longer. I figured I'd chat with her, be friendly, and then tell him that I appreciated his interest in my life, but that I just didn't click with her.

But then I met her.

I found Kelly stunningly beautiful. I hadn't been attracted to women for several years. I was stunned at how attractive she was to me. That wasn't supposed to happen to me anymore—I'm a gay guy, right? It was all so confusing.

I enjoyed talking to her too. We talked and talked; it was a bowling party, and I constantly needed to be reminded when it was my turn to bowl. We had common interests. She had been a music major in college, but had decided that music as a career wasn't for her. She worked at a bookstore—so she was a lover of music and a lover of books! And she was *beautiful*.

How could this be? Women for me had become scary—best kept at a distance. I tended to view women like the female spiders who kill their mate after becoming impregnated. Women weren't really to be trusted with your heart. They'd control you and stifle you and flatten you out until you were nothing but a pawn for whatever web they desired to spin for your life. And they'd always hurt you. Naturally this wasn't a healthy view, nor really conducive to romance.

But something about Kelly sliced a hole through all of the doubts and misgivings and fears I had of women. I didn't want the evening to end, and it seemed Kelly had enjoyed herself too.

I drove home with a tumult of emotions. How did it happen that I was suddenly and inexplicably attracted to this woman? What did this mean? Why did I feel such a thrill in conversing with her? And why did the thought of wanting to see her again consume me? I had butterflies in my stomach around her just like I had felt for my first love at Epcot. I thought I would never have these feelings again.

To be honest, I didn't want to have those feelings for a woman again. I had put a stake in the ground: I am a man who loves men. I'm *gay*. Women are nothing to me—just friends, never lovers, never allowed into my life to hurt me like I had felt I had been hurt before. And yet Kelly burned a hole through all of my defenses, all of my fears, all of my doubts. All of my defenses were built from stones made of ice. I erected walls of protection from the pain I experienced at the hands of women—unresolved, unhealed pain that closed my heart from ever letting a woman get close to me ever again. Kelly was so kind, so pleasant to talk to, and so beautiful to me that the walls I had erected around my heart started to melt.

A few days later I went to the bookstore where Kelly worked to try to make sense of all of this. I was nervous as I spotted her in the distance working in the music department, ringing up a customer buying a CD. She hadn't seen me yet, but she looked as beautiful as I remembered her. I lingered on the fringes until she finished her transaction, then walked toward her as she sorted through a stack of CDs.

"Excuse me, could you perhaps give me a hand finding a recording?" I said as I approached her, a bit out of sight.

She turned around, ready to help a customer, but then she saw me, and said, "What are *you* doing here?" She smiled.

"Well," I said, "I wanted to see you again. I had such a nice time talking with you the other day that I decided I'd come and pretend I wanted to buy a recording."

I really didn't know how guys talked to women they found attractive, but all I could do was try. I figured showing interest was the most important thing, and I hoped she'd be impressed that I drove to her town to see her. Or else she'd find it creepy. But I was willing to take the gamble so I could make sense of the feelings I had started to have since the party.

"I had a good time talking to you too. I'm just so surprised to see you," she said and added, "but it's nice to see you, too."

In between customers we chatted. It was so pleasant to be in her company. I made her laugh; she smiled and it made me happy. After about a half an hour or so, we both realized that she needed to get back to work, unhindered by my attentions.

"Could we get together again sometime?" I asked.

She looked up at me with a kindly smile and said, "Yes. I'd like that."

"So would I," I said, grinning from ear to ear. "I'd like that very much."

With that, I left, with promises to call her soon. I strode out to my car like a reborn man, with a feeling of joy that was hard to understand.

* * * * *

With the joy came confusion. Why, when I was getting ready to "come out" to my family and friends, had Kelly come into my life? This rocked my world and my certainty. I was in love with Jason—of that there was no doubt. But meeting Kelly rang a bell that wouldn't stop ringing, with vibrations that grew and rumbled through the foundation of the world I had been creating, causing it to crumble.

The weeks after meeting Kelly were turbulent ones. When we agreed to meet for lunch, I did feel like I was engaging in some sort of betrayal of Jason, but I rationalized this all by saying to myself, "Maybe Kelly and I will just become friends. And I'd eventually introduce her to Jason even." I was determined to tell Jason about her—and very soon. Yet I needed to see where this road would lead. Being attracted to a woman again after such a long time was unnerving but exhilarating too.

Kelly and I met for lunch on a wintry day in January. It was a joy to talk to her, and she seemed to enjoy my company as well. The time went by too fast.

I walked her to her car. The snow had fallen and left a dusting on her windshield.

"Here, let me clear that off for you," I said, surprised at how much joy it brought me to do that for her.

"Thank you, Dan," she said. "I had a really nice time."

"So did I," I said. "Could we do this again?"

"Yes, I'd like that."

"Me too."

The snow fell around her, leaving crystals of snow on her red wool jacket, pulled tight against her rosy cheeks.

"Can I give you a hug?" I asked, rather sheepishly.

She smiled in reply. "Yes, I'd enjoy that too."

We hugged, and I promised that I would call her again.

I waved as she went on her way, and then walked to my car to brush off the snow that had collected. My life was blanketed in mystery, just like the landscape around me. I had no idea what I was going to do.

* * * * *

I loved Jason. I had planned on sharing my life with him. But that plan had come about because I no longer was attracted to women. I was gay and wasn't supposed to be attracted to women. Here, unlooked for and unplanned, came a woman who not only was attractive to me; remarkably, she was attracted to me too! It was all horribly confusing. What I did know is that I needed to tell Jason about all of this.

The next time we saw each other I determined to tell him everything. I fixed dinner for him and that afternoon planned to tell him all that had been going on in my life. I remember it vividly. We had eaten dinner and were cuddling on my couch. I told him everything—I told him how irritated I had been at my friend for bugging me about meeting Kelly, how we met at the party, and that I was so surprised that I was attracted to her. I told him that meeting her renewed my long-dormant dreams of having a family. I told him I didn't know what to do about all of this, and asked him what he thought. He was silent for several moments as we lay next to each other. What he said astounded me.

"Dan," he said, "I know how much you have wanted to be a father. And I know how hard this life can be too. If you can have that life you dreamed of having, I want you to have it. You'd make a good father, you know." Tears welled up in his eyes and in mine. "I love you enough that I want you to have those dreams fulfilled, if there's any way possible." I held him tight, as we both cried.

The Ring

Jason did a remarkable thing. He cared for me more than he cared for himself. We were living outside of God's plan for human sexuality—I recognize that now. But in that moment he showed a Christ-like act of selfless, self-sacrificial love. When I look at same-sex couples, I always call to mind Jason and his love for me. Christians who affirm traditional sexual morality can often become judgmental and assume that the lives of same-sex couples are mired in selfish hedonism. This wasn't the case with Jason and me—we didn't have sex all that often anyway, and in this moment, I saw a pure love, a love like Jesus. No matter how lost a man may be, the image of God always calls to him, urging him to live out the nobility of his birthright. In that moment of selfless love, Jason loved me by laying down his hopes and dreams, for his friend. No greater love can be found than that. Yes, we were sinners, but we were stumbling through life the best way we knew how, as well as we understood, seeking out happiness where we thought it could be found. We didn't know any better, and yet in our relationship, he loved me with a Christ-like act of self-sacrificial love. I'll never forget it, and to my dying days I'll say that Jason is one of the best and most noble men I've ever known.

With Jason's leave and blessing, I started seeing Kelly with great trepidation. I expected it all to come crashing down at any moment just like all of my past attempts at dating. She'd figure out I wasn't attractive, or figure out that I was just a shadow of a man, rather than the man she thought I was.

But it never happened. She genuinely liked me, and I genuinely liked her. And if I thought she was beautiful the first day I met her, I didn't know how beautiful she really was. She was the most beautiful woman in the world to me—and still is. It all seemed too good to be true.

One month stretched into two, then we had been together for a half a year. The longest I'd ever dated a woman was six weeks. This seemed like a lifetime.

Summer came and with it adventures to Lake Michigan, to the quaint beach towns of Douglas and Saugatuck, where we toured art galleries and shops, grabbing a taste of gelato at a place called American Spoon and a drink at the local brewery. We took a trip north, wine tasting along Old Mission Peninsula, a finger of land that divides the Grand Traverse Bay in two. As we climbed the winding road that pierced the peninsula, we could see the deep blue water of the lake on either side of us. Row upon row of grapevines wound their way down the slopes, leading down to the water below. The sun was shining, the windows were down, the sunroof open. Kelly's hair was perpetually getting in her eyes, but we were happy. The weather was fine, the sky was blue, and we felt the warmth and glow of the sparkling white wines that flourish and do so well in northern Michigan. I was happier than I had ever been in my life.

The dog days of summer melted into fall. With it came trips to cider mills and walks through the woods, bedecked with falling leaves in the autumnal glow of a Michigan fall. Snow came, and we were still together. It seemed too good to be true. Christmas was soon upon us, and we went to a Christmas tree farm together, to pick out *our* tree. We walked through the trees, sipping hot cocoa as we compared this tree to that one, until we finally picked out just the right one. I cut it down and hauled it out to the car.

I set the tree up at home, with a fire roaring in the fireplace. Nat King Cole crooned on the speakers, while the snow fell outside. There was something so different with Kelly than with Jason. It was richer; it was more ful-filling—it was more mysterious than being with a man. I began to understand the beauty of the differences in the sexes. Life with Jason was easy; times with Kelly could be more challenging, but in the challenge of trying to understand the way a woman thinks was a surprised-and-unlooked-for thrill. Something C.S. Lewis wrote echoes what I learned in my time with Kelly. He writes of a moment in John Milton's *Paradise Lost* when Eve first awakes. She sees herself reflected in a pool before she sees Adam, and she is struck by her own beauty. Indeed, when she sees Adam, she's at first disappointed—she turns back to the beauty of her own reflection in the pool. Yet she listens and heeds the voice of God, pointing her to her true companion. Lewis says that once she crosses this bridge, "she lives to learn that being in love with Adam is more inexhaustible, more fruitful, and even better fun, than being in love with herself."[1] That's the way it was for me too; after Kelly, love with a man doesn't hold a candle compared to what it was like to experience man's true sexual complementarity.

After Christmas, and the turn of the year, we began reflecting on our relationship. We got along splendidly. I was the first man Kelly met whom she ever imagined set-tling down with. She once said that I had shown her that

---

[1] C.S. Lewis, "Religion: Reality or Substitute?" in *Christian Reflections*, ed. Walter Hooper (Grand Rapids: William B. Eerdmans, 2014), p. 48.

it was possible for two people to fit together, like lock and key. Such was my love for her.

But there was a problem with our future together. Though I wanted a family, Kelly had never wanted children. It was one of the only sources of conflict between us. We rarely fought or quarreled. The question of children, however, needed to be resolved. We didn't discuss it much, but after winter stretched to spring, and summer came, it seemed we needed to make a decision.

Those were difficult conversations. We found ourselves at an impasse. When I suggested the possibility that maybe we could have a relationship, and I'd forgo my dreams of children, she didn't like that idea—she thought I'd resent her the rest of my life.

We decided to take a break. It was August, and we came to a point of decision: What was the point of going on if we couldn't come to agreement about children?

I realized I was so in love with her that if I saw her often, I'd always fall back in love with her all over again. I wanted her in my life, more than anything in the world. If I was going to have any chance of seeing things clearly, I'd need a long break from seeing her. We took a year off from seeing each other so each of us could weigh our options. It was dreadfully painful for me.

I don't think anyone understood why I was so miserable following our breakup. I was living a horribly painful life. Only a handful knew that Kelly was more than just a regular breakup. She was the first woman I had ever met whom I thought I could really share my life with.

There was a part of me that believed after a year and a half with Kelly, I had somehow been miraculously transformed into a ladies' man. But that wasn't really the case. Kelly was a woman I loved. She didn't represent all women for me. It was her—specifically her—whom I fell in love with, all of her, and it was all of what made her uniquely herself that I loved.

I tried dating other women. The litmus test for me was if they were remotely attractive. I asked out some women, but these dates never went anywhere. How could they? I was still in love with Kelly. I limped through the year, as best I could. I leaned on friends who promised all would be well.

Yet my heart was heavy. I was as in love with Kelly as ever. As the months progressed I reflected on what to do. I began praying too.

Kelly seemed like a gift to me. If there's a gift, there must be a giver. I didn't believe that it was an accident that Kelly came into my life; I was healed in so many ways in the year and a half that we were together.

Saint Paul asks the Romans, "Do you not know that God's kindness is meant to lead you to repentance?" (Rom 2:4). I found in Kelly a renewed belief in God's kindness, and the gift of her in my life slowly wooed me back to Jesus. I approached him with as much trepidation as I had begun dating Kelly. I would only go to church occasionally, but the seed of belief was planted again.

So I prayed, asking God what to do about my sorrow surrounding Kelly. I don't believe I had an answer, but I sought him out. It seemed, though, that I was left to make up my own mind. In all of my reflection, I always came to the same conclusion: the only woman I could ever love, or ever wanted to love, was Kelly. Of all the women in the world, of all women who had come before, or who might come after, I would choose Kelly above all others. I didn't care about children. I weighed hypothetical children in the balance on one hand, and the tangible reality of Kelly on the other. My love didn't ebb with the passage of time. It had only grown and blossomed. I was miserable without her and had been so happy with her.

What I needed to do was to resolve the question once and for all. I wanted to share my life with Kelly, and I needed to tell her that I did and make it as clear as day.

I made a plan. I bought a ring—not an engagement ring; we hadn't seen each other or hardly spoken in the past year. But it was a beautiful ring, with thirty-two tiny little diamonds on it, in a pattern that I knew she would love. I called her up and asked to see her again and planned to give her the ring.

I told her I would bring food for lunch from her favorite restaurant. We planned to meet at 12:30, and so I ordered flowers to be delivered, precisely at 1:00. "Be sure it's not earlier, not later!" I told them.

A few days later I drove to her house, filled with great hope and a little fear, but whatever might happen, I could finally move on with my life. I just hoped and prayed that it would be with her.

Unrequited Me

On September 10, 2007, just a few days after I saw her, I wrote in my journal, "This chapter didn't turn out the way I had hoped." A few days later, reeling in pain, I described the day in my journal:

September 18, 2007

It's safe to say that in my 37 years on this earth, these past few weeks have been the most painful moments I've experienced. I'm certain that I will have greater pain in my life than this—I still haven't lost anyone from my immediate family, nor any of my closest friends. But for now, this is the apex, or perhaps more accurately the nadir, and it's been difficult. I suppose some could try to dismiss the intensity of the pain I feel since it's "just a break-up," but it's so much more than that for me, since it's a death of a vision and hope I had that I had found my soul mate after at least 20 years of yearning to find her. Through this intense pain, however, I feel that I am learning lessons about life, and I have seen the hand of God working in my life.

As I drove the half hour home from her house, my brother Steve called me to see how I was doing. As I spoke with him, I began weeping like I had never done before nor knew possible. At that moment, another phone call came in, which I obviously couldn't answer. On the arc of my life, that moment—the moment when that second call came—is the most intense moment of pain I have ever felt in my life.

Exhausted, I went straight to bed when I came home, but awoke again at 11:00 P.M. or so. Even though it was late, I returned the call I missed earlier that night. My friend Bob answered the phone, and I sensed a strain in his usually lighthearted voice. It didn't take long for me to understand why. His wife was going in the next day for an emergency hysterectomy, and he wanted to know if I could sit with him while she was in surgery.

It seemed impossible to consider such a thing, still so deep in the pain of losing Kelly. Yet it seemed to me that God was showing me what he wants us to do with our pain and suffering: he wants us to use our suffering to enter into the suffering of others. There were connections between our pain, his and mine. That night, I lost the person who I had hoped more than anything would become my soul mate. His pain was linked to a fear that he would lose his soul mate of over forty years. The timing of his call to me, exactly coinciding with the darkest moment of my life, was no coincidence to me either. It was as if God was saying, "I know your pain—live in it, feel it, embrace it fully, and minister to your fellow man through it."

I did sit with him the next day, and thankfully his wife was fine. It was good for both of us to be together, and he was very grateful—and so was I. In sharing our sorrows, each of our sorrows was eased.

As I reflected on this in my journal, I wrote,

I definitely subscribe to the Catholic view of redemptive suffering, suffering willingly embraced and offered up as a sacrifice on behalf of someone else. It's an intriguing proposition that Paul lays out in the following passage: "I find joy in the sufferings I endure for you. In my own flesh

I fill up what is lacking in the sufferings of Christ for the sake of His Body, the Church" (Col. 1:24). I believe that Christ invites us to participate in the redemption of the world through our suffering, and in some small way I saw this sitting with my friend Bob.

As I move forward, the ache in my heart ebbs and flows. I still feel very raw, and I'm still very confused and hurt and there is little joy to be found of late. Clearly through the grace of God, I made a decision that every time I feel a stab of pain, or grieve the loss of a future I had hoped for with all my heart, that I would embrace that pain and sorrow, and offer it up on behalf of Kelly. I can't necessarily share Paul's noble words and say that I find joy in the pain, but when I consciously offer that pain up for Kelly, I find myself saying, "Bring it on!" I willingly endure it, and find that indeed I can embrace it, and in so doing, I find it is much more tolerable for me, since now it has a purpose. Anytime I think of her, I pray for her, that she would be wooed by the savior of the world, that the Hound of Heaven would doggedly pursue her, and that she would be filled with the love of Christ. I pray for healing for her, and that she would have a life filled with joy. In my more noble moments, I strive to pray that the man she ends up with will cherish and treasure her as much as I had hoped to do. It seems at those moments, I always tend to whisper a desperate prayer that that man be me.

This morning, I awoke with a profound sense of loss and loneliness, coupled with a palpable longing for companionship. I realize this is the season that I am living in right now, and I'm sure I'll feel this again tomorrow and the next day and the day after that. I feel as if I've begun a hard journey, climbing into the unknown, since I don't know where the road will take me, or how far I need to journey. I feel like Sam and Frodo traveling in a desolate and barren land. But this is our lot in life often, is it not? I feel that for the first time in my life, I truly know what my cross is, and I will take it up each day and bear it on behalf of Kelly. I think that's the only way that I will find my way out of this morass, and the only way I can make sense of the pain I feel, on a nearly constant basis. But oh, dear God! I pray that you heed the deepest desire of my heart, that you would call Kelly to yourself. Please may it be so! I pray that you would answer the cry of my heart, and answer it speedily and quickly! Draw her to you, dear God, and heal the wounds of her heart, just as I ask you to do the same for me.

It's uncomfortable rereading that these many years later. It sounds a bit melodramatic to me now—yet the desire to transform the suffering I was feeling, and to make of it something positive, to try and mold it into an expression of love, was genuine. I realize now that all of this pain was allowed by God, in part because he was planting the seeds of my return to the Catholic faith. The water that fertilized my homecoming was suffering.

I didn't know what pain was until I lost Kelly. Even now, as I think back on those feelings, their echo makes me flinch. I don't want to ever go through that sort of pain again. A poem I wrote at the time expressed the pain I felt in losing her.

Schism

It is like a death, this loss of you,
A loss I do not understand.
Yet this I know:
You love me not.

Your love for me has
Shriveled and dried.
Scorched by a hellish sun,
Desiccated to a gritty dust.

I grasp at the remnant of my dreams,
But they pour through my fingers,
Blown by a bitter wind,
Irretrievably scattered into the chasm between us.

I don't think those around me understood why the loss of her devastated me so much. But most of them didn't know that I had despaired of ever being married, or having a family, because I didn't find women attractive or desirable. Yet after the death of the dream I thought would bring happiness to me, I started to see glimmers that all of the suffering I had ever lived with might actually have meaning and purpose. For the pain I suffered was doing God's work; I was beginning to learn one of the most important lessons we can ever learn: the cross we receive is always the cross we need.

The Wound of Living

When I lost Kelly, I began reading everything I could get my hands on about suffering. I looked first at my shelf, and one of the books I turned to was Peter Kreeft's *Making Sense Out of Suffering*, a book I had picked up and read several years before.

I wrote:

October 9, 2007

I've been rereading an excellent book by Peter Kreeft called *Making Sense Out of Suffering*. There's one paragraph in particular that rang forth like a bell for me.

"All our sufferings are transformable into his work, our passion into his action. That is why he instituted prayers, says Pascal: to bestow on creatures the dignity of causality."[1]

Kreeft goes on:

We are really his body; the Church is Christ as my body is me. That is why Paul says his sufferings are making up in his own body what Christ has yet to endure in his body (Col 1:24).

Thus God's answer to the problem of suffering not only really happened 2,000 years ago, but it is still happening in our own lives. The solution to our suffering is our suffering! *All our suffering can become part of his work, the greatest*

[1] Peter Kreeft, *Making Sense Out of Suffering* (Ann Arbor, Mich.: Servant Books, 1986), p. 136.

work ever done, the work of salvation, of helping to win for those
we love eternal joy.[2]

That last bit of text in italics was something I had underlined years ago when I first read this book. But as you
can imagine, it means much more to me now, since there
is someone who I love dearly, and for whom my greatest desire is that she might find eternal joy. If I can be a
part of winning that for her, I'd be the happiest man on
the planet.

I had plenty of opportunities to practice what I learned
from Peter Kreeft, for things would remain painful and
dark for a long time. I often found myself on the verge of
tears. Part of my solace came through poetry, especially
this poem by the Dominican priest Father Paul Murray:

A Note on Human Passion

Sacred or profane—it does not matter—
one must not anaesthetize
or dull the pain
but instead sustain
the splintered heart's
helpless yet terrifying
and sharp desire
never to be healed
of the wound of living.[3]

"The wound of living" seemed to be all that I was experiencing. But I refused to anesthetize it. I wanted to travel
through it, as best I could. I was inspired to follow C. S.
Lewis' example as dramatized in the film *Shadowlands*,

<hr />

[2] Ibid. (italics added).
[3] Paul Murray, *The Absent Fountain* (Dublin: Dedalus Press, 1991), p. 28.

which portrays Lewis' wife's death from cancer, and the grief he experienced. In a poignant moment of the film, Lewis reflects on the loss of his mother to cancer as a young boy, and the loss of his wife, Joy Davidman, to the same disease so many years later.

I recalled the scene in my journal:

> Sometimes when I feel the pain, I wish I could numb it, turn it off, or excise it from my heart, but I can't, and honestly, I really don't want to do that. I think that's incredibly unhealthy—to willfully choose to ignore the pain one is feeling isn't good at all. I am living in it, each day, and I'm not going to kill it because I don't like it. I think there is much yet for me to learn. As is the case for me so often, I think of C.S. Lewis. One of the best quotes from one of my favorite movies, *Shadowlands*, speaks to how I feel: "Why love, if losing hurts so much? I have no answers anymore: only the life I have lived. Twice in that life I've been given the choice: as a boy and as a man. The boy chose safety, the man chooses suffering. The pain now is part of the happiness then. That's the deal."[4]
>
> I'm not choosing safety.

"Safety" for me would have been to turn my back on God again, or to go and find another boyfriend—or maybe see if things could work out with Jason again. But I had turned a corner. I had discovered the truth that my feelings didn't define me—I wasn't a gay man, but simply a man, like any other. I now trusted that God gave us his commandments because of his love for us, like signposts warning us to stay away from the many tempting byways splitting off from the path that leads to the blessed life. At

---

[4] *Shadowlands*, directed by Richard Attenborough, written by William Nicholson (New York: Savoy Pictures, 1993).

this point, the only path that made any sense to me was the path of Christ, and that meant in part suffering, just like Lewis learned.

Yet despite my noble impulses to "offer it all up" for Kelly, and to not try to dull the pain I felt, there were lessons God still was teaching me. He's always teaching us; he's always cleaning us up—and the process is always painful. I needed to see how much of the pain I was feeling was rooted in the dark parts of my heart.

What I saw there was ugly:

Saturday, December 15, 2007

I was mistaken when I said earlier this week that I felt like the storm was passing. I was lulled into thinking that a calm breeze in the air meant the worst was over. It seems that the storm has begun anew, but with increased intensity and with new forces at work.... I feel as if I'm in the middle of a volcanic thunderstorm where the air is filled with acrid stench. It turns out there is sulphur in my heart. I have found myself filled with an intense hatred towards Kelly, the intensity of which I have never felt before in my life.... I am tempted to live in that hatred and to feed it and feel nothing but vitriol towards her.

These feelings have taken me by surprise, but they shouldn't, should they? I am after all a mere man, a son of Adam, a fallen creature. The natural response of a man is to feel anger and hatred towards anyone who has harmed him.... It's awful, isn't it? I think this could be the most profound struggle I will need to face in all of this: to love her anyway....

I've been thinking a lot about grace lately.... In the past, I would have really beaten myself up for feeling like I do about Kelly right now and telling myself that I need to stop those feelings at whatever the cost. Stifling is better than living in a moment of hatred, right? I'm not so convinced of that now. My growing understanding of grace is this: God KNOWS us, and knows how we are and knows our weaknesses and strengths. Grace to me is a God who says, "I understand your weakness—I love you anyway." He of course says to us to go and sin no more, but this I know: God understands why I'm feeling hatred towards Kelly right now. He doesn't excuse it or condone it, but he certainly understands it. As for me, I think it's part of the process of healing, and in some anthropological framework, I think I need to go through this phase, and work through it, and fight it, to wrestle with it. God is there, and understands better than anyone the profound pain and heartbreak I've felt over this.... I'm not proud of it, but God understands. And He forgives me. Where sin is, grace abounds (cf. Rom 5:20). Thank God.

There exists in all of us, I believe, that petulant child who wants the world to be exactly as we wish it, and when we don't get our way, we throw tantrums. The rage in my heart is just such a tantrum. I demand that she loves me.... I have found that unrequited love can produce the most intense feelings of hatred. I don't think there's an uglier thing than love turned to hatred. In *The Four Loves*, C. S. Lewis talks about love transformed into hatred. He would argue that it was never love in the first place, but just selfish desire springing from our needs.... Right now, that has reared its awful, ugly head and I see it for the monster it is.

As usual, Lewis provides great insight for me:

> Need-love cries to God from our poverty; Gift-love longs to serve, or even to suffer, for God; Appreciative love says: "We give thanks to thee for thy great glory." Need-love says of a woman, "I cannot live without her"; Gift-love longs to give her happiness, comfort, protection—if possible, wealth; Appreciative love gazes and holds its breath and is silent, rejoices that such a wonder should exist even

if not for him, will not be wholly dejected by losing her,
would rather have it so than never to have seen her at all.[5]

It's clear that what I'm feeling right now is motivated by
"need-love" and is rooted in my pride at being rejected by
her and by desiring to have what she provided me.

It would seem that these words of Lewis were written
for me:

> Love anything, and your heart will certainly be wrung and
> possibly be broken. If you want to make sure of keeping
> it intact, you must give your heart to no one, not even to
> an animal. Wrap it carefully round with hobbies and little
> luxuries; avoid all entanglements; lock it up safe in the
> casket or coffin of your selfishness. But in that casket—
> safe, dark, motionless, airless—it will change. It will not
> be broken; it will become unbreakable, impenetrable,
> irredeemable. The alternative to tragedy, or at least to
> the risk of tragedy, is damnation. The only place outside
> Heaven where you can be perfectly safe from all the dan-
> gers and perturbations of love is Hell.[6]

I'm not interested in damnation, so I'm not going to
keep my love in a coffin. But right now, my heart is a
volcano erupting from the depths of my soul. Not a pretty
sight. May God help me to love her.

Probably the most difficult lesson for me to learn was how
many of my desires for her happiness were tainted by some
perverse sense of myself being "the noble one". All that talk
of "offering up my suffering" for her salvation revealed the
taint of self-righteousness and self-aggrandizement within
me. As I would pat myself on the back, I'd say to myself,
"Look how noble I am." Sometimes the feeling of "being
the noble one" becomes a drug to ease our pain.

[5] C. S. Lewis, *The Four Loves* (New York: Harcourt Brace, 1960), p. 17.
[6] Ibid., p. 121.

Yet even so, those feelings and desires were genuine, even though tainted by the weakness that comes from my humanity. What good can we ever do that is free from the taint of pride, or desire for adulation, or simply the good feelings "being noble" brings us?

I have become more convinced since then of the grace of God. He accepts even our feeble and tainted attempts at doing good, since he knows our weaknesses. It is a great comfort to realize that any good we do is Christ in us, actually doing the good. If there has ever been a noble impulse in me, it didn't come from me; so when I look back on those moments of wishing for Kelly's happiness and salvation, the good that was there was Christ in me. The selfish part, the part that used the noble feelings as a drug to ease the pain—well, that's me, plain and simple. And when you look your weakness straight in the face, sometimes, all you can do is chuckle at how predictable you are. You've got to have a sense of humor about acquiring virtue, a sense of humor that comes from knowing that on our own, we're pretty much a mess.

And here's the thing too: when we know that any good we ever do is the grace of God in our lives, we can choose the good intentions that come our way, and trust that God will give us the strength to follow them. I really started to learn what it meant to actually love Kelly long after we broke up. It was only then that I saw her as she really is: a beloved daughter of God whose happiness meant more than anything in the world to me. God used the pain of her loss like a purifying fire that helped me see her the way he saw her, and then gave me the desire, as well as the grace, to offer up my loneliness on behalf of her happiness—and eventually for others too, a sure sign that I was starting to grow up. It's remarkable, really—and so countercultural that it could only come from God. I was finally learning what love was all about.

Courage

The loss of Kelly made me think of my whole life differently. I began thinking about homosexuality not so much through the lens of sexuality, but rather through the lens of suffering. The more I read of the Catholic understanding of redemptive suffering, the more I was able to make sense of why God had allowed same-sex attractions in my life, and the sadness I felt after things didn't work out with Kelly. Somewhere along the way I read Pope Saint John Paul II's apostolic letter on suffering, *Salvifici Doloris*; there I finally began to understand what my same-sex attractions were a sign of—I didn't have a sexual orientation toward men. Rather, I realize I live with a sexual *disorientation*, which is the lack of something within me that should be present. It is a sign that I suffer from the privation of the good of experiencing my true sexual orientation.

Pope Saint John Paul II put it this way:

> Man suffers on account of evil, which is a certain lack, limitation or distortion of good. We could say that man suffers *because of a good* in which he does not share, from which in a certain sense he is cut off, or of which he has deprived himself.... Thus, in the Christian view, the reality of suffering is explained through evil, which always, in some way, refers to a good.[1]

[1]John Paul II, apostolic letter *Salvifici Doloris*, On the Christian Meaning of Human Suffering (February 11, 1984), no. 7, https://w2.vatican.va/content /john-paul-ii/en/apost_letters/1984/documents/hf_jp-ii_apl_11021984 _salvifici-doloris.html (italics in original; hereafter cited as *SD*).

As I considered the meaning of suffering in man's life, I realized that one reason God had allowed these unwanted attractions in me, and the suffering I endured because of them, was because through my suffering, God invited me to love others. Pope Saint John Paul II says, "Love is ... the fullest source of the answer to the question of the meaning of suffering. This answer has been given by God to man in the Cross of Jesus Christ."[2]

I learned more than this. Not only is our suffering an invitation to love. Suffering that is allowed by God becomes our vocation, which finally gives a meaning to the question why God allows suffering to exist in the world:

> For it is above all a call. It is a vocation. Christ does not explain in the abstract the reasons for suffering, but before all else he says: "Follow me!" Come! Take part through your suffering in this work of saving the world, a salvation achieved through my suffering! Through my Cross. Gradually, *as the individual takes up his cross,* spiritually uniting himself to the Cross of Christ, the salvific meaning of suffering is revealed before him. He does not discover this meaning at his own human level, but at the level of the suffering of Christ. At the same time, however, from this level of Christ the salvific meaning of suffering *descends to man's level* and becomes, in a sense, the individual's personal response. It is then that man finds in his suffering interior peace and even spiritual joy.[3]

These thoughts helped me to be "renewed by the transforming of my mind" (cf. Rom 12:2) about homosexuality. It only made sense through understanding the beauty of the cross. I kept writing and writing, and felt I needed to write a book.

[2] *SD* 13.
[3] *SD* 26 (italics in original).

I told my godparents about what I had been doing. They invited me to attend the Courage Apostolate's national conference in 2009, held at Villanova University outside Philadelphia. The Courage Apostolate is a public association of the faithful that provides pastoral care and support for men and women who experience same-sex attractions (SSA) and who have made a free choice to live chaste lives following the teachings of the Catholic Church. Terence Cardinal Cooke, then Archbishop of New York, became convinced in the early 1980s that such a ministry was necessary, and he turned to Father Benedict Groeschel and Father John Harvey, O.S.F.S., to make plans for it. The first Courage members met in Manhattan in late September 1980, and Father Harvey led the apostolate for nearly thirty years. Today the apostolate includes chapters throughout the United States and in more than a dozen countries overseas.

My godparents had been involved with Courage for many years, because their own son lives with attraction to the same sex. They eventually became the leaders of EnCourage, the arm of the Courage Apostolate that serves the pastoral needs of friends and families of those who live with SSA. Thus, when they heard that I was considering writing a book, they suggested I come to the national conference to see what advice and counsel I might get on publishing my thoughts.

I had no intention of or interest in returning to the Church of my youth. My entire family had left the Church when I was only eleven, and to me Catholicism was beautiful but alien. Yet over time, everyone in my family had come back to the Catholic Church. One of my brothers had even become a priest, but I was stubborn in my resistance. I didn't feel comfortable in the Catholic Church.

The Mass at Villanova University was startlingly different than the megachurch I had been attending. Incense clouded the air, issuing from a golden thurible, swung by a robed man leading a cavalcade of other robed men: deacons, dozens of priests, a handful of bishops, and at the end of the procession, Justin Cardinal Rigali, the Archbishop of Philadelphia. They called him a "prince of the Church". It was all so strange to my Protestant eyes and ears. The organ pipes swelled, and the men and women gathered together in one voice, filling the vaulted ceilings with their song, a refreshing change from the praise band at my church.

The liturgy started. "The grace of our Lord Jesus Christ and the love of God and the fellowship of the Holy Spirit be with you all!"

I knew the response. "And also with you."

"My brothers and sisters, to prepare ourselves to celebrate these sacred mysteries, let us call to mind our sins."

"Ah yes. My sins," I thought. "They're the reason I'm here in the first place. My lifetime of foolishness and weakness has led me to this point. It's good to call them to mind before we worship God."

Cardinal Rigali began, "I confess to Almighty God," then with one voice the men and women gathered there joined him. I looked out at them, as we said the words together. These men and women were my brothers and sisters. They knew what I had lived with; they knew all about what it meant to live with attractions to the same sex. They knew about the heartbreak, the loneliness, the doubts, the isolation I had felt. And they knew about the challenges and sins, and guilt and regret, that existed in my life.

"I confess to Almighty God, . . . and to you, my brothers and sisters, that I have sinned through my own fault, in my thoughts and in my words, in what I have done, and what I have failed to do; and I ask blessed Mary, ever virgin, all the angels and saints, and you, my brothers and sisters, to pray for me to the Lord our God."[4] It was beautiful, saying these words with one voice. And I wanted these men and women "to pray for me, to the Lord our God". And it was good to say publicly this act of confession. It felt cleansing. It seemed appropriately humble to say such things to God. It was strange to ask Mary to pray for me, but I thought it could only help to ask—maybe she could hear me, and maybe she could pray for me, but if not, what harm was done by asking?

Cardinal Rigali's homily was filled with grace, kindness, and compassion. They were words of mercy and forgiveness, like the words Christ spoke to the woman caught in adultery two thousand years ago. " 'Woman, where are they? Has no one condemned you?' She said, 'No one, Lord.' And Jesus said, 'Neither do I condemn you; go, and do not sin again' " (Jn 8:10–11).

I meditated on Cardinal Rigali's words as the Liturgy of the Eucharist began. I gazed up at the dome of the church, my eyes wandering along its marble pillars and alcoves, then to the altar, where a crucified Christ hung. My eyes rested on the crucifix, confronted by the garish display: Christ died for me—for my sins that fill me with so much sorrow, the sins that led me here. He died for me—*in that way*, because he loved me. It was good to see his crucified body, but it pained me. I looked away.

"Lord, I am not worthy to receive you, but only say the word, and my soul shall be healed." Healing of my soul— that's what I desired, more than anything. I had been the prodigal son for so long, feeling unworthy of love, from anyone, including God. Healing is what I wanted; and as I looked around me, hearing everyone in the church say these words, I knew this was what they longed for too.

---

[4] This Mass was said before the change of liturgy.

"Lamb of God, you take away the sins of the world: have mercy on us. Lamb of God, you take away the sins of the world: have mercy on us. Lamb of God, you take away the sins of the world: grant us peace." I was humbled as I heard those words, repeated three times. These weren't empty, repetitious words. I looked back on my long life of addiction and sin, and was filled with great sorrow.

The reception of the Eucharist began. I sat in my pew as I watched my brothers and sisters process to the altar and receive Communion. And suddenly, a longing deep in my heart was kindled to be among them, truly to be family with them.

Before the Mass began, I wasn't a practicing Catholic. But somewhere during the hour-long Mass, I decided to be reconciled with the Church. There was such joy here, such peace. And the singing! Ah, the singing of praise and thanksgiving by broken men and women like me! They belted it out, with such joy—that was what cinched it. These men and women from Courage were filled with unspeakable, boundless joy that overflowed and poured out from them. I wanted what they had.

All of my wanderings, all of my rebellion, all of my choices had sent me in the wrong direction. Like the prodigal son, I had taken my inheritance and squandered it. Yet little did I know that the first step I took toward truly living in my Father's house was the step I took when I left it. All along the way, God, my loving Father, knew that those steps would lead me to this moment, to this homecoming where I would come back to the Church of my Baptism. I was dumbfounded as I stood at the end of Mass, singing the closing hymn, watching as the priests, bishops, and Cardinal Rigali exited the church.

I walked out of church carrying a secret, a secret I wanted to tell someone. I can't describe how much joy I felt at that moment. I needed to tell someone.

As we neared the door to the church, our pace slowed. Everyone was speaking with Cardinal Rigali, who stood at the exit. I watched as men and women reached for Cardinal Rigali's hand—he had some sort of special ring. I couldn't hear what they said. Was it, "Thank you, Your Eminence," or "Thank you, Your Excellency," or "Your Highness"? I couldn't tell, so I didn't bother with it. I awkwardly kissed the ring on his hand though, and then said to him, "You know what?"

"No, what's that?" he said, with a kindly smile.

"I just decided to come back to the Catholic Church, during Mass. I've been away for a long time, but it's good to be back, where I belong."

His smile broadened. "Well, I'm happy for you. God is good, and he is always calling us to himself." Like the father in the Parable of the Prodigal Son (see Lk 15:11–32), who was always on the lookout for his wayward son, he added, "Welcome home."

I looked for my godparents. They needed to know. They had been at my Baptism, they had prayed for me throughout my life—they had invited me to the Courage Conference; it was they whom God chose to help bring me home.

They were elated and overjoyed. After we hugged and spoke of the joy we felt, I knew there was someone else I needed to tell. I needed to tell someone in my family, and the first person I called was my brother, Father Steve.

The Return of the Prodigal Son

Now, if you've been away from the Catholic Church for over thirty years, and decide that you're going to come back, it's handy to have a brother who is a priest. I called him up and told him the good news—then asked him what my next step needed to be.

"Well," he said, "since you were baptized into the Church, and received First Communion before we left, all you need to do is make a good confession, and you'll be reconciled with the Church."

With that, we said our good-byes and spoke briefly about how good God is.

Confession took place that night in the chapel. I entered the church and saw priests scattered throughout the sanctuary. Someone played music quietly at the piano.

I saw a priest who was free, and walked up to him nervously. "Father," I said, "I haven't been to confession in over thirty years. I'm not quite sure what to do."

He guided me through the process with fatherly love and compassion. I told him everything. Everything, from the very beginning—all of my moments of shame, all of my moments of addiction, all the furtive search for happiness in the dead ends of sexual pleasure. I poured out a lifetime of sin and sorrow in one liberating moment of emancipation and release.

And then he raised his hand above my head and said the most glorious words anyone has ever said to me: "God, the Father of mercies, through the death and Resurrection of his Son has reconciled the world to himself and sent the Holy Spirit among us for the forgiveness of sins; through the ministry of the Church may God give you pardon and peace, and I absolve you from your sins in the name of the Father, and of the Son, and of the Holy Spirit."

I had never felt so free, so liberated in all my life. These weren't empty words; I experienced joy—abundant, ebullient, and overpowering joy—as he said those words. The words of the priests have power, given to them from Christ while he was still among us, after he was raised from the dead, a power unimaginable: the power to forgive sins.

As a Protestant, I didn't understand what confession and forgiveness of sins was all about. I thought all I needed to do to receive God's forgiveness was to tell him I was sorry. But here, humbling myself before a priest who acted in the Person of Christ—this was what confession was supposed to be. Those hands, raised above my head, were hands of a priest who had been ordained by the laying on of hands, hands that were linked with a thousand sets of hands, reaching back in an unbroken chain of apostolic succession through two thousand years of mankind, stretching back to the moment when the resurrected Christ appeared before his disciples, and said to them, " 'Peace be with you. As the Father has sent me, even so I send you.' And when he had said this, he breathed on them, and said to them, 'Receive the Holy Spirit. If you forgive the sins of any, they are forgiven; if you retain the sins of any, they are retained' " (Jn 20:21–23).

As I left the priest to go back to my pew, I knew truly that all of my sins had been forgiven, through the grace of Christ and power of the priest to forgive sins. I knew this just as surely as the Roman centurion who, on the day of Christ's last breath on the Cross, as Saint Matthew tells us, said, "Truly this was the Son of God!" (Mt 27:54). I knew that here, at last, my sins had been forgiven.

I went to bed, with joy and peace in my heart, looking forward to the next day when I would finally be able to partake of the Body and Blood of Jesus Christ in the Eucharist.

* * * * *

Mass was in the late morning. I couldn't keep my joy contained—all morning long at the conference I told anyone who would listen that I had just come back to the Church. A few of them invited me to sit with them at Mass, and I looked forward to sitting with my newfound friends for my first Eucharist in thirty years.

But I was running late for Mass. As I entered, the Mass was just beginning. I couldn't spy my new friends, but I saw my godparents sitting in the back pew. So I slid in next to them. Their faces were full of joy. We hugged, and suddenly my godfather said to me, "Dan, we've been asked today to carry up the gifts. Would you like to carry the gifts with us?"

I didn't understand what he meant. I looked around me, wondering what he meant by "the gifts".

"Sure," I said, "but I don't know what you mean by 'the gifts'."

"Well, Dan, what I mean by the gifts is the bread and wine to take up for Communion."

As he said those words, I was stunned.

"Yes!" I exclaimed. "Yes, of course!"

My godparents and I have often reflected on that moment, how God had orchestrated all of the events of my life to lead to this moment. As we sat there, together in that pew, I realized that if I had gotten there just a little bit earlier, I would have sat with my newfound friends. But instead, my plans to be early had been waylaid—all because my loving Father desired to show me, and my godparents, how much he loved and cared for us.

I recalled the words of Proverbs 16:9:

> A man's mind plans his way,
> but the LORD directs his steps.

From my birth, as well as from my Baptism and the seeming random choice of Bob and Susan Cavera as my godparents—all of it, all of my wandering, all of my doubts, all of my fears, even my time when I had left God behind— the Lord God, the Host of Hosts, the King of Kings, had directed my steps to this moment. He had directed my steps even that very morning, guiding me to the pew next to my godparents, who were witnesses to my spiritual birth. Now they were witnesses to my spiritual rebirth, and together we would walk to the altar, carrying the bread and wine that would become Jesus' Body and Blood that I would consume for the first time in thirty years.

It boggles the mind. No one can tell me there isn't a God. I have seen his hand in my life. I had wrestled with God my entire life. I doubted his promises, the promises of Jeremiah 29:11, but now, I saw that they were true. Indeed I could now understand how God had plans to prosper me and not to harm me, plans that gave me a hope and a future.

As I walked up to the altar, alongside my godparents who were there so many years ago at my First Communion, I thought of the times when I had scoffed at the words of Christ in Matthew: "Ask, and it will be given you; seek, and you will find; knock, and it will be opened to you. For every one who asks receives, and he who seeks finds, and to him who knocks it will be opened. Or what man of you, if his son asks him for bread, will give him a stone?" (Mt 7:7–9).

Once I thought all God had given me were stones, but I now saw that he had always been guiding me to this moment. The prodigal son was coming home. And there was a feast set before me to celebrate my homecoming. I would receive the Bread of Life—and in his inexpressible mercy, to just show me how much he really did love and care for me, and my godparents, he made sure that we were the ones who carried the bread and wine up to the altar.

It is a wondrous thing to partake of the Body and Blood of Christ. Christ—truly present, in the flesh, in the transformation of the fruit of the earth and vine, and the work of human hands, into his Body and Blood.

The rest of the Courage conference was a joyous blur. I hated to leave my new friends. No—not my friends, my new family. For the men and women of Courage are my family—part of the vast family of believers across the earth, and across time. It is a glorious thing to have rejoined the Church, built on the Rock of Peter, to be under the dome of the Church against which "the gates of Hades shall not prevail" (Mt 16:18).

I know I'm safe now. I'm finally home, and I know I'm where I belong. G. K. Chesterton wrote once about his own conversion to Catholicism that the Church "is much larger inside than it is outside".[1] Such has been the case with me. You don't know the Catholic Church is bigger than the universe, until you go through her doors, and there discover the peace that surpasses all understanding.

---

[1] G. K. Chesterton, *The Catholic Church and Conversion* (San Francisco: Ignatius Press, 2006), p. 81.

PART TWO

RECLAIMING REALITY

Reclaiming Sexual Reality

I think being straight is overrated. I consider myself a pansexual.

—A Catholic high school student
in Flint, Michigan

Only what is true can ultimately be pastoral.

—Congregation for the Doctrine of the Faith,
*Letter to the Bishops of the Catholic Church
on the Pastoral Care of Homosexual Persons**

Somehow or other we must become fully conscious of the real world, seeing reality as a whole and living wholly in it.

—Frank Sheed, *Theology and Sanity*†

One of the most important questions of my life has been wondering how best to view my attractions to men. I've been on a lifelong search for answers that have made sense of my experience, and in that search, I have been

---

*Congregation for the Doctrine of the Faith, *Letter to the Bishops of the Catholic Church on the Pastoral Care of Homosexual Persons* (October 1, 1986), no. 15, http://www.vatican.va/roman_curia/congregations/cfaith/documents/rc_con_cfaith_doc_19861001_homosexual-persons_en.html.

†Frank Sheed, *Theology and Sanity* (San Francisco: Ignatius Press, 1993), p. 30.

concerned most of all with finding and discovering what is really and objectively true. I have always wanted to live my life based on reality, on the way things really are. On the one hand, the way things "really are" is that I am sexually attracted to men. But despite what the gay rights movement said about me (that my feelings and attractions reveal my true sexual identity), I never felt convinced by their arguments. "Being gay" never really made sense to me. Defining reality based on my feelings seemed a rather unconvincing premise upon which to build a life. My father taught me this at a very early age. In the planetarium where he worked, I would often sit next to him as he gave presentations to visiting school children. My favorite part of every program was the moment when he made the star projector spin speedily, round and round, making it feel as if all of us in the auditorium were spinning. The dome of the planetarium filled our vision, and though we knew we were seated firmly in chairs, it felt as if we were dizzily careening through space. As the gathered children enjoyed the experience, my father would use the moment to teach them about Nicolas Copernicus' revolutionary discovery that the earth revolves around the sun, not the other way around, as most men had believed throughout history. "Feelings are important," he would say, "but they don't always tell us the truth." My search for sexual reality has been motivated by the same desire of Copernicus' search for the truth of the universe. I want to live my life according to reality, not based on what I *feel* reality to be. Though I'm not a philosopher, here in Part Two I have collected my thoughts on the nature of reality in the realm of human sexuality, and how viewing my sexuality through a search for objective reality has helped shape my own understanding of myself. I believe that society is in need of a return to sexual sanity, rooted in embracing and accepting the truth that the sole sexual identities that are objectively true are male and female, designed for union with each other. For me, accepting this truth has been liberating. I hope it can help others like me, who aren't satisfied with the labels modern man has made up about sex and sexual identity.

Is homosexuality normal?

In my opinion, few people have spoken more honestly about reality and homosexuality than Camille Paglia. Though she is a self-identified pagan lesbian feminist, she says,

> Homosexuality is not "normal." On the contrary, it is a challenge to the norm; therein lies its eternally revolutionary character. Note I do not call it a challenge to the *idea* of a norm. Queer theorists have tried to take the post-structuralist tack of claiming that there is no norm, since everything is relative and contingent. This is the kind of silly bind that word-obsessed people get into when they are deaf, dumb, and blind to the outside world. Nature exists, whether academics like it or not. And in nature, procreation is the single, relentless rule. That is the norm. Our sexual bodies were designed for reproduction.
>
> However, my libertarian view, here as in regard to abortion, is that we have not only the right but the obligation to defy nature's tyranny. The highest human identity consists precisely in such assertions of freedom against material limitation. Gays are heroes and martyrs who have given their lives in the greatest war of them all. Fate, not God, has given us this flesh. We have absolute claim to our bodies and may do with them as we see fit. To develop and expand our sensory responses is a pagan strategy, reverent in its own way toward nature. Homosexual potential is in everyone, and evidence suggests that under the right

circumstances it will out. But the instinctual imperative to
mate is also in all of us.[1]

I disagree with Paglia's pagan worldview, but at least I
think she's honest about human sexuality. She's arrived
at the same conclusion I have in my search for sexuality
reality: our sexual bodies are designed for reproduction.
I disagree, however, that "the highest human identity consists precisely in ... assertions of freedom against material
limitation [i.e., 'nature's tyranny']." Quite the contrary: I
believe that man's greatest freedom comes from living
in accordance with the truth of sexuality revealed to us in
the nature of our bodily design. One of the many reasons
I joined the Catholic Church is her unambiguous embrace
of the objective reality of man's sexual nature, as revealed
to us in our bodies. The way we exist in the world, divided
between male and female, becomes foundational to the
Church's teaching on sexual morality and the virtue of
chastity. The Church's doctrine of morality is foremost
a doctrine rooted in the nature of man's objective being.

The Catholic philosopher Josef Pieper has helped me
understand the importance of man's way of "being" as a
guide to truth and reality. He writes,

> There is a statement in Goethe, "All laws and moral prin-
> ciples may be reduced to one—the truth. Truth is the
> "proclamation of being", says [Saint] Hilary, and [Saint]
> Augustine says, "Truth is that which manifests what is."
> So he who undertakes to reduce morality to truth, and,
> following this arrow, probes more deeply, beyond "truth"
> or rather through it, necessarily reaches being. All laws and
> moral principles may be reduced to being.[2]

[1]Camille Paglia, "Rebel Love: Homosexuality", in *Vamps & Tramps: New
Essays* (New York: Vintage Books, 1994), pp. 70–71.

[2]Josef Pieper, "Reality and the Good", in *Living the Truth: The Truth of All
Things and Reality and the Good* (San Francisco: Ignatius Press, 1989), pp. 112–13.

Man has a certain way of being that is objectively true. Homosexuality, as Paglia rightly points out, is in opposition to our true nature. We all *know* this, intuitively, whether we want to acknowledge it or not. *I* certainly knew this intuitively when I first became aware of my attractions to other boys in my class. The idea that my feelings define my sexual identity more than my body does has never made much sense to me at all. For a time I tried to think of myself as gay, but it took a lot of gerrymandering of my brain to believe that homosexuality is as innate a trait to me as the color of my skin, or to believe that I'm not designed for sexual union with a woman. As a man, I'm confronted with the physical reality of my body every day. My body, and the sexual organs that are part of my body, are designed for union with a woman, and designed for the propagation of the species through procreation. That's my sexual nature, and every other man's nature. Indeed, men who call themselves gay can father children with women who call themselves lesbians, and sometimes do. In so doing, they are living out their sexuality in accordance with the real nature of things.[3]

Nature matters, and that is as true for human beings in their created reality as it is for the physical environment we inhabit. We care immensely about the environment—care that it is restored to its most pristine and unpolluted nature,

[3] As a case in point, consider the story of Catherine Hall, a woman who identifies as a lesbian, who attempted to conceive a child with a man who views himself as gay. Describing their situation, she said, "It's true that we are trying to have a baby together, but he's not my boyfriend. I don't know what to call him. Our relationship is impossible to define. Last September, A and I moved from London to Milan. He's here on business. I'm here because I'm trying to conceive a child with him. People often assume that we're a couple, but we're not. He's a gay man and I'm a lesbian. We are, in one sense, simply friends, but at the same time we are something much more." Catherine Hall, "My Future Family", *Guardian*, February 6, 2009, https://www.theguardian.com/lifeandstyle/2009/feb/07/family4.

pining for a return to primeval purity. With man's sexuality, however, society seems to want to ignore our nature, in favor of supposedly new and improved constructions and designs. I believe in the realm of human sexuality; we are wise to follow our instincts with regard to our concern for the natural world. Pope Benedict XVI often spoke of the parallels between care of the environment and care for the true nature of man, what he called a "human ecology". Speaking to the German Bundestag in 2011, he said,

> How can reason rediscover its true greatness, without being sidetracked into irrationality? How can nature reassert itself in its true depth, with all its demands, with all its directives? ... If something is wrong in our relationship with reality, then we must all reflect seriously on the whole situation and we are all prompted to question the very foundations of our culture.... We must listen to the language of nature and we must answer accordingly. Yet I would like to underline a point that seems to me to be neglected, today as in the past: there is also an ecology of man. Man too has a nature that he must respect and that he cannot manipulate at will. Man is not merely self-creating freedom. Man does not create himself. He is intellect and will, but he is also nature, and his will is rightly ordered if he respects his nature, listens to it and accepts himself for who he is, as one who did not create himself. In this way, and in no other, is true human freedom fulfilled.[4]

These words have brought me immense freedom! When we respect our created nature, we experience true human freedom. When we oppose or question or seek to change our created nature, we necessarily live in dissonance with

[4] Address of His Holiness Benedict XVI at the Reichstag Building, Berlin (September 22, 2011), https://w2.vatican.va/content/benedict-xvi/en/speeches/2011/september/documents/hf_ben-xvi_spe_20110922_reichstag-berlin.html.

reality. The consequences of living in denial of objective reality are inevitably frustration and confusion. The person who is confused about his sexual identity, in order to be truly free, to be truly liberated, must accept himself *as he truly is*. We are creatures, who have been made by God. No man is his own special creation. In acknowledging and accepting his sexual identity, and the orientation of sexuality that is part of that identity, a man finds his true nature, and thus his true self.

The Gender Spectrum: A Rainbow of Possibilities

Today, people are told by self-appointed experts that their bodily reality doesn't tell them who they are, as sexual beings. Society is inundated with an ideology that says that who people feel themselves to be, or who they're attracted to, defines their sexual identity more reliably than their body does. People searching for answers to their questions about sexual identity will be told that human sexuality exists on a spectrum. This is the "new reality" that we are told we must believe.

At the website for an organization simply called "Gender Spectrum", you will read that the notion of male and female is something that "Western culture *has come to view*" as a "binary concept, with two rigidly fixed options: male or female, both grounded in a person's physical anatomy."[5]

The notion of male and female, the website continues, is merely the result of a "quick glance between the legs", which becomes a "gender label that the child will carry

[5]"Understanding Gender", Gender Spectrum, accessed March 15, 2016 (italics added), https://web.archive.org/web/20160318002945/https://www.genderspectrum.org/quick-links/understanding-gender/.

96   RECLAIMING REALITY

for life". Gender fluidity, the website claims, "conveys a wider, more flexible range of gender expression or identity, with interests and behaviors that may change, even from day to day." Truly liberated children, they claim, are "gender fluid" because they "do not feel confined by restrictive boundaries of stereotypical expectations of boys and girls".[6]

The people behind Gender Spectrum proclaim that "instead of the static, binary model produced through a solely physical understanding of gender, a far richer tapestry of biology, gender expression and gender identity intersect in a multidimensional array of possibilities."[7]

When I hear of this "richer tapestry" of gender ideology, I think of what Josef Pieper called the "excellent original form of classical theology's idea of man, which has in many respects become faint and—worse still— many times painted over." Pieper calls the Christian idea of man the "ultimate human exemplar" and argues that "it is absolutely essential for our lives that we again see this idea of man clearly and that we affirm it."[8] One of the tasks of the Church today is to counter the confused tapestry of the gender spectrum with man's true form and nature as male and female.

The seeds of today's "gender spectrum" were planted in the early days of the gay revolution. In his 1971 book *Homosexual Liberation*, John Murphy wrote that homosexuality "should be discussed as an acceptable life style in any kind of sex education program, at any age".[9] He writes elsewhere in the same book:

[6] Ibid.

[7] Ibid.

[8] Josef Pieper, *The Christian Idea of Man* (South Bend, Ind.: St. Augustine's Press, 2011), pp. 7–8.

[9] John Murphy, *Homosexual Liberation: A Personal View* (New York: Praeger Publishers, 1971), p. 19.

Education must be revised to include the depiction of homosexuality and lesbianism as life styles that exist, rather than as unacknowledged secrets. It seems sensible to begin this as soon as possible, preferably in conjunction with present sex education programs. Shocking at first (even to many homosexuals, including myself), this proposal should not be feared as indoctrination; it is no more dangerous than the heterosexual propaganda that has jammed children into increasingly irrelevant roles.[10]

One need only turn to the pages of the *Washington Post* to know that Murphy's vision for the education and indoctrination of our children has been realized in our schools. In 2014, the paper published an article called "When No Gender Fits: A Quest to Be Seen as Just a Person". The article tells the story of an eighteen-year-old girl, Kelsey, who identifies as "agender" or "non-binary". We're told, "It's what Kelsey feels comfortable with."[11] Kelsey's been told that how she *feels* is the most important guide to the truth about her sexuality.

Her story reveals how gender theory has been inculcated in our schools, becoming accepted as authoritative in matters of sexual identity:

The most recent person Kelsey told was Kristen, a childhood friend. Kristen was religious, from a conservative family, but she'd nodded along when Kelsey said their Advanced Placement psychology textbook should define gender on a spectrum rather than as a binary.[12]

[10]Ibid., p. 179.
[11]Monica Hesse, "When No Gender Fits: A Quest to Be Seen as Just a Person", *Washington Post*, September 20, 2014, https://www.washingtonpost.com/national/when-no-gender-fits-a-quest-to-be-seen-as-just-a-person/2014/09/20/1ab21e6e-2c7b-11e4-994d-202962a9150c_story.html.
[12]Ibid.

Few things reveal the agenda to teach gender theory to even the youngest children as clearly as "The Genderbread Person" worksheet does, distributed in schools across the country.[13] (See Illustration 1.)

According to the "Genderbread Person", sexual identity can be plotted on a grid, determined primarily by one's feelings. The bodily reality of sex, so central to our existence as creatures who exist as a union of body and soul, is relegated to the least important place. The reality spoken by the doctor at the moment of our birth is mocked now as just a "quick glance between the legs".

The language of the Genderbread Person lures a young person confused about who he is, like a forbidden fruit of secret wisdom:

> Gender isn't binary. It's not either/or. In many cases it's both/and. A bit of this, a dash of that. This tasty little guide is meant to be an appetizer for gender understanding. It's okay if you're hungry for more. In fact, that's the idea.

Against the temptation of gender ideology stands the constant teaching of the Church, as reflected in the words of Pope Saint John Paul II: "The words of the Book of Genesis contain that truth about man which is confirmed by the very experience of humanity. Man is created 'from the very beginning' as male and female: the life of all humanity—whether of small communities or of society as a whole—is marked by this primordial duality."[14] Male

---

[13] "The Genderbread Person v3.3", It'sPronouncedMetrosexual.com, accessed March 15, 2016, http://itspronouncedmetrosexual.com/wp-content/uploads/2015/03/Genderbread-Person-3.3-HI-RES.pdf.

[14] *Letter to Families from Pope John Paul II* (February 2, 1994), no. 6, https://w2.vatican.va/content/john-paul-ii/en/letters/1994/documents/hf_jp-ii_let_02021994_families.html.

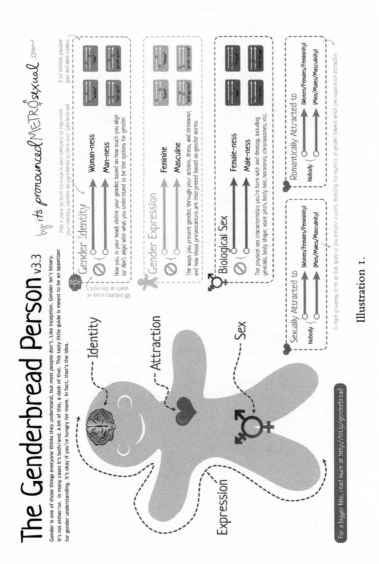

Illustration 1.

and female aren't outdated views of mankind—they are the answer to modern man's confused understanding of human sexuality.

Abuse of Language, Abuse of Power

Gender ideologues are an example of the "innovators" C. S. Lewis warned us about in *The Abolition of Man*, undermining objective reality and natural law, which Lewis terms the "Tao" (the Chinese word for the "way"):

> Either we are rational spirit obliged for ever to obey the absolute values of the *Tao*, or else we are mere nature to be kneaded and cut into new shapes for the pleasures of masters who must, by hypothesis, have no motives but their own "natural" impulses. Only the *Tao* provides a common human law of action which can overarch rulers and ruled alike....
>
> I am not here thinking solely, perhaps not even chiefly, of those who are our public enemies at the moment. The process which, if not checked, will abolish Man, goes on apace among Communists and Democrats no less than among Fascists. The methods may (at first) differ in brutality. But many a mild-eyed scientist in pince-nez, many a popular dramatist, many an amateur philosopher in our midst, means in the long run just the same as the Nazi rulers of Germany. Traditional values are to be "debunked" and mankind to be cut into some fresh shape at the will (which must, by hypothesis, be an arbitrary will) of some few lucky people in one lucky generation who have learned how to do it. The belief that we can invent "ideologies" at pleasure, and the consequent treatment of mankind as mere specimens, preparations, begins to affect our very language.[15]

---

[15] C. S. Lewis, *The Abolition of Man* (London: Geoffrey Bles, 1967), pp. 50–51.

Our times reveal how prescient Lewis was. New ide-
ologies have indeed begun "to affect our very language".
Nowhere is this more evident than in the terminology
invented by the gay rights movement. "Homophobic"
was a term invented in 1972 by George Weinberg to
become a bludgeon, wielded against anyone who doesn't
approve of same-sex relationships, or who appeals to
objective reality about the sexual nature of man that says
that sexual intimacy and sexual complementarity necessarily go together.[16] Society has been trained by the
gay rights movement to now speak of "sexual minorities", and to believe that "gay rights" are the "new civil
rights movement", though many African Americans take
umbrage with the comparison.[17] Where we once spoke
of "sexual preference", the ideologues of the gay rights
movement have forced society today to speak of "sexual
orientation" instead. This change had a philosophical and
political motive behind it: The former way of speaking,
of course, doesn't support the proposition that people are
born and innately "gay". The latter term does. Similarly,
what was once viewed as a "sex change operation" has
now been deliberately transformed into "gender confirmation surgery", suggesting that since the body doesn't fit the
mind, the body needs to be changed, rather than the mind
helped to accept the reality of the body. Internet headlines
tell us that a "man" can now become pregnant and bear
children; and if "he" chooses to nurse the child that sprung
from "his" womb, we're told we must call this practice

[16] See George H. Weinberg, *Society and the Healthy Homosexual* (New York:
St. Martin's Press, 1972).

[17] See Karen Grigsby Bates, "African-Americans Question Comparing Gay
Rights Movement to Civil Rights", National Public Radio, July 2, 2015,
http://www.npr.org/2015/07/02/419554758/african-americans-question
-comparing-gay-rights-movement-to-civil-rights.

"chest-feeding".[18] We're told that a family is now what anyone wants a family to be, and that marriage can now be between any two people who happen to have fallen in love with each other. Like the proverbial slowly boiled frog, we've allowed the very bedrock of civilization— the nature of man and of the family—to be transformed through the slow, but purposeful degradation of words into instruments of propaganda, wielded by brilliant sophists bent on changing reality. Indeed, one recent book, chronicling a man's "transition" into life as a woman, bears the revealingly honest title *Redefining Realness*.[19]

In his work *Abuse of Language, Abuse of Power*, Josef Pieper writes, "Public discourse itself, separated from the standard of truth, creates on its part, the more it prevails, an atmosphere of epidemic proneness and vulnerability to the reign of the tyrant. Serving the tyranny, the corruption and abuse of language becomes better known as propaganda."[20] Pieper argues that the abuse of language as propaganda contains a latent form of violence. The word becomes a *weapon*. "All of this is not outside our own experience," he says. We associate this sort of propaganda with the political machine of dictators; yet the weaponizing of the word "can be found wherever a powerful organization, an ideological clique, a special interest, or a pressure group uses the word as their 'weapon'".[21] The gay rights movement deftly uses the power of propaganda, the word wielded as

---

[18]Jessi Hempel, "My Brother's Pregnancy and the Making of a New American Family", *Time Magazine*, September 12, 2016, http://time.com/4475634/trans-man-pregnancy-evan/.

[19]Janet Mock, *Redefining Realness: My Path to Womanhood, Identity, Love and So Much More* (New York: Atria Books, 2014).

[20]Josef Pieper, *Abuse of Language, Abuse of Power*, trans. Lothar Krauth (San Francisco: Ignatius Press, 1992), p. 31.

[21]Ibid., p. 32.

a weapon, against anyone they perceive stands in the way of their aims. Just recently, a group of "progressive organizations" fomented a propaganda war against Christian and other religious organizations who still uphold traditional marriage, in opposition to same-sex marriage, by labeling such organizations as "hate groups".[22] In some countries like Sweden, it is becoming illegal to even preach about homosexuality as being immoral.[23]

In his discussion of the abuse of language, Pieper recalls the battle Plato waged his entire life with the sophists, whom Plato saw as dangerous, for they "fabricate a fictitious reality".[24] Nothing could be more fictitious than the "reality" the gay rights movement has fabricated: that human sexuality is not truly divided between male and female, but rather is divided between gay and straight, and that the body is merely raw material from which man can create his own sexual way of being. In the context of the

[22] "A coalition of progressive groups on Thursday started a campaign to label social conservative organizations that oppose lesbian, gay, bisexual and transgender rights as hate groups." "LGBTQ Advocates Seek to Label Conservative Opponents as Hate Groups", NBCnews.com, April 14, 2017, http://www.nbcnews.com/feature/nbc-out/lgbtq-advocates-seek-label-conservative-opponents-hate-groups-n746671.

[23] Ake Green, a Pentecostal pastor in Sweden who preached a sermon on the immorality of homosexuality, was sentenced to one month in jail for engaging in "hate speech". Albert Mohler, president of Southern Baptist Theological Seminary, commented on the case, saying, "The logic of this prosecution is driven by the ardent determination of homosexual activists to make all criticism of homosexuality illegal. The logic of many hate crimes statutes plays right into this ideological strategy. By silencing all opposition, advocates for the normalization of homosexuality have the public square entirely to themselves, with defenders of biblical sexuality and the traditional family left without a voice and risking prosecution for any language or argument deemed offensive by the guardians of political correctness." Albert Mohler, "Criminalizing Christianity: Sweden's Hate Speech Law", ChristianHeadlines.com, accessed May 2, 2017, http://www.christianheadlines.com/columnists/al-mohler/criminalizing-christianity-swedens-hate-speech-law-1277601.html.

[24] Pieper, *Abuse*, p. 34.

success of the gay rights movement in transforming the words and language we use surrounding human sexuality and human rights, I find Pieper's warning against modern sophistry like we see in the realm of human sexuality chilling:

> That the existential realm of man could be taken over by pseudorealities whose fictitious nature threatens to become indiscernible is truly a depressing thought. And yet this Platonic nightmare, I hold, possesses an alarming contemporary relevance. For the general public is being reduced to a state where people not only are unable to find out about the truth but also become unable even to search for the truth because they are satisfied with deception and trickery that have determined their convictions, satisfied with a fictitious reality created by design through the abuse of language. This, says Plato, is the worst thing that the sophists are capable of wreaking upon mankind by their corruption of the word.[25]

In accepting the language of the gay rights movement, society has succumbed to a tyranny of words, consciously designed to transform civilization. And the greatest victims of this abuse of language, and the fictitious realities they promote, are our children. So-called experts use language that confuses children when they are most impressionable. They speak authoritatively about "new realities" as if they were obvious and noncontroversial. The children unfortunately accept these theories without question. One young girl told me that she thought "being straight was overrated" and that she identified as a "pansexual". Sadly, when kids are told that they can pick and choose their sexuality on a grid, from a rich rainbow-colored tapestry of possibilities, it's unsurprising that some will believe they can.

[25] Ibid., pp. 34-35.

Against this confused view of freedom, the Church stands as a bulwark, proclaiming that true freedom comes from accepting our true nature:

> *Faced with theories that consider gender identity as merely the cultural and social product of the interaction between the community and the individual, independent of personal sexual identity without any reference to the true meaning of sexuality, the Church does not tire of repeating her teaching:* "Everyone, man and woman, should acknowledge and accept his sexual identity. Physical, moral and spiritual difference and complementarities are oriented towards the goods of marriage and the flourishing of family life."[26]

There are two words, and two words alone, that describe man's sexuality, uttered by God himself:

> *Male* and *female* he created them, and he blessed them and named them Man when they were created. (Gen 5:2; italics added)

We must save our language if we wish to teach our children, and the society in which we live, who they really are, and how to love God and to pursue the path that God has marked out for human flourishing. The most important step in the restoration of the true order of sexual reality is to reclaim the dignity of the Word, the Logos, the Word made flesh, the only Word that has the power to convey reality. Where words have become an instrument of deception and manipulation, they must become instruments of truth and healing. We must reclaim the dignity of the Word.

We need to start using the right words again.

---

[26] Pontifical Council for Justice and Peace, *Compendium of the Social Doctrine of the Church: To His Holiness Pope John Paul II, Master of Social Doctrine and Evangelical Witness to Justice and Peace* (June 29, 2004; repr., April 2005), no. 224, http://www.vatican.va/roman_curia/pontifical_councils/justpeace/documents/rc_pc_justpeace_doc_20060526_compendio-dott-soc_en.html (italics in original).

Reclaiming the Dignity of the Word

Words are the most important thing we have. A few words, one word, can change history. Imagine that the correct words had been chosen by those people who are in charge of our lives. A few well-thought-out words and things might have been different. Unfortunately, they have chosen all the wrong words.

—Mr. Shikagawa, in *The Pearl Diver**

Words can be sadly mistreated and misused; but they could not be false unless they could also be true. Language may become a suspicious instrument on the tongues of fools and charlatans, but language as such retains its power to signify and communicate the Truth.

—Thomas Merton, *The Ascent of Truth*†

Words are grown so false, I am loath to prove reason with them.

—William Shakespeare, *Twelfth Night*

The divine word which you are called to speak in the world is the word spoken first by God in the moment of

*Jeff Talarigo, *The Pearl Diver* (New York: Anchor Books, 2005), p. 150. Used by permission of Doubleday, an imprint of the Knopf Doubleday Publishing Group, a division of Penguin Random House LLC. All rights reserved.

†Thomas Merton, *The Ascent of Truth* (New York: Harcourt, 1981), p. 28. Copyright © 1951 by The Abbey of Our Lady of Gethsemani and renewed 1979 by The Trustees of Merton Legacy Trust. Reprinted by permission of Curtis Brown Ltd. and Houghton Mifflin Harcourt Publishing Company. All rights reserved.

creation (cf. Gen 1:2–3). You too are sent into the darkness ... to speak the Word which is Jesus Christ.

—Pope Saint John Paul II‡

God spoke, and all that is came to be.

In the beginning was the Word, and the Word was with
God, and the Word was God. He was in the beginning
with God; all things were made through him, and without
him was not anything made that was made. In him was
life, and the life was the light of men. The light shines
in the darkness, and the darkness has not overcome it
(Jn 1:1–5).

Out of the void of disorder and chaos, God's Word, the
Logos himself, brought order through separation and distinction; for the Book of Genesis tells us that "God separated the light from the darkness. God called the light Day,
and the darkness he called Night." The water was named
the "Seas", and "the dry land Earth". The "lesser light" and
"the stars" were made so to guide men in darkness, and to
give them knowledge of days, seasons, and years. All this
God beheld and judged, and he "saw that it was good"
(1:4–5, 10, 16, 18).

And God spoke again, as a communion of Persons: "Let
us make man in our image, after our likeness". From the
dust of the ground, the Lord God made man, and breathed
the breath of life into him (1:26; 2:7).

‡Address of the Holy Father John Paul II to the Society of the Divine Word
(June 30, 2000), http://w2.vatican.va/content/john-paul-ii/en/speeches/2000
/apr-jun/documents/hf_jp-ii_spe_20000630_divine-word.pdf.

Yet Adam walked in the Garden of Eden alone. Thus, God, who beholds what he has made and judges rightly, said, "It is not good that the man should be alone" (2:18).

> So the LORD God caused a deep sleep to fall upon the man, and while he slept took one of his ribs and closed up its place with flesh; and the rib which the LORD God had taken from the man he made into a woman and brought her to the man (2:21–22).

And Adam beheld in wonder the beauty of she who was to rule the earth by his side; and like the God in whose image he was made, Adam spoke, and called her by name—his words echoing through the newly formed earth like the rushing of wind, an avalanche of joy cascading through every rock and glen and valley of creation:

> "This at last is bone of my bones
>   and flesh of my flesh;
> she shall be called Woman,
>   because she was taken out of Man" (2:23).

And all creation rejoiced, and the angels gave glory to God, and the one Adam, once alone—thence made two— once more became one, rejoined again, a joyous union of flesh and flesh and bone and bone:

> Therefore a man leaves his father and his mother and clings to his wife, and they become one flesh. And the man and his wife were both naked, and were not ashamed. . . .
>   God created man in his own image, in the image of God he created him; male and female he created them. (2:24–25; 1:27)

Light and darkness, day and night; Brother Sun and Sister Moon; heavens above, the sea and earth below—these are all the right words. And towering above them stands their template: male and female, man and woman, for which all else was made. All else shall pass away, yet these two shall remain.

* * * * *

For Christians, the words we use matter. As English-speaking Catholics around the world know, words matter so much to the Church that a rather unfamiliar word was added to the Nicene Creed in 2011; "consubstantial with the Father" replaced what the Church had said about Jesus Christ since Vatican II, "one in being with the Father". The change more accurately reflected the real nature of the relationship between the Father and the Son, and thus the theology of the Church.[1] Words naturally matter to Christians, because Christianity is a religion founded on the incarnate Word of God, Jesus Christ, the Logos. God is literally the "Author" of creation, the first maker of words. He brought the world into existence through the words he spoke. "Reality," Pope Benedict XVI says in reference to the creation of man in Genesis, "is born of the word."[2] Because God chose the word as the means by which he brought the universe into existence, human language itself has a creative power. That

---

[1] Another example of how words matter is the Great Schism of 1054 between the Eastern and Western churches, which resulted from a disagreement over the meaning represented in a word, used by the Latin Church in the Nicene Creed. The word "filioque" reflected the Latin Church's belief that the Holy Spirit proceeded from both the Father and the Son. The Eastern Church argued that "and the son" was not true, since they believe that the Holy Spirit proceeds only from the Father. See Aidan Nichols, O.P., *Rome and the Eastern Churches: A Study in Schism* (San Francisco: Ignatius Press, 2010).

[2] Benedict XVI, Post-Synodal Apostolic Exhortation on the Word of God in the Life and Mission of the Church *Verbum Domini* (September 30, 2010), no. 9, http://w2.vatican.va/content/benedict-xvi/en/apost_exhortations/documents/hf_ben-xvi_exh_20100930_verbum-domini.html.

means man is a word maker too. Just as God is the Author of creation, and gave names to the created realities of the world, God gives the same task to man, his image and likeness. When God created the animals, God brought them to Adam "to see what he would call them; and whatever the man called every living creature, that was its name" (Gen 2:19). God gave him the divine prerogative of giving things their right and proper names. The *Compendium of the Social Doctrine of the Church* says of this moment,

> All of creation in fact has value and is "good" (cf. *Gen* 1:4, 10, 12, 18, 21, 25) in the sight of God, who is its author. Man must discover and respect its value. This is a marvelous challenge to his intellect, which should lift him up as on wings (cf. John Paul II, Encyclical Letter *Fides et Ratio*, proem: *AAS* 91 [1999], 5) towards the contemplation of the truth of all God's creatures, that is, the contemplation of what God sees as *good* in them. The Book of Genesis teaches that human dominion over the world consists in *naming things* (cf. *Gen* 2:19–20). In giving things their names, man must recognize them for what they are and establish with each of them a relationship of responsibility (cf. *Catechism of the Catholic Church*, 373).[3]

God saw that what he made was good, distinguishing and separating the created world by calling everything he made by name; so too does man see, behold, and judge things for what they are. In order to be like God, to act as his image and likeness, man must call things by their right names, a task that is part of the prophetic role of man in

[3] Pontifical Council for Justice and Peace, *Compendium of the Social Doctrine of the Church: To His Holiness Pope John Paul II, Master of Social Doctrine and Evangelical Witness to Justice and Peace* (June 29, 2004; repr., April 2005), no. 113, http://www.vatican.va/roman_curia/pontifical_councils/justpeace/documents/rc_pc_justpeace_doc_20060526_compendio-dott-soc_en.html (italics in original).

the world.[4] Unlike God, however, man has the freedom to portray truth as well as falsehood through the words he creates.

I believe an essential task of the Church's prophetic role in the world is to help the world see that the words they have made up about man's sexual identities aren't adequate to reflect the truth and dignity of the human person, or the richness of human sexuality. The Church's teaching clarifies and gives light to the truth of human sexuality and the true identity of the human person by considering humanity solely as male and female, created with those identities by God. In the divine task of "giving things their names", we should take special care for the labels we give to ourselves, particularly concerning sexuality, which comprises the realm in which man images the selfless, self-giving Trinitarian love of the Father and the Son, a love so overflowing with fecundity and life-creating love that it is another Person, the third member of the Blessed Trinity, the Holy Spirit.[5] It is within

---

[4] "The Christian faithful are those who, inasmuch as they have been incorporated in Christ through Baptism, have been constituted as the people of God; for this reason, since they have become sharers in Christ's priestly, prophetic, and royal office in their own manner, they are called to exercise the mission which God has entrusted to the Church to fulfill in the world, in accord with the condition proper to each one." CCC 871 (quoting CIC [Codex Iuris Canonici], can. 204 §1; cf. LG [Lumen Gentium] 31).

[5] For an understanding of the echo of Trinitarian love within marriage, Angelo Cardinal Scola is helpful: "We can now contemplate, in precise terms, the full meaning of love, one which maintains all its constitutive factors and dimensions in unity. In the end, what does this singular *mystery* (sexual difference cannot be directly represented in concepts!) of man and woman reveal to us? It is an echo, in the human creature, of that unfathomable mystery from which Jesus Christ has lifted a corner of the veil: the difference in perfect unity that exists in the Trinity, the three persons who are one God. The most appropriate word, coined by Christian thought, for indicating this impenetrable mystery is 'communion.' *Communio personarum* exists in perfection in the Three in

man's sexual difference that it can truly be said that the words of God in creating man were fulfilled: "Let *us* make man in *our* image" (Gen 1:26; italics added). Only in the communion and unity of man and woman can man fully be understood as the *imago dei*. Before the Fall of Man, when Adam still saw reality clearly, our first father recognized the extravagant love of God in creating woman as the complement of man. The woman was a "word" of God, which could be read by Adam—in beholding her and recognizing her as "bone of his bone, flesh of his flesh" (cf. Gen 2:23), his own identity and vocation were revealed to him. Just as God brought the animals to Adam and named them by "recogniz[ing] them for what they are" and then "establish[ed] with each of them a relationship of responsibility", so was the case when Adam beheld Eve for the first time.

I have often wondered how many people today have sufficiently pondered the importance of the first recorded words of man in Scripture. In a religion that is born of the Word, created through the Logos, which Pope Benedict XVI said is the *"creative Reason"* of God,[6] the first words spoken by man I believe are the most important words

---

One, because the Father gives himself completely to the Son without keeping anything of his divine essence for himself. The Father generates the Son. The Son himself gives back the same, perennial divine essence. This exchange of love between the two is so perfect as to be *fruitful* in a pure state: it gives rise to another person, the Holy Spirit (*donum doni*). Unity and difference coexist in this perennial event of being and letting be, which (inconceivable to us) implies a difference in perfect identity. This difference, the most radical possible even though it in no way threatens the identity of the Three who are one God, is also at the root of creation from God." Angelo Cardinal Scola, *The Nuptial Mystery*, trans. Michelle K. Borras (Grand Rapids: William B. Eerdmans, 2005), pp. 131–32.

[6]Benedict XVI, *Verbum Domini*, no. 8 (italics in original).

a man has ever spoken. They are holy, sacred, and prophetic: "She shall be called *Woman*, because she was taken
out of *Man*" (Gen 2:23; italics added). In the Church's
teaching, these are the only sexual identities that reflect the
creative wisdom and design of God, the only words rich
enough and precise enough to encompass the fullness of
what it means to be sexually differentiated creatures, made
in the image of the Triune God. It would sound strange
to say of the Genesis account that "God created Adam as a
straight man", or that "out of the rib of Adam, God created
a woman with a *heterosexual orientation*"; yet the thinking
of gender ideology causes us to do precisely that. Applied
to the Creation story, the inadequacy of words like "heterosexual", "homosexual", "gay", or "straight" to describe
the dignity of man's sexual identity becomes clear. These
words are weak and wanting: it would be indecent to say
of the sexual nature of Jesus Christ, the New Adam, that
he was a "straight man", or to say of Mary, the New Eve,
the Virgin Mother of God, that she realized her "heterosexual identity" in giving birth to her Son. The idea of
viewing Jesus, or his Mother, through the grid of man's
understanding of sexuality seems sacrilegious—as with
Christ, so too with us.

Among the most quoted passages from the documents
of Vatican II is *Gaudium et Spes*, no. 22: "The truth is that
only in the mystery of the incarnate Word does the mystery of man take on light.... Christ, the final Adam, by
the revelation of the mystery of the Father and His love,
fully reveals man to man himself and makes his supreme
calling clear.... For by His incarnation the Son of God has
united Himself in some fashion with every man. He worked
with human hands, He thought with a human mind, acted
by human choice and loved with a human heart. Born of

the Virgin Mary, He has truly been made one of us, like us in all things except sin."[7]

It is only through the incarnate Word that man can understand who he is. Pope Benedict XVI said, "In the light of the revelation made by God's Word, the enigma of the human condition is definitively clarified."[8] All men are men like Christ, in all things, except sin. Jesus Christ redeemed man's sexuality, by becoming man, and by his life, death, and Resurrection, he showed us that the fulfillment of man's sexuality is not limited to, or even primarily defined by, man's sexual attractions, or the physical gratification of the sexual urge. Rather, human sexuality encompasses far more than *attractions*, or *orientation*, or *feelings*. In contrast to the Church's complex, rich, and deep understanding of human sexuality, the world's lexicon of sexual identities reduces sexual identity to the realm of urges and feelings, which by their very nature are fickle, fluid, and changeable.

The teaching that has helped me swim against the tide of the world's thinking about sexuality is the Church's wisdom and constant witness about the nature of man, expressed so clearly in Pope Saint John Paul II's encyclical *Veritatis Splendor*, the "Splendor of Truth":

> It must certainly be admitted that man always exists in a particular culture, but it must also be admitted that man is not exhaustively defined by that same culture. Moreover, the very progress of cultures demonstrates that there

[7] Second Vatican Council, Pastoral Constitution on the Church in the Modern World *Gaudium et Spes* (December 7, 1965), no. 22, http://www.vatican.va /archive/hist_councils/ii_vatican_council/documents/vat-ii_cons_19651207 _gaudium-et-spes_en.html.

[8] Benedict XVI, *Verbum Domini*, no. 6.

is something in man which transcends those cultures. This "something" is precisely human nature: this nature is itself the measure of culture and the condition ensuring that man does not become the prisoner of any of his cultures, but asserts his personal dignity by living in accordance with the profound truth of his being. To call into question the permanent structural elements of man which are connected with his own bodily dimension would not only conflict with common experience, but would render meaningless *Jesus' reference to the "beginning"*, precisely where the social and cultural context of the time had distorted the primordial meaning and the role of certain moral norms (cf. Mt 19:1–9). This is the reason why "the Church affirms that underlying so many changes there are some things which do not change and are *ultimately founded upon Christ,* who is the same yesterday and today and for ever" (*Gaudium et Spes,* 29). Christ is the "Beginning" who, having taken on human nature, definitively illumines it in its constitutive elements and in its dynamism of charity towards God and neighbour (cf. Saint Thomas Aquinas, *Summa Theologiae* I–II, q. 108, a. 1).[9]

I was struck recently how quickly society has changed its understanding of human sexuality. After one of my talks, a woman who is nearly eighty came up to speak with me. She has been married for more than fifty years and has many children and grandchildren. "I am so grateful I grew up when I did," she said.

You see, when I was in junior high, I had a crush on a girl in my class. We were best friends, and we would

[9]John Paul II, encyclical *Veritatis Splendor* (August 6, 1993), no. 53 (italics in original), http://w2.vatican.va/content/john-paul-ii/en/encyclicals/documents /hf_jp-ii_enc_06081993_veritatis-splendor.html.

often cuddle, and sometimes that cuddling went even further. We often experimented sexually with each other,
but I never thought of myself as a "lesbian" or "bisexual".
No one knew those words back in the forties and fifties,
when we were growing up. We were just two girls, who
became curious about sex, and one thing led to another,
but what we did together didn't make us think we were
somehow a different kind of girl. I bet now, though, if
we were growing up today, we might wonder if we were
lesbians. Maybe we would have thought that what we
did together made us lesbians. What if I "came out" back
then? I probably would never have married my husband,
and never had the children and grandchildren God has
blessed me with.

Thankfully, she wasn't influenced by the culture of her
time into thinking that she was something other than
just a girl, unlike the children of today, who can so easily
become confused as to their true nature, because of the
words and categories of sexual identities the world has told
them they need to use. I was trapped by that confusion
for a time, but now I see reality clearly again. I reject the
words modern man has made up about sexual identities,
and instead rely on the constant teaching of the Church to
see myself as I really am.

As Christians who worship the incarnate Word of
God, called to share the Good News of the Gospel to the
whole world, I believe we are called to reclaim the dignity
and truth of the words written in Genesis and echoed by
Christ himself, when he said, "Have you not read that he
who made them from the beginning made them male and
female?" (Mt 19:4; cf. Gen 1:27). These are our sole sexual
identities as indicated by both reason and revelation. As
Christians, we are on a rescue mission, and as followers
of the incarnate Word of God, part of that rescue mission

involves the words we use. Through our words, we can point the lost and confused to safety and liberating freedom *to be who they truly are*, by proclaiming that the sole truth of their sexual identity is as a man or a woman, and in the process, help them understand why this is so liberating. The Psalmist says, "Your word is a lamp to my feet and a light to my path" (Ps 119:105). Man can build a firm foundation for his life only if he builds on the Word of Christ, the Logos, the creative wisdom of God, rather than the confusing words man has made up about sexuality.

The Invention of Homosexuality and Heterosexuality

As we will see in the next chapter, one of the fundamental aims of the gay rights movement has been to transform the debate about human sexuality from discussions about *behavior* to sexual *identity* by making up words as an attempt to describe new sexual ways of being in the world. Karl Ulrichs (1825–1895) was one of the first people to do this. With his new lexicon of sexual identities, he desired to prove to the world that "nature pleases itself with thousands of [sexual] gradations", and that these gradations, including his own sexual attraction to men, are as normal and essential a mark of human sexuality as the love of a man for a woman that exists in marriage.[10] One scholar says that "Ulrichs established the science of sexuality on the invention of a new classificatory language.... Behind the invention of new words ... was a new affirmation of

---

[10] Karl Ulrichs, *Formatrix: Anthropologische Studien über urnische Liebe* [1865], in *Forschungen über das Rätsel der Mannmännlichen Liebe* (Leipzig: Max Spohr, 1898), pp. 54, 42–43. As quoted in Ralph M. Leck, *Vita Sexualis: Karl Ulrichs and the Origins of Sexual Science* (Chicago: University of Illinois Press, 2016), p. 41.

sexual heterogeneity.... For the first time, sexual diversity was understood ontologically,[11] as part of the vast geography of nature."[12]

The neologisms used by Karl Ulrichs in 1862 to describe his own attractions to men, *Urning* and *Uranism*, have long fallen by the wayside, yet Ulrichs' nomenclature influenced one of his correspondents, Karl-Marie Kertbeny, to coin the words "homosexual" and "heterosexual", which clearly persist to this day.[13] Writing in the *Gay and Lesbian Review* about the influence of the nomenclature created by Ulrichs and Kertbeny, Douglas Sadownick observed, "Later 19th-century sexual modernists incorporated these categories, adding others to establish an encyclopedic classification system honoring the range of sexual variation that we recognize today."[14]

---

[11] "Ontology" refers to a philosophic understanding of *what something is*, by recognizing its most essential nature, which means we see and understand the one quality of something that must be present in order for it to be understood to be the sort of thing it is. For example, I play trombone, and own several trombones—ontologically speaking, a trombone, by its very nature, exists in the world to be used by a trombone player to make music in the way a trombone produces music: with a player buzzing his lips into a sliding metal tube, terminating in a bell-shaped flare. Ontologically speaking, it's impossible for a trombone to be anything other than a trombone. *Being* a trombone is what defines what a trombone *is*. That's what "ontology" is all about. Ulrichs' new words, like *Urning*, were designed to make a case that people exist in the world with an essential nature of being an *Urning*, a word he used for himself, with a definition he often revised, eventually settling on its meaning as a woman trapped in a man's body. This is the way he viewed himself, and by creating a word to describe how he felt, he desired to make a claim that being an *Urning* was as ontologically true as existing in the world as male or female. This view of human sexuality would later be termed "essentialism". We'll speak briefly about that in the next chapter. See Leck, *Vita Sexualis*, p. 41.

[12] Ibid., pp. 38–39.

[13] See ibid., p. 58.

[14] Douglas Sadownick, "Against Foucault", *Gay and Lesbian Review*, December 31, 2016, http://www.glreview.org/article/against-foucault/.

Those promoting gender ideology and the inventors of new words and new sexual identities have understood a fundamental truth of all successful revolutions: to achieve the goals of any revolution, and to change the way society thinks, the language of society must be transformed. Julia Penelope, linguist, self-labeled lesbian, and gay rights activist, wrote,

> What we say *is* who we are. Creating a universe of discourse that reflects a different way of perceiving the world requires understanding how the language we use indicates how we think and our awareness of the conceptual framework we've learned.[15]

Penelope also said, "Language is power, in ways more literal than most people think. When we speak, we exercise the power of language to transform reality."[16]

This is the claim of modern man concerning sexual identity: "I have the power to transform reality through the language I use. I am my own master, completely autonomous and self-creating. What I say I am *is who I am*." Modern society has embraced the existentialist claims put forth by Simone de Beauvoir: "One is not born, but rather, becomes a woman"[17]—that is, anyone can become a woman, anyone can become a man, anyone can create new sexual ways of being; our bodies place no limitations on us, nor do our bodies reveal reality to us. Modern thinkers believe that "male and female" are obsolete notions of man that must be torn down, so that something new and

---

[15] Julia Penelope, *Speaking Freely: Unlearning the Lies of the Fathers' Tongues* (New York: Pergamon Press, 1990), p. 108.

[16] Ibid., p. 125.

[17] Simone de Beauvoir, *The Second Sex*, trans. Constance Borde and Sheila Malovany-Chevallier (New York: Vintage Books, 2011), p. 283.

better can be erected in their place. The new edifice is built on the foundation of a new language, created to disseminate this "new and improved" vision of reality. We are living in an age of a modern Tower of Babel: "Come, let us build ourselves a city, and a tower with its top in the heavens, and let us make a name for ourselves" (Gen 11:4). There is nothing new under the sun: we desire to be like gods, and have taken the name of God for ourselves, defiantly proclaiming, "I AM WHO I AM" (Ex 3:14).

By focusing on man's feelings, the world's view of human sexuality as LGBTQIA+[18] leads people away from the truth of their real nature as beloved sons and daughters of God, born male and female. Man requires a firm foundation upon which to base his life, and the only foundation firm enough to build upon is the Word of God. "Those who build their lives on [God's] word build in a truly sound and lasting way," said Pope Benedict XVI. "The word of God makes us change our concept of realism: the realist is the one who recognizes in the word of God the foundation of all things."[19] He said, too, that when "we listen to this word, we are led by the biblical revelation to see that it is the foundation of all reality".[20]

In my experience, very few people have heard the Church's teaching about the inadequacy of sexual labels like "homosexual" and heterosexual" to describe man's sexuality. The Church's 1986 *Letter to the Bishops of the Catholic Church on the Pastoral Care of Homosexual Persons* says this:

---

[18]LGBTQIA+: An acronym that seeks to represent myriad sexual identities, such as lesbian, gay, bisexual, transgender, queer/questioning, intersex, and asexual. The "+" refers to any other sexual labels not represented by one of the letters within the acronym.

[19]Benedict XVI, *Verbum Domini*, no. 10.

[20]Ibid., no. 8.

The human person, made in the image and likeness of God, can hardly be adequately described by a reductionist reference to his or her sexual orientation. Every one living on the face of the earth has personal problems and difficulties, but challenges to growth, strengths, talents and gifts as well. Today, the Church provides a badly needed context for the care of the human person when she refuses to consider the person as a "heterosexual" or a "homosexual" and insists that every person has a fundamental Identity: the creature of God, and by grace, his child and heir to eternal life.[21]

The Church views sexual identity not through a lens of sexual gratification or sexual or romantic attractions, or through a lens of "orientation", but rather through a lens that understands the true meaning and purpose of human sexuality. Men, for example, will only understand their sexual identity when they see it primarily through the lens of imaging the fatherhood of our Father in heaven. The male sexual identity is directed toward fatherhood, where "being a father" is not limited to biological fatherhood—this is evidenced by the priestly witness of so many men, and most powerfully by Saint Joseph, the earthly father of Jesus. Just as Jesus Christ served as a spiritual father for so many while he walked on the earth, single men or men in infertile marriages can be fathers too, in their own way: by investing in the lives of others, protecting the weak and sick, working with youth, visiting the imprisoned, and caring for the elderly and the poor. As men, we will only realize our sexual nature when we embrace our sexual

[21] Congregation for the Doctrine of the Faith, *Letter to the Bishops of the Catholic Church on the Pastoral Care of Homosexual Persons* (October 1, 1986), no. 16, http://www.vatican.va/roman_curia/congregations/cfaith/documents/rc_con_cfaith_doc_19861001_homosexual-persons_en.html.

identities as being one directed toward fatherhood—
whether that be physical fatherhood or spiritual fatherhood of some sort. Sex, as a man, is only partially about
physical sexual intimacy and pleasure, and is truly only a
part of our sexual identity as men when it exists in marriage with a woman, open to life. This is one reason why I
believe speaking of men as "heterosexual" (or "homosexual") is such an inadequate definition for our sexual identity: it focuses too much attention on the genital and erotic
component of man's sexuality. The same holds true for
women, whose sexual identity is most deeply connected
with motherhood, and whose perfect exemplar is Mary,
the Mother of God. Like fatherhood, women can fulfill
and live out their sexual identity toward motherhood in
manifold ways, other than biological motherhood. Realizing that my sexual identity isn't really primarily about
sex or *romance* has helped me see that words like "gay" are
just too limiting to be of any real value to reflect the true
dignity of man's sexuality.

As Christians, called to be the light of the world, we're
not always confident that our vision of reality is something
we really need to—or should—share with others. Writing
in the journal *Communio*, then–Cardinal Ratzinger issued
challenging words to Christians: Do we *really* believe the
Christian view of reality, and do we believe it's good news
for the world? "Christians", he says,

> have no confidence in their own vision of reality. They
> hold fast to the faith in their private devotion, but they do
> not dare to presume that it has something to say to man-
> kind as such or that it contains a vision of man's future and
> his history. From original sin to redemption, the whole tra-
> ditional structure seems too irrational and unreal for them
> to dare to bring it into public discussion.... They hold

the opinion that theology is merely an internal affair.... Because Christians are so weak in faith, the search for new myths will continue.[22]

It's my confidence in the Church's vision of reality that causes me to question and challenge the words and sexual identities made up by the world. People will only be liberated from the "new myths" that view humanity as LGBTQIA+ if Christians no longer stand silent. We cannot remain reluctant to speak about the beauty of the Church's teaching on sexuality and sexual identity for fear that it will appear "unloving", "irrational", or "unreal". We need to love the world enough to speak about the Christian vision of sexual reality, confident that God's creation of man as male and female is truly part of the Gospel of Jesus Christ we are called to proclaim to a lost and confused world. We need to be a light for the world and speak passionately about the richness of the Church's understanding of human sexuality. We can't place the Good News of the Church's teaching on human sexuality under a bushel any longer, for the world desperately needs the truth we have. We need to start having conversations with those we love about God's beautiful plan for man's sexuality, confident that it *really* is good news.

The Canadian bishops are a good model for how to talk about the Church's thinking about sexual identity labels. In their 2011 document *Pastoral Ministry to Young People with Same-Sex Attraction*, they explain why they use the term "same-sex attraction" instead of words like "gay" or "lesbian":

[22]Joseph Ratzinger, "Freedom and Liberation", in *Joseph Ratzinger in Communio, Volume 2: Anthropology and Culture*, ed. David L. Schindler and Nicholas J. Healy (Grand Rapids: William B. Eerdmans Publishing, 2013), p. 55.

In this document the expression "person with same-sex attraction" refers to one who feels an erotic and emotional attraction, which is predominant and not merely episodic, towards persons of the same sex, whether with or without sexual relations. The terms "gay" and "lesbian" are not used to define people in the Church's official teachings and documents. Although these words are common terms in current speech, and many people use them to describe themselves, they do not describe persons with the fullness and richness that the Church recognizes and respects in every man or woman.[23]

Christians shouldn't be "clanging cymbals" (cf. 1 Cor 13:1) in our discussions about sexual identity. But we should be confident that by speaking about "the fullness and richness that the Church recognizes and respects in every man or woman", we are speaking words of liberating truth for all men and women. As Christians called to be the "salt of the earth", we should sprinkle our conversations with words of truth about human sexuality. We don't need to educate ourselves on every sexual identity label that exists. Rather, we need to educate ourselves about the richness and beauty of the Church's vision for human sexuality so that we can propose it as a truly beautiful alternative to the world's view. When we do this, we can begin to realize that every sexual identity of modern man is impoverished in some way, and thus every label contains an invitation to consider the fullness of God's creative wisdom in establishing man as male and female. We can plant seeds of truth by the words we use. Instead of "gay" or "lesbian", we can do as the bishops of Canada advise, and say in

[23] Episcopal Commission for the Doctrine of the Canadian Conference of Catholic Bishops, *Pastoral Ministry to Young People with Same-Sex Attraction* (June 2011), http://www.cccb.ca/site/images/stories/pdf/ministry-ssa_en.pdf.

our conversations "people who live with same-sex attractions"; or for those who consider themselves transgender, we can speak of those who are confused about their sexual nature or identity. If you do this, at some point, someone will probably ask why you talk that way, which then becomes an opportunity to engage him in a conversation and evangelize him with the good news of the Church's vision of human sexuality. I find conversations like these are best done in a convivial setting, over a cup of coffee, or a shared meal—or best of all, with a pint of craft beer. In a world so used to shouting, conversations like this can only ever really occur among friends.

For me, I long to have these conversations, since I have found the Church's teaching so liberating. Where once I was ready to "come out" and viewed myself as a gay man, I realize now that to truly *be who I am*, I need to see myself the way God sees me, which is the way the Church sees me, as a man. Like Jesus at the tomb of Lazarus, Christ called to me to "come out" from the world's views of human sexuality, and that has made all the difference. Pope Francis' meditation on that moment in John's Gospel has shaped my view of my time when I lived life the way I wanted to live, as a gay man:

> Before the sealed tomb of his friend Lazarus, Jesus "cried with a loud voice: 'Lazarus, come out!'. And the dead man came out, his hands and feet bound with bandages, and his face wrapped with a cloth" (vv. 43–44). This cry is an imperative to all men, because we are all marked by death, all of us; it is the voice of the One who is master of life and wants that we all may "have it abundantly" (Jn 10:10). Christ is not resigned to the tombs that we have built for ourselves with our choice for evil and death, with our errors, with our sins. He is not resigned to this! He invites us, almost orders us, to come out of the tomb in which our

sins have buried us. He calls us insistently to come out of the
darkness of that prison in which we are enclosed, content
with a false, selfish and mediocre life. "Come out!", he says
to us, "Come out!". It is an invitation to true freedom, to
allow ourselves to be seized by these words of Jesus who
repeats them to each one of us today. It is an invitation to let
ourselves be freed from the "bandages", from the bandages
of pride. For pride makes of us slaves, slaves to ourselves,
slaves to so many idols, so many things. Our resurrection
begins here: when we decide to obey Jesus' command by
coming out into the light, into life; when the mask falls
from our face—we are frequently masked by sin, the mask
must fall off!—and we find again the courage of our original face, created in the image and likeness of God.[24]

By truly "coming out", and embracing the word and
identity God gave me, as a man, I have found my true
face. My life has been marked by sin, by shame, by pride,
by my desires to live my life according to my own whims,
to define my "own concept of existence, of meaning, of
the universe, and of the mystery of human life".[25] In my
pride, I became a slave to myself and my passions—but in
the light of the truth of the Church's teaching on human
sexuality, the mask has fallen from my face, and I see
myself as I really and truly am: as a beloved son of God,
made as a man, like Adam, like Jesus and every other man
who has ever walked upon the face of the earth.

[24]Pope Francis, Angelus (April 6, 2014), https://w2.vatican.va/content
/francesco/en/angelus/2014/documents/papa-francesco_angelus_20140406
.html.
[25]This is Justice Kennedy's feeble view of true liberty, enshrined in Casey v.
Planned Parenthood, 505 U.S. 833 (1992). "At the heart of liberty is the right
to define one's own concept of existence, of meaning, of the universe, and of
the mystery of human life."

Why I Don't Call Myself Gay

And Simeon blessed them and said to Mary his mother, "Behold, this child is destined for the fall and rise of many in Israel, and for a sign that is spoken against."

> —Luke 2:34

We think primarily in earthly categories.

> —Pope Saint John Paul II[*]

If I feel attracted to the same sex, does it mean I'm gay?

> —A Catholic high school student in the diocese of Pittsburgh

The word "gay" has always rubbed me the wrong way. I never understood exactly what is meant by it.

> —James Baldwin[†]

It seems to me that we should naturally be suspicious of the words a man chooses to describe his sexuality: it's the

---

[*]John Paul II, Apostolic Letter to the Youth of the World on the Occasion of International Youth Year *Dilecti Amici* (March 31, 1985), no. 5, http://w2.vatican.va/content/john-paul-ii/en/apost_letters/1985/documents/hf_jp-ii_apl_31031985_dilecti-amici.html.

[†]"Go the Way Your Blood Beats: An Interview with James Baldwin", interview by Richard Goldstein, *The Village Voice*, June 26, 1984, in *James Baldwin: The Last Interview and Other Conversations* (New York: Melville House Publishing, 2014), p. 59.

biggest area where he lacks objectivity. The biggest reason I refuse to call myself gay is simple: I don't think that it's objectively true.

In my own search for how best to understand myself and my sexuality, I've been fascinated by the thinking of other men and women living with same-sex attractions who never felt that words like "gay" were useful for them either— people like Gore Vidal, who never considered himself to "be gay", even though he had many lovers who were men. In an essay called *Sex Is Politics*, he wrote, "I have often thought that the reason no one has yet been able to come up with a good word to describe the homosexualist (sometimes known as gay, fag, queer, etc.) is because he does not exist."[1] I agree with him, completely. Conventional wisdom today would argue that he was in denial, or suffering from internalized homophobia (both are charges that have been leveled against me before); but his thinking makes perfect sense to me, based on the twofold expression of human nature, as male and female, and that man as a fallen creature can experience a variety of attractions and desires.

Like me (and like Camille Paglia, as we saw earlier), he saw the dividing line of humanity between male and female, not gay or straight:

> The human race is divided into male and female. Many human beings enjoy sexual relations with their own sex; many don't; many respond to both. This plurality is the fact of our nature and not worth fretting about.[2]

Gore Vidal also rejected the category of the "heterosexual" person. "There is no such thing as a homosexual

[1] Gore Vidal, "Sex Is Politics", in *United States: Essays 1952–1992* (New York: Broadway Books, 2001), p. 550.
[2] Ibid.

person," he wrote, "any more than there is such a thing as a heterosexual person. The words are adjectives describing sexual acts, not people."[3] His words, written in 1979, are surprisingly consistent with the teaching that the Church would issue in 1986, which we've already mentioned in the previous chapter:

> The human person, made in the image and likeness of God, can hardly be adequately described by a reductionist reference to his or her sexual orientation.... Today, the Church provides a badly needed context for the care of the human person when she refuses to consider the person as a "heterosexual" or a "homosexual" and insists that every person has a fundamental Identity: the creature of God, and by grace, his child and heir to eternal life.[4]

Vidal said some rather stunning things about homosexuality, including criticism of the gay movement's new vision of sexual identity when he said, "Gay militants now assert that there is something called gay sensibility, the outward and visible sign of a new kind of human being."[5]

It makes no sense to me that I'm a "new kind of human being", a different species of sexual creature because I have attractions to men, and have engaged in sexual acts with other men. My innate maleness and sexual identity as a man hasn't changed because of my inclinations or behaviors. I made a choice, when I was sexually active, to engage in sexual behaviors that brought me pleasure. For the most part, they happened to be with men. I suppose in this,

---

[3] Ibid.

[4] Congregation for the Doctrine of the Faith, *Letter to the Bishops of the Catholic Church on the Pastoral Care of Homosexual Persons* (October 1, 1986), no. 16, http://www.vatican.va/roman_curia/congregations/cfaith/documents/rc_con_cfaith_doc_19861001_homosexual-persons_en.html.

[5] Vidal, "Sex Is Politics", p. 550.

Vidal and I are of like mind. The difference is that I have found that engaging in those sexual behaviors led me away from happiness, not toward happiness, which is one of the reasons I have come to embrace the Catholic Church's understanding of human sexuality. We may disagree on the morality of sexual acts among men, but we both agree that the concept of the "gay person" doesn't comport with the reality of man's nature.

Like Vidal, the novelist James Baldwin, who also engaged in romantic and sexual relationships with men, didn't use the word "gay" either:

> The word "gay" has always rubbed me the wrong way. I never understood exactly what is meant by it. I don't want to sound distant or patronizing because I don't really feel that. I simply feel it's a world that has very little to do with me, with where I did my growing up. I was never at home in *it*. Even in my early years in the Village, what I saw of that world absolutely frightened me, bewildered me. I didn't understand the necessity of all the role playing. And in a way I still don't.[6]

Asked whether he ever considered himself gay, he said, "No. I didn't have a word for it. The only one I had was 'homosexual' and that didn't quite cover whatever it was I was beginning to feel.... It was really a matter between me and God."[7] So too with me.

Essentialism or Social Construction?

There was a (rather forgotten) debate in the mid to late twentieth century about sexual identity, a debate that I

[6] "Interview with James Baldwin", p. 59.
[7] Ibid.

think it wise to revive today: Do homosexual persons, as such, really exist *as homosexuals*, or is homosexuality, and the entire spectrum of sexual identities, a product of man's imagination, and the result of social constructs? The debate centered in large part around the way we should use words (and thus *think)* about sexuality: Should we speak of people as *being* homosexual, heterosexual, gay, or straight, or rather is it more accurate to speak of people who have homosexual or heterosexual attractions and then act on them? The idea is shocking today, accustomed as we are to accept as a given the notion of human sexuality divided between "straight" and some variation of "not straight". Yet the debate isn't something to scoff at, for it has deep philosophical roots.[8] Even the French philosopher Michel Foucault, himself a man unabashedly honest about his sexual attractions for men, wrote of the invention of the homosexual as a type of person:

> As defined by the ancient civil or canonical codes, sodomy was a category of forbidden acts; their perpetrator was nothing more than the juridical subject of them. The nineteenth-century homosexual became a personage, a

[8] For reference to the debate between essentialists and social constructionists, see the anthology *Forms of Desire: Sexual Orientation and the Social Constructionist Controversy*, ed. Edward Stein (New York: Routledge, 1992). Stein summarizes the two sides of the debate in his introduction: "In simplest terms, essentialists think that the categories of sexual orientation (e.g., heterosexual, homosexual and bisexual) are appropriate categories to apply to individuals.... This follows from the essentialist tenet that there are objective, intrinsic, culture-independent facts about what a person's sexual orientation is. In contrast, the social constructionist denies that there are such facts about people's sexual orientation in the absence of a social construction of that orientation. Thus, social constructionism, if true, has deep ramifications for the historical, scientific, sociological, philosophical, anthropological and psychological studies of sexuality because these studies often assume that the objects of their investigations are natural rather than cultural entities" (pp. 4–5).

past, a case history, and a childhood, in addition to being a type of life, a life form, a mysterious physiology. Nothing that went into his total composition was unaffected by his sexuality.... It was consubstantial with him, less as a habitual sin than a singular nature. We must not forget that the psychological, psychiatric, medical category of homosexuality was constituted from the moment it was characterized.... The sodomite had been a temporary aberration; the homosexual was now a species.[9]

The noted, and at times controversial, sex researcher Alfred Kinsey advised against categorizing people as "being homosexual", despite reporting much higher rates of same-sex erotic activity in the general population than anyone had ever imagined:

For nearly a century the term homosexual in connection with human behavior has been applied to sexual relationships, either overt or psychic, between individuals of the same sex.... It would encourage clearer thinking on these matters if persons were not characterized as heterosexual or homosexual, but as individuals who have had certain amounts of heterosexual experience and certain amounts of homosexual experience. Instead of using these terms as substantives which stand for persons, or even as adjectives to describe persons, they may better be used to describe the nature of overt sexual relations, or of the stimuli to which an individual erotically responds.[10]

The gay rights activist Dennis Altman acknowledged Kinsey's argument, and alluded to Gore Vidal's views and

[9] Michel Foucault, *The History of Sexuality, Volume 1: An Introduction*, trans. Robert Hurley (New York: Vintage Books, 1990), p. 43.

[10] A. C. Kinsey, W. B. Pomeroy, and C. E. Martin, *Sexual Behavior in the Human Male* (Philadelphia: W. B. Saunders, 1948), p. 656.

the debate between the essentialists and the social constructionists in his book *The Homosexualization of America*:

> The very term "homosexual" is a product of the nineteenth
> century and is one that many people in the Freudian tra-
> dition have seen as essentially a limitation and restriction
> of a universal bisexuality. Gore Vidal, for example, claims
> that the word should always be used as an adjective and
> never a noun, because it describes particular acts rather
> than particular people, and Kinsey, too, stressed that one
> should never speak of homosexuals as if such an identity
> were inherent rather than the product of social labeling.[11]

Altman naturally gravitated to an essentialist framework: fundamental to the aims and goals of the gay rights
movement was convincing society that homosexuality is as
inherent and essential an aspect of man's nature as his skin
color and ethnicity. As Altman proclaimed triumphantly
elsewhere in his book, published in 1982, less than fifteen
years after the Stonewall riots: "The greatest single victory
of the gay movement over the past decade has been to shift
the debate from behavior to identity."[12]

Ideas Have Consequences

The reframing of sexuality from behavior to *identity* has
brought about a lot of confusion in the world, especially
among young people, like a high-school-aged boy in
Pennsylvania who submitted a handwritten question to
me at a presentation I gave at his parish. It read simply: "If
I have attractions to the same sex, does it mean I'm gay?"

---

[11] Dennis Altman, *The Homosexualization of America* (Boston: Beacon Press, 1982), pp. 42–43.
[12] Ibid., p. 9.

I'm grateful I was there to tell him what the Church would say to him: that his sexual attractions don't define him—his created nature, as a young man made in the image and likeness of God, is what defines him. But sadly, because of the "greatest single victory of the gay movement", and the reframing of homosexuality from *behavior* to *identity*, this young man lives in a world where by definition he thinks he might just be gay—simply because he happens to feel attractions to the same sex. Whether or not he's "gay" or "bisexual" could be in question—but whatever he is, he is necessarily something other than straight, because he lives in a society where one's sexual identity is defined by *feelings* and *desires*. In the current view of sexuality, since he's had attractions to the same sex, by definition, he isn't straight. If he knows anything about the world, he at least knows *that*. So the question I pose is this: Have we treated this young man with justice by creating a world in which he has to ask this question in high school? Does this division of the world into *straight* and *not-straight* bring him freedom or anxiety? Understanding or confusion? Is this way of sexual identification truly *liberating*? Do our sexual labels help him to be honest with himself and with others if he feels he must use the word "gay" to describe himself?

Consider this email from someone who wrote me not long ago:

Dear Daniel:

I have a problem that I was hoping you might be able to address.

Since I have SSA I have often called into question my masculinity. As much as I try to hide it, I know that many people perceive me as feminine when they first meet me, which leads them to believe I am gay. As much as I hate this perception, I know I can't fault people for thinking this because I know the signs are there. I don't enjoy cars, sports, drinking, women, ESPN, playing the guitar, etc. Things that most masculine men are "supposed" to like/ do/enjoy....

It does hurt me when people call me "gay". I hate that word so much.... For whenever I am referred to as being "gay" I feel like I'm being slapped with a label. "Oh, he's this ..." or "Oh, he's just that ..." is what I essentially hear from people. Like I've been discarded into a box and suddenly they know everything about me. I certainly know that you've spoken out about one considering calling themselves "gay" as it reduces their identity tenfold and not as a child of Christ. I couldn't agree with this more. But it's still hard to deal with.[13]

How does the liberation of the gay rights movement reach down into this man's life? This poor fellow, just by living and moving about in life in the way he does, has been defined by others with a label he hasn't chosen for himself. "I hate the word so much," he says, for it means that others relegate him to an identity shaped by their own expectations and assumptions they've made up about him. "Being gay" is no longer even just about the person having the desires: the "gay" person has become a *type* in the mind of society and culture, and if you're a man who fits into whatever mold society says a gay man is like, people will start asking questions like, "That friend of yours, is he gay?" This man has unjustly been put in a box labeled "gay" because he's perceived a certain way, solely based on his interests and mannerisms. He's so tormented by all of this that he began working with a speech therapist to somehow lower his voice. How sad and tragic I find this to be!

[13] Personal email, September 1, 2015.

Thomas Merton wrote, "Your idea of me is fabricated with materials you have borrowed from other people and from yourself."[14] How true this is about the man who wrote to me and countless others who are unjustly labeled by those around them. My heart breaks for him. Merton writes, "Objective truth is a reality that is found both within and outside ourselves, to which our minds can be conformed. We must know this truth, and *we must manifest it by our words and acts*."[15] I think one of our missions as Christians in the world today is to heed these words of Thomas Merton about sexuality: we need to manifest sexual truth by using the right words again, and resisting the wrong ones, the ones that trap people into identities based on their desires—or our misshapen, polluted, and impoverished perceptions of sexual identities marked on a grid between gay and straight, rather than the reality that we are made male and female, and made for each other.

It takes a courageous man to swim against the tide of cultural fashion. The entire world says to this fellow, "Why don't you just accept yourself for who you truly are?" I believe by rejecting the world's division of man into gay or straight, he has done just that—he knows who he truly is: a man. I admire him immensely. This is yet another reason I refuse to call myself a gay Christian. I desire to be a sign of contradiction in the world that would put him in a box, because of how he talks and walks. This man hasn't benefited from the supposed liberties provided to man through the gay rights movement; he's not free to shape his life, without having a label slapped on him. And since he does, in fact, find men attractive, that's another reason he's forced to confront the label and identity forced

---

[14] Thomas Merton, *No Man Is an Island* (New York: Harcourt Brace Jovanovich, 1955), p. 194.
[15] Ibid., p. 190 (italics added).

upon him by those around him: *because* he's attracted to men, their assumptions about him must be right. The way to counter the shackles and prison of labels like this is to start reclaiming objective reality again, and help men like him to see themselves as they truly are: men, with the same identity, vocation, responsibility, and dignity as every other man who's ever lived.

Thomas Merton's writings about sincerity and reality have shaped my own thinking about my sexuality and have informed my convictions that speaking of people as "gay people" doesn't reflect reality or their inherent dignity as children of God. These words of Merton are one reason why I've written this book:

> We owe a definite homage to the reality around us, and we are obliged, at certain times, to say what things are and to give them their right names and to lay open our thought about them to the men we live with....
>
> But the fact that men spend so much time talking about nothing or telling each other lies that they have heard from one another ... shows that our minds are deformed with a kind of contempt for reality. Instead of conforming ourselves to what is, we twist everything around, in our words and thoughts, to fit our own deformity.
>
> The seat of this deformity is in the will. Although we may speak the truth, we are more and more losing our desire to live according to the truth. Our wills are not true, because they refuse to accept the laws of our own being: they fail to work along the lines demanded by our own reality.[16]

I don't say I'm gay, because I accept the laws of my own being. I'm not a gay man, nor is any man. As Christians, called to be emissaries of the Word, we must say what

[16] Ibid., pp. 190–91.

things are again, and to give them their right names again, the names given them by God at the foundation of the world—reiterated by Jesus himself while he still walked among us, incarnate, in the flesh, as a man: "Have you not read that he who made them from the beginning made them male and female?" (Mt 19:4).

* * * * *

Before we conclude, I know that some readers will ask me why I don't think we should say that people are gay, since Pope Francis has spoken of people as "gay" before. When asked about the press conference when he said the now-famous comment, "If someone is gay and is searching for the Lord and has good will, then who am I to judge him?", Pope Francis said that he "was paraphrasing by heart the Catechism of the Catholic Church where it says that these people should be treated with delicacy and not be marginalized. I am glad that we are talking about 'homosexual people' because before all else comes the individual person, in his wholeness and dignity. And people should not be defined only by their sexual tendencies: let us not forget that God loves all his creatures and we are destined to receive his infinite love."[17]

Interestingly, in the same press conference, he said something else, which has largely been ignored: "I still haven't found anyone with an identity card in the Vatican with 'gay' on it."[18] The notion of man having an

---

[17] Pope Francis, *The Name of God Is Mercy* (New York: Random House, 2016), pp. 61–62.

[18] Apostolic Journey to Rio de Janeiro on the Occasion of the XXVIII World Youth Day: Press Conference of Pope Francis during the Return Flight (July 28, 2013), https://w2.vatican.va/content/francesco/en/speeches/2013/july/documents/papa-francesco_20130728_gmg-conferenza-stampa.html.

"identity card" has featured prominently in Pope Francis' pontificate. He has used the metaphor on many occasions, perhaps because his own Argentinian identity card is very important to him. He may be the head of state of the Holy See, but when his passport and Argentinian national identity card expired in 2014, Pope Francis asked officials from the Argentinian embassy to come to the Vatican to renew them. He has no need of them; yet they are important enough to his own identity that Pope Francis still carries the identity card of Argentina, the place where he was born and raised.[19] Pope Francis has said that "the Beatitudes are 'the Christian's identity card' ",[20] and said that our "identity card" can be "found in the fact that mankind was created 'in the image, in the likeness of God' ".[21] But most valuable of all to our discussion here is a comment Pope Francis made during another press conference on a plane, this time from the Central African Republic to Rome: "It is idolatry when a man or a woman loses his or her 'identity card' as a child of God, and prefers to seek a god more to their liking."[22] Pope Francis may have said

[19] "Pope Renews Argentine Passport, Identity Card", *Catholic News Service*, February 18, 2014.

[20] Pope Francis, Morning Meditation in the Chapel of the *Domus Sanctae Marthae*: "The Christian Identity Card" (June 9, 2014), https://w2.vatican.va /content/francesco/en/cotidie/2014/documents/papa-francesco-cotidie _20140609_christian-identity-card.html.

[21] Pope Francis, Morning Meditation in the Chapel of the *Domus Sanctae Marthae*: "Two Identity Cards" (February 10, 2015), https://w2.vatican.va/content /francesco/en/cotidie/2015/documents/papa-francesco-cotidie_20150210_two -identity-cards.html.

[22] Apostolic Journey of His Holiness Pope Francis to Kenya, Uganda, and the Central African Republic: In-Flight Press Conference of His Holiness Pope Francis from the Central African Republic to Rome (November 30, 2015), https://w2.vatican.va/content/francesco/en/speeches/2015/november /documents/papa-francesco_20151130_repubblica-centrafricana-conferenza -stampa.html.

things that have confused people about homosexuality, but he is not confused on what our true "identity card" reveals to us—he has said he is a son of the Church, and has reiterated time and time again the Church's timeless teaching on sexual morality and the nature of man, created in the image of God as male and female, made for each other.

In closing this chapter, I will leave the final word to Pope Francis:

> Modern contemporary culture has opened new spaces, new forms of freedom and new depths in order to enrich the understanding of this difference. But it has also introduced many doubts and much skepticism. For example, I ask myself, if the so-called gender theory is not, at the same time, an expression of frustration and resignation, which seeks to cancel out sexual difference because it no longer knows how to confront it....
>
> God entrusted the earth to the alliance between man and woman: its failure deprives the earth of warmth and darkens the sky of hope. The signs are already worrisome, and we see them.[23]

I believe one of those signs that deprive "the earth of warmth and darkens the sky of hope" is the division of mankind into "gay" and "straight"—which is why I don't call myself gay.

[23] Pope Francis, General Audience (April 15, 2015), https://w2.vatican.va /content/francesco/en/audiences/2015/documents/papa-francesco_20150415 _udienza-generale.html.

The Empty Promises
of Coming Out

For some persons, revealing their homosexual tendencies
to certain close friends, family members, a spiritual director, confessor, or members of a Church support group
may provide some spiritual and emotional help and aid
them in their growth in the Christian life. In the context
of parish life, however, general public self-disclosures are
not helpful and should not be encouraged.

—United States Conference of Catholic Bishops*

Despite what we've so often been told, *being gay* is always—
and always will be—a *choice*. Attractions to the same sex
come unbidden and unchosen. What we do with those
erotic attractions, however, and how we allow them to
shape our view of ourselves, is always a choice. No one "is
gay" until he or she chooses to be gay, usually followed by
the ritual of "coming out".

I remember when I chose to be gay. It was in 2000
or 2001; I hadn't experienced any attractions for women
for quite some time, but still somehow clung to the hope

*United States Conference of Catholic Bishops, *Ministry to Persons with a
Homosexual Inclination: Guidelines for Pastoral Care* (Washington, D.C.: United
States Conference of Catholic Bishops, 2006), under "Church Participation",
http://www.usccb.org/about/doctrine/publications/homosexual-inclination
-guidelines-pastoral-care.cfm.

that I could be a father, just so long as I could find one woman to be attracted to. I tested my sexual attractions in an unusual way, but which made perfect sense to me at the time. I went on a research expedition to a strip club, wondering if somehow seeing a naked woman—in the flesh—could possibly stir some sort of arousal in me.

I sat down in a corner of a strip club off of I-94, near Chicago, and a woman soon walked over to me, scantily clad, wondering if I was interested in a lap dance. I watched her with the eye of a research scientist—was there anything remotely sexually interesting for me? Nothing, whatsoever, so I declined her offer, and then proceeded to comment on the weather. It was a beautiful summer day, and soon our conversation turned toward gardening. We found we both enjoyed planting heirloom tomatoes, and I learned a trick from her for freezing vegetables that I still use to this day. The only sexually attractive people at the strip club were some of the men there, ogling the strippers. Having just talked about gardening with a nearly naked woman who wanted to give me a lap dance, I decided then that I must truly be gay.

I entered the gay world not long after by visiting a friend living in Chicago who had gone to my Christian high school. He was out and proud as a gay man, and he offered to initiate me into the gay community, so I spent a long weekend with him in Boystown, the gay district in Chicago. Not long after that, I finally found a man to have sex with, and within a year or so I was dating Jason, planning to share my life with him. I essentially viewed myself as living out my life as a gay man, just waiting for the right time for the next inevitable step: to announce to my family and friends that I was gay, through the ritual of "coming out".

Yet from the very beginning, "being gay" seemed very strange to me. This did not come from some sort of psychological angst or denial about my sexual attractions, or continuing moral hang-ups—I had gladly turned my back on God, and embraced the sexual liberty of leaving behind what I viewed at the time as his absurd commandments. No, my problem with the idea of "the gay person" stemmed primarily from an intellectual and philosophical evaluation of what it means "to be gay". Though I felt a certain liberation at first when I went to Boystown and started to view myself as a member of the gay community, it never seemed to me that I had found my "true community", or my "true family", just because I had decided for myself that I was now a gay man. As time passed, the more I contemplated the idea of being a part of the LGBT community, I started to wonder what that even *meant*—building a sense of community based on a shared experience of whom one found sexually attractive, or the sort of person you enjoyed having sex with, seemed a weak foundation upon which to build a sense of community. My "straight" friends didn't do this. Their sense of community was built around common interests, around church communities, or around school activities, work, or even around things like Boy Scouts, as was the case with my family growing up. Whenever I spent time with other gay guys, I became quickly bored and annoyed with our conversations, which so often seemed to involve countless double entendres and sexual innuendoes, and often was characterized by adopting an exaggerated flamboyance and way of talking that was very odd to me.

It seemed to me that by entering the gay community, I would be entering into an exclusive niche of people who had cordoned themselves off from the rest of the world based on their collective decision that the most important defining element of their lives was their sexuality, and their perceived sense of sexual identity. There also seemed to be a lot of role-playing in the gay community, where people adopted ways of behaving and thinking that were prescribed to them.[1] The more I wrestled with the idea of "being gay", the more I realized it had very little to do with my experience, or how I wanted to live my life. This growing disillusionment with the notion of seeing myself now "as a gay man" was one reason I delayed "coming out". It seemed an injustice to my own personal dignity to place myself in a box that didn't seem to fit who I was or how I viewed the world. I realized there was very little about the gay community that appealed to me. Sure, we had a common bond that we all lived with same-sex attractions and enjoyed sexual pleasure with members of the same sex, but there was where the similarities ended for me. My true community was the community I had built over a lifetime: my friends, family, and coworkers. The least interesting aspect of my community of friends, the one area that no one really cared all that much about, except in a rather cursory way, was *sex* and *sexual identity*, which seemed to me just the opposite of the gay community. Everything in the gay community

---

[1] For example, there are many subdefinitions of "gay" identities that are often rooted in body types, or ages: twinks are skinny young men with very little body hair who are typically under thirty; twunks are the same age, but with more muscle mass, yet still without much body hair; daddies are older men who are often desired by younger men where "daddy-son" fantasies are commonplace; bears are men who are hairy and often overweight; a polar bear is an older hairy man with silver or gray hair; cubs are young, chubby men with hair; otters are young, fit men with very hairy bodies; wolves are younger men with hair and with very muscular bodies—the divisions go on and on, and subcommunities within the gay community often spring up around these taxonomical differences. The label of "gay" becomes even more exclusively confining with these additional identities, based on an objectification of men based solely on their physical attributes. Added to these categories is a dizzying array of sexual preferences or fetishistic desires, each with its own prescribed term and often role associated with the label.

always somehow revolved around sex and sexual identity, and for me, it became quickly boring, and an odd foundation on which to build a sense of community. Thus, "being gay" seemed a strange way upon which to base my life and so coming out made little sense to me.[2]

Over the years, I've been intrigued by the writings of many people who felt similarly about "coming out" based on questioning the construction of the gay identity, as a *type* of person. I resonate with William H. DuBay's thoughts on gay identity in his book *Gay Identity: The Self Under Ban*. "I remember the moment I decided I was gay," he says. "It was April 1971 and I was standing outside the

---

[2]Admittedly, there are sadly many cases when people lose their family and friends after they "come out" and thus lose their historic community. I don't want to diminish the experience of those who have found a community of friends in the gay community, after having been rejected—or feeling rejected—by their family, friends, or church. When and where this has happened, families and the church community need to repent and ask forgiveness for their failings. There is still much work to be done in reaching out in love to those in the gay community who have been hurt by people in a particular church community, and thus have felt forced to leave, in search of a new community to call home. I once had such an awful experience with a judgmental priest in the confessional that I left without receiving absolution and wept as I drove away, reeling from a priest who in no way reflected the mercy and compassion of Christ. It was a spiritually abusive moment, and I am not alone in having experienced such moments in the confessional; and moments like these often lead people away from the Church. Here, as in all things, Christ must be our model: like with the woman at the well, or the woman caught in adultery, every church community, especially the Catholic Church and her priests, needs to invite all who are sexually broken into the only true community that builds up man: the church family, centered around Christ, and in the Catholic Church, centered around the Eucharist. Here is where every church community's understanding of true human community can help build up those healthy components of true communion that exist within the gay community, and help those in the gay community to leave behind those unhealthy parts of the gay community that seem endemic to the culture. For a discussion of these problems, from someone who writes as a member of the gay community, see Michael Hobbes, "Together Alone: The Epidemic of Gay Loneliness,", *Huffington Post Highline*, March 2, 2017, http://highline.huffingtonpost.com/articles/en/gay-loneliness/.

newly opened gay community center in downtown Seat-
tle, hesitating to go in." For him, walking through those
doors would mean walking into a new life, a new identity
as a gay man, and "life would never be the same.... Step-
ping through that door with heart pounding," he said, "I
felt I was making a statement about myself and about the
society in which I lived."[3] Not long after, he "came out"
and announced to his family and friends that he was gay.

DuBay, however, like me, would later reject the labels
"gay" or "homosexual", calling them "highly loaded, stig-
matic terms that severely alter our perceptions of people,
making us believe that people act differently because they are
different."[4] Writing in the *LA Times* in 1994, he denounced
the "vicious and lazy way of thinking that divides the whole
world into two kinds of persons, gay and straight".[5] This
lazy way of thinking, DuBay argues—and here I agree with
him—"has corrupted our language."[6]

Let me be clear: DuBay has no moral issues with men
having sex with men; he and I do not share the same
view of sexual morality. He believes that same-sex attractions and behavior are a natural and normal way of being
human, and he acts on those desires because he enjoys
them and finds nothing morally wrong with them. To act
on those desires is, for him, a *choice* he has freely made: "I
have been in a same-sex relationship for half my life, but
I reject the label [of gay]. I do this not because I don't have

[3] William H. DuBay, *The Gay Identity: The Self Under Ban* (Jefferson, N.C.:
McFarland, 1987), p. 130.

[4] William H. DuBay, "Gay Identity", QueerByChoice.com, June 12, 2012,
http://www.queerbychoice.com/dubay_gayidentity.html.

[5] William H. DuBay, "Sexuality Is Not Just 'Gay' or 'Straight': Gay Rights:
A Movement That Identifies a Person by Sexual Behavior Is Limiting, Not
Liberating", *Los Angeles Times*, August 26, 1994, http://articles.latimes.com
/1994-08-26/local/me-31298_1_sexual-behavior.

[6] DuBay, "Gay Identity".

any choice but because I like it. Is that hard to understand? It is a very big difference."[7]

For DuBay—and for me—it seems ill conceived to "come out" and identify as a different kind of person, based on something like sexual attractions or one's sexual proclivities. It is a mistaken construct of man that would create more than fifty supposedly discrete forms of sexual identity, based on the vagaries of man's sexual appetites and behaviors.[8] Man is a complex creature, and in the realm of human sexuality, he will be confronted with a remarkable array of varied appetites and feelings; yet the desires, appetites, and behaviors of man don't change the sort of innate creature he is. It's only the confused thinking of modern man that refashions human nature in such a way as to make man into a different sort of creature whose identity would be based primarily on sexual attractions and feelings.[9] This way of thinking claims that any feelings-based sexual identity must be treated as an objective reality and therefore must be considered normal and healthy. Finally, according to this logic, the next step is that this identity must somehow be adopted and claimed through the ritual of "coming out". "Coming out" has become a secular sacrament of sorts, portrayed as a rite of passage into a new life of freedom and liberty, and the only way anyone with same-sex attractions can ever truly be at peace in the realm of human sexuality. This is not true.

[7] William H. DuBay, "More on Gay Behavior", *Civic Language Comments on Current Affairs and Building Social Capital* (blog), July 3, 2013, http://www.impact-information.com/wordpress/?p=243.

[8] ABC News has identified fifty-eight gender options. See Russell Goldman, "Here's a List of 58 Gender Options for Facebook Users", ABCNews.com, February 13, 2014, http://abcnews.go.com/blogs/headlines/2014/02/heres-a-list-of-58-gender-options-for-facebook-users/.

[9] See ibid.

From the very beginning of the gay rights movement, gay rights activists have convinced young men and women into "coming out" by posing it as their only path to human fulfillment, honesty, and freedom. Consider this passage from a book published in 1979 for young people, called *A Way of Love, A Way of Life: A Young Person's Introduction to What It Means to Be Gay*:

> Young gays inwardly struggle with whether or not to share knowledge of their sexual orientation with family or friends. Certainly being honest about being gay seems to have obvious advantages. It eliminates the need to live a double life. Always being on guard to keep "the big secret" under wraps can take a lot of effort and imagination, not to mention outright deception. We all try to be reasonably honest and truthful with those we love. The price we often pay for hiding our sexual orientation is to grow apart from family and friends as we erect a barrier between us and them. Under these circumstances existing relationships can be strained.[10]

The book then quotes a young man who says, "The very worst thing is to be closeted. A teen-ager will become a loner that way, even if he or she lives with a family. I mean, living two lives, always hiding!"[11]

Similar advice is given today by movements such as the "It Gets Better Campaign", which positions itself as an anti-bullying organization. Yet the book associated with the campaign, edited by Dan Savage and Terry Miller, is called *It Gets Better: Coming Out, Overcoming Bullying, and*

[10] Frances Hanckel and John Cunningham, *A Way of Love, A Way of Life: A Young Person's Introduction to What It Means to Be Gay* (New York: Lothrop, Lee and Shepard Books, 1979), p. 63.

[11] Ibid.

Creating a Life Worth Living.[12] Life gets better, they seem to be saying, only after you come out; doing so is a necessary ingredient to "creating a life worth living". In the process, coming out becomes a way to take a stand against bullying, something everyone rightly abhors.

"Coming out" becomes then far more than merely sharing with others about your attractions to the same sex. When you come out, you join the ranks of a noble struggle against oppression and injustice. This exerts a seductive form of pressure on young people, as the sociologist Robert Endleman describes:

> In some young adults, who are still struggling to define their sexuality, their sexual and gender identity, and who have been "trying on" homosexuality, as it were, as one possibility, the drive of the movement activists and their associated "therapists" to get the individual positively to embrace his homosexual self and solidify his homosexuality, is not in fact the liberating force its proponents claim, but in many cases the reverse, another form of tyranny. For one can be tyrannized into a nonconformity position, as well as into a conforming one—especially where there are so many obvious "secondary gains" to be accrued from such a resolution—the exhilarating feeling of solidarity with an "oppressed" but now militant minority, the thrill of battle against "evil," even the very danger of confrontation in the external world (so much more palatable than confrontation with one's own much more mysterious inner demons).[13]

I find his argument very convincing as to why "coming out" becomes so tempting for many young people.

---

[12] Dan Savage and Terry Miller, *It Gets Better: Coming Out, Overcoming Bullying, and Creating a Life Worth Living* (New York: Dutton, 2011).

[13] Robert Endleman, *Psyche and Society: Exploration in Psychoanalytic Sociology* (New York: Columbia University Press, 1981), p. 258.

It is easy to see how the presentation of coming out as joining a mission to overturn injustice, and becoming a member of an oppressed minority with a right to demand protection and special rights, can be seductive to young people, especially those who feel marginalized and isolated because of their experience of same-sex attractions. One book on coming out says "you are a hero for coming out".[14] Who doesn't want to be a hero, especially if you can do it by coming out, which is posed as the most courageous and honest act one could ever do for himself? Imagine how alluring this can be for a young person, confused about his sexuality, wondering if there's something amiss in his own sexual identity. Instead of wrestling with these questions, or seeking help for the wounds that led to his attractions to the same sex—or even considering that there *are* wounds that led to his attractions—now, by coming out publicly, he becomes part of a movement, a part of an oppressed class, part of a "sexual minority". The pain of silence becomes a pathway toward being a part of a mission for social change. This can be an intoxicating temptation for a person considering coming out.

Pope Saint John Paul II, quoting the Synod Fathers in his *Christifideles Laici*, states, "The sensitivity of young people profoundly affects their perceiving of the values of justice, nonviolence and peace. Their hearts are disposed to fellowship, friendship and solidarity. They are greatly moved by causes that relate to the quality of life and the conservation of nature. But they are troubled by anxiety, deceptions, anguishes and fears of the world as well as by

---

[14]Christopher Lee Nutter, *The Way Out: The Gay Man's Guide to Freedom No Matter If You're in Denial, Closeted, Half In, Half Out, Just Out or Been Around the Block* (Deerfield, Fla.: Health Communications, 2006), p. 38.

the temptations that come with their state."[15] It makes sense then why some young people are drawn to joining a cause fighting for the rights of "sexual minorities", instead of wrestling with the mysterious inner wounds within their psyche that led to their same-sex attractions. They are urged to ignore voices like the Church, which teaches that homosexuality has a "psychological genesis",[16] and instead are urged to "come out", and take pride in something that once caused them to question their own sexual identity.[17] And beyond this, implicit in the idea of "the closet" is that when a person "comes out", it's only then that he is finally able to live freely, "as he really is". One author claims, "Coming out may be difficult and stressful

---

[15]John Paul II, Post-Synodal Apostolic Exhortation on the Vocation and the Mission of the Lay Faithful in the Church and in the World *Christifideles Laici* (December 30, 1988), no. 46, http://w2.vatican.va/content/john-paul-ii /en/apost_exhortations/documents/hf_jp-ii_exh_30121988_christifideles-laici .html.

[16]*CCC* 2357.

[17]For an example of the sorts of theories of causation young people who "come out" are urged to ignore—and an example of what has been helpful for me in wrestling with my own "mysterious inner demons" surrounding SSA— consider psychologist Bob Schuchts' brief explanation of how one's psycho-sexual development can divert from a normal path toward experiences of SSA: "When a child develops and matures in a healthy way, he will naturally gravi- tate to opposite-sex attractions during the stage of *sexual exploration*. In normal development, the adolescent will mature physically, emotionally, and spiritu- ally. He will learn a balanced self-mastery over sexual desires, even in times of heightened arousal and attraction. The maturing person will also develop an integrated social identity. Without healthy development during this stage, dis- ordered desires are frequently expressed compulsively in fantasy, masturbation, pornography, sexual promiscuity, or isolation. Same-sex attraction, formed in earlier stages, is often manifested during this time, especially among adoles- cents with low confidence, negative body image, a history of sexual abuse, and unhealed identity wounds". Bob Schuchts, "Restoring Wholeness in Christ", in *Living the Truth in Love: Pastoral Approaches to Same-Sex Attraction*, ed. Janet E. Smith and Father Paul Check (San Francisco: Ignatius Press, 2015), p. 61 (italics in original).

at the time, but it is a rebirth. You are at the very beginning of a new life, one in which you will, for the first time
in a very long time, be able to live in freedom, honesty,
and pride."[18]

William DuBay illustrates what some people believe is
to be gained by claiming homosexuality as an identity that
defines one's life:

> The concept of homosexuality as a disease has given way
> to the concept of homosexuality as a *condition*. Either
> way, the myth serves the purposes of social control by
> placing the cause of the emotion somehow beyond the
> experience itself, underlying it as an inherent condition,
> somehow permanently set in early childhood and remain-
> ing stable throughout one's life. This inherent condition
> we sometimes call "sexuality," "sexual orientation" or
> "sexual preference," but the meanings we give it are much
> more substantive. It is much more than a liking or a pref-
> erence in the sense of a choice. It is rather the *explanation*
> of why we prefer. Many people refer to this condition as
> "my sexual identity," clearly indicating the sense of having
> a condition that sets them apart from others.
>
>   Gay-identified persons carefully cultivate and cher-
> ish this sense of having a differentiation condition. They
> tend to reinterpret their own biographies and give new
> meanings to their accomplishments, disappointments, and
> failures in light of this perception. "I always knew I was
> different," some people say, "long before I experienced
> any homosexual feelings." For many people, the con-
> dition of being gay occupies a major part of their self-
> concept. The process goes from feeling gay and doing gay
> to being gay.[19]

[18] Michelangelo Signorile, *Outing Yourself: How to Come Out as Lesbian or
Gay to Your Family, Friends and Coworkers* (New York: Simon and Schuster,
1996), p. XXX.

[19] DuBay, *Gay Identity*, p. 7 (italics in original).

Endleman said something similar:

> "Coming out" signals one's finally recognizing one's "true" nature, concealed up till now beneath societally enforced charades of heterosexuality. (One then retrospectively rewrites one's whole biography to accord with this conversion illumination.)[20]

This is part of the lure and temptation of "being gay" and "coming out": when one comes out, one is able to stick a sign in the ground that says, "This is who I am." For a young person trying to discover who he is, having one thing on which he can blame all the unhappiness of his life, by which he can explain all his doubts and his feelings of being different with its associated feelings of isolation—and to which he can pin all his hopes and dreams—is a tantalizing temptation. But in the long run, this seemingly easy way out isn't the answer—rather, it's an empty promise, offered to young people by those who have rejected God's plan for humanity. Father John Hardon wrote that religious instruction, "especially of adolescents, should take into account their tendency to identify with surrounding customs as an expression of personal autonomy".[21] "Coming out" is a powerful expression of personal autonomy for a young person confused about his sexual identity; and who most likely has suffered great pain, often in silent despair, wondering where to find hope and happiness. We need to work hard in our schools and parishes to understand the suffering of those who live with same-sex attractions, or those who live with confusion about their sexual identity. And they need help to understand that "coming

---

[20] Endleman, *Psyche and Society*, p. 321.

[21] John Hardon, S.J., *The Catholic Catechism: A Contemporary Catechism of the Teachings of the Catholic Church* (New York: Doubleday, 1981), p. 355.

out", or embracing the world's view of sexuality, will not bring them the happiness they desire.

Examples of men and women who learned this lesson the hard way abound within the Courage Apostolate. One of my good friends from Courage who came out in high school made the astute observation that "coming out" was really a "going in" to a prison that trapped him—and others—into a false view of himself.

A Courage chaplain recently told me the story of a college student in his Courage chapter who, like the young man above, decided in high school to come out as gay. Believing "this is who he was", he claimed the identity and happily came out. When he did so, however, he found that other boys weren't really interested in being close friends with him. He was popular with the girls—they all liked having the stereotypical "gay friend", and he stepped into that role—but what he longed for was close friendships with other boys. He realized that by coming out, he had been labeled as "the gay guy", and as a result, the other boys in his school didn't really have any interest in spending time with him. When he went to college, where he knew no one, he went back to being just him, another young man, among a sea of other young men and women. He found the supposed liberation of "being out" actually prevented him from having the friendships with men that he so deeply craved. Since claiming his true sexual identity, simply as a man, he's been able to nurture and build the friendships with other men he longed for in high school.

My situation is similar. I have not found public knowledge of my attractions helpful to me—in fact, quite the opposite has been true. Indeed, part of the reason I became public about this part of my life was so that others might consider a different viewpoint on the wisdom of "coming out".

Since my attractions to men have become well known to those in my circle, I find it remarkable how some of my friends have reinvented my past life, simply because they now seem to view me as a gay man.

One of my close friends stumbled on my writings and asked me about them. In our conversation, we discussed the women I had dated in the past. Now, in his eyes, this became me "exploring my sexuality", with the implication that the reason things didn't work out was because I was really gay. My past is like a green screen in a television studio onto which some of my friends have projected the backdrop they've made up about me and my life. It's all rather unfortunate, but I think this happens quite often to people when they come out. I hope my experience can be viewed as a cautionary tale to others.

Then there are the temptations that naturally come when one is "out of the closet". I once read someone say that there are temptations to sin by "being in the closet", and this was given as a reason people should "come out". I chuckled at the absurdity of the statement—if there are temptations associated with a man keeping his sexual desires for men secret, well, they are nothing compared to the temptations of "being out".

The first time in my life when a man offered to come home and have sex with me only happened after he talked to me about my essay "Why I Don't Call Myself a Gay Christian". He is a friend of mine who identifies as gay. Having read my essay, he wanted to know more about my thoughts on homosexuality. I told him what I thought and what I believed—and then he offered to come home with me and have sex. It didn't matter to him that I had just told him that I'm striving my darnedest to live a chaste life. He was interested in sex with me and apparently viewed me now as being on the market. Keeping my sexual attractions private was a very helpful tool in living chastely and avoiding temptations like that—and it's one very important reason why men especially should keep this part of their lives out of the public eye.

Some people suggest that "not coming out" is equivalent to living a lie. One commenter on a blog discussing this issue wrote,

> If someone asks me "Are you gay?" I would be lying if I said "No." Anyone who is same-sex attracted would be lying. You can't pretend like you're not gay just because it isn't your preferred label. You could answer by saying, "Yes, but I prefer the term same-sex attracted." But if [to answer] "No" to the question "Are you gay?" would be a lie for a same-sex attracted person (and I'm pretty sure almost everyone would think so) ... then "gay" means "same-sex attracted" in the straightforward sense, and one can't escape a reality just by refusing to identify with it.[22]

This is muddled thinking about the nature of reality and what constitutes a lie. No one is guilty of lying by giving a negative response to the rather impertinent question "Are you gay?" Yet here, concerns over being deceitful often relate to questions of one's romantic future. A challenging aspect of living with same-sex attractions, particularly for young people, is worrying about what to say to friends and family about the question of dating and marriage. I lived with these worries for a time too. But I learned that the easiest and most honest thing I could ever say was "I leave my future in God's hands. I don't feel called to marriage, but I'm open to marriage if it is God's will."

---

[22]A Sinner, comment on Ron Belgau, "What Does 'Sexual Orientation' Orient?", *Spiritual Friendship: Musings on God, Sexuality, Relationships* (blog), September 28, 2013, https://spiritualfriendship.org/2013/09/27/what-does -sexual-orientation-orient/.

No one lies by "not coming out". Indeed, *honesty* is the primary reason no one should ever "come out". By not identifying as a gay man, I recognize the truth that I'm made for a woman, just as Adam was made for Eve. Let me be clear—that truth doesn't make me desire women, or turn off my desires for men, nor does it make me pine for marriage like I once did. In fact, I tend to expect I'll be single the rest of my life. But it seems to me that if I desire to have appropriate humility before God my Creator, I must accept and recognize that I am a man made for union with a woman. And that truth means that God may actually have a wife in store for me, at some point in my life. Now, that's not anything I really desire at all. In fact, the idea of sharing my life with a woman sort of gives me the heebie-jeebies. I'm not keen on the idea of marriage, but I have enough faith in Divine Providence that if God desires for me to be married, he would also inspire a desire in me for the woman he would will for me to marry. Here it is helpful for me to recall what we learn in Genesis: *God brought Eve to Adam.* I'm not really interested in finding an Eve, so I'm not looking for one, but I know that God might will that for me, and if he does, one sign will be that I will recognize her as a gift from God, as Adam did when he saw Eve and said, "This at last is bone of my bones and flesh of my flesh" (Gen 2:23). It doesn't look like that will happen in my life, but humility before my Creator keeps me open to the possibility. I don't fret about "keeping up appearances" anymore—I realize that was all wasted worry. It's the most honest thing in the world for me to say to prying questions, "I don't know what God has in store for me, and I leave my future in his capable hands." And then I leave it at that. That's far more honest about my true nature than for me ever to say to anyone, "Well, I'm not dating a woman *because I'm gay*."

"Coming out" leads to belief in what is ultimately an unreal condition—it paints a false image of the human person and traps people into sexual identities that are disconnected with reality. Even so, a certain amount of discreet disclosure is wise. It's hard—and I think pretty near impossible—to go through life without sharing with anyone about your same-sex attractions. As stated in the chapter opener, the United States Conference of Catholic Bishops wisely understands the need for this and suggests the best way to go about it:

> For some persons, revealing their homosexual tendencies to certain close friends, family members, a spiritual director, confessor, or members of a Church support group may provide some spiritual and emotional help and aid them in their growth in the Christian life. In the context of parish life, however, general public self-disclosures are not helpful and should not be encouraged.

I have followed the bishops' wise advice and found it very beneficial. Being open about my same-sex attractions with my family, certain close friends, and some priests, as well as my friends at Courage who are a support group for me, has helped me in my desire to live a chaste life. Not coming out publicly as a gay man has helped me keep my same-sex attractions in perspective. I like to think of same-sex attractions in my life sort of like the solar system. People who come out place a high importance on their sexual attractions—they move their identity as gay to the center of their solar system. If they're Christian, it doesn't necessarily replace the identity they have as a child of God—but it seems to me that it becomes for them like a binary star system, with two "suns" around which all aspects of their lives orbit. Everything in their lives, they believe, is shaped by and revolves around their gay identity, even if they acknowledge that it's not the strongest identity they have. I think of my attractions very differently.

I place my identity as a man and a beloved son of God at the center of my life, and everything else in my life—interests, career, dreams, even my same-sex attractions—finds its place in relation to that central truth. My attractions to men aren't at the center of my life, but they certainly influence the rest of my life in some ways—sort of like every planet's gravitational pull impacts all the other planets in the solar system and even pull on the sun. But I don't place much importance to them in shaping my life—and this is a deliberate choice. Same-sex attractions have as much power over my life as I allow them to have. This is one reason I have chosen not to be gay, and not to come out as a gay man. No doubt my same-sex attractions impact other areas of my life, but I believe I place them in a far healthier place by refusing to "come out" and thereby placing "being gay" at the center of my life. That holds no interest for me.

I'd rather know myself—and be known—as just a man, just the way God created me.[23]

---

[23] It's the virtue of chastity that helps me see myself as I really am, and helps me live my life based on reality. We'll talk about that in Part Three.

PART THREE

HOW TO RUN THE RACE: LIVING OUT THE DAILY BATTLE FOR CHASTITY

Jesus Is Our Holiness

If anyone strives to be delivered from his troubles out of love of God, he will strive patiently, gently, humbly and calmly, looking for deliverance rather to God's Goodness and Providence than to his own industry or efforts.

—Saint Francis de Sales[*]

For it is impossible for a man to win a triumph over any kind of passion, unless he has first clearly understood that he cannot possibly gain the victory in the struggle with it by his own strength and efforts, although in order that he may be rendered pure he must night and day persist in the utmost care and watchfulness.

—Saint John Cassian[†]

When I think of my battle for chastity, I think about the words of Saint Paul when he said, "I do not understand my own actions. For I do not do what I want, but I do the very thing I hate.... For I know that nothing good dwells within me, that is, in my flesh. I can will what is right, but I cannot do it. For I do not do the good I want, but the evil I do not want is what I do" (Rom 7:15, 18–19).

[*] St. Francis de Sales, *Introduction to the Devout Life*, ed. W. H. Hutchings (London: Rivingtons, 1882), p. 247.
[†] St. John Cassian, *Conference of Abbot Serapion*, chap. 13, in vol. 11 of *A Select Library of Nicene and Post-Nicene Fathers of the Christian Church*, 2nd series, ed. Philip Schaff and Henry Wace (New York: Christian Literature, 1894), p. 345.

Through painful experience, Saint Paul learned the most important lesson a man striving to live chastely can ever learn: that only Jesus can save us from our miserable state: "Wretched man that I am! Who will deliver me from this body of death? Thanks be to God through Jesus Christ our Lord!" (Rom 7:24–25).

Saint Paul's life, and his "thorn in the flesh" (see 2 Cor 12:7), brings me great hope in my own struggles for the virtue of chastity.

Saint Paul writes,

> Three times I begged the Lord about this, that it should leave me; but he said to me, "My grace is sufficient for you, for my power is made perfect in weakness." I will all the more gladly boast of my weaknesses, that the power of Christ may rest upon me. For the sake of Christ, then, I am content with weaknesses, insults, hardships, persecutions, and calamities; for when I am weak, then I am strong. (2 Cor 12:8–10)

Saint Paul doesn't tell us what his "thorn in the flesh" was, nor does the Church provide a definitive explanation. Yet, as a man who has been so good at living an *unchaste* life, I take comfort that the Doctor of the Church Saint Alphonsus Liguori taught that Saint Paul's thorn in the flesh was a temptation to unchastity.

He writes:

> Even Saint Paul ... groaned under temptations against chastity.... He three times prayed to the Lord, to deliver him from these temptations; but in answer the Lord told him, that his grace was sufficient for him.... God permits even his servants to be tempted, as well to try their fidelity, as to purify them from their imperfections.[1]

---

[1] St. Alphonsus Liguori, *Sermons for All the Sundays in the Year*, trans. Nicholas Callan, D.D. (Dublin: James Duffy and Sons, 1882), p. 357.

There are three important lessons I believe we can learn from Saint Paul's battle against this thorn in the flesh, and apply to the battle for purity and chastity. First, God, and God alone, brings about our victory. We must not rely on our own efforts here. Second, we need to have patience with ourselves and with our fragile human nature, and trust that God has allowed a temptation or a struggle in our lives in order to "purify" us from our "imperfections". That means we must be gentle with ourselves when we stumble, and be humble enough to know who we are and what our nature is. Third, we must persevere and never give up trying, never give into despair, and always cling to hope and have faith in the truth that Jesus is our holiness.

Jesus Is Our Holiness

Saint John Cassian teaches us that though God's grace is needed for any good we do, it is especially necessary for living out the virtue of chastity. In his *Conferences,* he writes:

> And therefore though in many things, indeed in everything, it can be shown that men always have need of God's help, and that human weakness cannot accomplish anything that has to do with salvation by itself alone, i.e., without the aid of God, yet in nothing is this more clearly shown than in the acquisition and preservation of chastity.[2]

He continues in the same theme, and like Saint Alphonsus he speaks of Saint Paul's thorn in the flesh in the context of fighting for chastity. He teaches us that

[2] St. John Cassian, *The Third Conference of Abbot Ciueron,* chap. 6, in vol. 11 of Schaff and Wace, *Select Library of Nicene and Post-Nicene Fathers,* p. 424.

there is no carrying out of our purpose, unless the power to perform it has been granted by the mercy of the Lord,... the opportunity for doing everything that we wish does not lie in our own power.... While without our own consent the regularity of our routine is broken and we yield something to weakness of the flesh, we may even against our will be brought to a salutary patience. Of which providential arrangement of God the blessed Apostle [that is, Saint Paul] says something similar: "For which I besought the Lord thrice that it might depart from me." And He said to me: "My grace is sufficient for you: for my strength is made perfect in weakness": and again: "For we know not what to pray for as we ought."[3]

Saint Augustine imparts the same truth: "It is God's gift which is indispensable for the observance of the precepts of chastity. Accordingly, it is said in the Book of Wisdom: 'When I knew that no one could be continent, except God gives it, then this became a point of wisdom to know whose gift it was'"[4] (see Wis 8:21). And again, Saint Augustine says, "In order ... that this victory may be gained, grace renders its help."[5]

Therefore, the greatest lesson we can ever learn in our battle for the virtue of chastity is to trust and believe the words of Christ: "apart from me you can do nothing" (Jn 15:5). When we battle for chastity, and so often fail, we must cling to the promise of Christ made to Saint Paul, realizing that God's grace is sufficient. We learn this through our weaknesses and failures. It is weakness that teaches us that *Jesus is our holiness.*

[3] Ibid.

[4] St. Augustine, *On Grace and Free Will*, chap. 8, in *Saint Augustin: Anti-Pelagian Writings*, vol. 5 of *A Select Library of the Nicene and Post-Nicene Fathers of the Christian Church*, 1st series, ed. Philip Schaff (New York: Christian Literature, 1887), p. 447.

[5] Ibid.

Blessed Columba Marmion, an Irish saint known for his wise spiritual counsel, wrote in a letter of spiritual direction,

> Do not let yourself be discouraged by your miseries; the Good God leaves you some miseries to convince you thoroughly that you can do nothing. He does not wish us to be able to attribute to ourselves whatever good we can accomplish. *Jesus is our holiness;* we must be very faithful and wait for Him to act in us.[6]

Thomas Merton has helped me understand this too. He knew his own weakness in chastity—like Saint Augustine, before he entered the Church, he fathered a child out of wedlock. He understood the battle that wages inside all of us.

> Real self-conquest is the conquest of ourselves not by ourselves but by the Holy Spirit. Self-conquest is really self-surrender.
>
> Yet before we can surrender ourselves we must become ourselves. For no one can give up what he does not possess.
>
> More precisely—we have to have enough mastery of ourselves to renounce our own will into the hands of Christ—so that He may conquer what we cannot reach by our own efforts.[7]

Be Gentle and Patient with Yourself

Saint Francis de Sales is the loving teacher who helps me be gentle with myself. In a letter of spiritual direction, he wrote to a young woman that she must be patient with herself in her battles against her passions. How I wish I

[6] Columba Marmion, *Union with God*, p. 96 (italics in original). See also p. 29.
[7] Thomas Merton, *Thoughts in Solitude* (New York: Farrar, Straus and Giroux, 2011), p. 18.

could have heard this when I was a young man, first wrestling with sexual sin and temptation:

> It is not possible that you can be so speedily mistress of your soul, and keep it so absolutely under your hand at the first time. Be content with gaining from time to time some little advantage over your ruling passion. One must bear with others; but in the first place one must bear with one's self, and have patience with one's being imperfect.[8]

He told his spiritual daughter and coworker, Saint Jeanne-Françoise de Chantal,

> If you happen to do something that you regret, be neither astonished nor upset, but, having acknowledged your failing, humble yourself quietly before God and try to regain your gentle composure. Say to your soul: "There, we have made a mistake, but let's go on now and be more careful." Every time you fall, do the same.[9]

He goes on to encourage her with words that have helped me immensely in my own battles:

> But most important, my dear daughter, don't lose heart, be patient, wait, do all you can to develop a spirit of compassion. I have no doubt that God is holding you by the hand; if He allows you to stumble, it is only to let you know that if He were not holding your hand, you would fall. This is how He gets you to take a tighter hold of His hand.[10]

---

[8] St. Francis de Sales, *Practical Piety, Set Forth by St. Francis de Sales, Bishop and Prince of Geneva, Collected from His Letters and Discourses* (Louisville: Webb and Levering, 1853), p. 193.

[9] *Letters of Spiritual Direction: Letters of Francis de Sales and of Jane de Chantal*, selected by Wendy M. Wright and Joseph F. Power, trans. Péronne Marie Thibert (New York: Paulist Press, 1988), p. 158.

[10] Ibid.

The longer I have lived, the more comfort I have taken in the need to grab ahold of the hand of Christ with a firmer grip as each year passes. In his work *On Hope*, Josef Pieper quotes the medieval theologian Paschasius Radbertus, who said, "Christ is held by the hand of hope. We hold him and are held. But it is a greater good that we are held by Christ than that we hold him. For we can hold him only so long as we are held by him."[11] I often recall a moment in my life when I slipped and stumbled after several years of sexual sobriety. I went on retreat soon after, sharing my sorrows and regrets with one of the kindly priests from the Community of Saint John in Peoria, Illinois. He told me words I've never forgotten. "Sometimes," he said, "God allows a fall so that we might learn to cling to him ever more tightly."

I think much of our struggles to overcome difficult habits or sins is rooted in impatience with *ourselves*. But here, we need to understand that God made man a certain way, and that we are not the sort of creatures who can be "perfect" just by willing ourselves to be so. Saint Irenaeus reminds us that "humanity slowly progresses, approaches perfection and draws near to the uncreated God."[12]

Saint Irenaeus also said that "people who do not wait for the period of growth, who attribute the weakness of their nature to God, are completely unreasonable. They understand neither God nor themselves." He adds, "At the outset they refuse to be what they were made: human beings who are subject to passions. They override the law of human nature; they already want to be like God the Creator before they even become human beings."[13]

[11] Josef Pieper, *On Hope*, trans. Mary Frances McCarthy, S.N.D. (San Francisco: Ignatius Press, 1986), pp. 33–34.

[12] Irenaeus of Lyon, *Against Heresies* 4.38, in *Theological Anthropology*, trans. and ed. J. Patout Burns, S.J. (Philadelphia: Fortress Press, 1981), p. 25.

[13] Ibid.

We have to remember that we're pilgrims, on a journey, and that we all progress at our own pace. Pope Saint John Paul II said, "Chastity is a difficult, long term matter; one must wait patiently for it to bear fruit, for the happiness of loving kindness which it must bring. But at the same time, chastity is the sure way to happiness."[14] Thomas Merton puts our struggles for chastity in perspective. He says, "A man is known, then, by his end. He is also known by his beginning. And if you wish to know him as he is at any given moment, find how far he is from his beginning and how near to his end. Hence, too, the man who sins in spite of himself but does not love his sin, is not a sinner in the full sense of the word."[15] That has helped me so much in being patient with myself when I recognize how weak I am.

There's a beautiful little book called *My Daily Life* that has helped me immensely in understanding the human condition. I stumbled on it in an Adoration chapel during a time when I despaired of ever being free from sins of unchastity. I read a line that has become a creed for me when I am tempted to despair at my own faults:

> *Jesus is far more reasonable with you than you are with yourself.* He does not expect you to be today the better person you can be next year. It will take you a year to gain the wisdom, prudence and strength that will be yours a year from now.[16]

This is essential in the spiritual walk. Jesus is reasonable, patient, and gentle with us because he knows that we are

[14] Karol Wojtyła, *Love and Responsibility* (San Francisco: Ignatius Press, 1993), p. 172.

[15] Thomas Merton, *Thoughts in Solitude* (New York: Farrar, Straus and Giroux, 1999), p. 10.

[16] Anthony J. Paone, S.J., *My Daily Life* (Brooklyn, N.Y.: Confraternity of the Precious Blood, 1970), p. 31 (italics added).

on a journey to become who we were created to be. He knows the weakness of our nature. We must likewise be patient and strive to see ourselves as God sees us. And this takes humility. As the same author says,

> The first qualification you will need to achieve this spiritual development, is humility. Humility is the virtue which disposes a man to: 1) face reality as it is, 2) change what can be changed, and 3) learn to make the most of what cannot be changed. Without humility you cannot live a realistic life.[17]

A few pages later, the author mapped out a path that I have followed ever since in my battle for chastity, which I commend to anyone despairing of ever having mastery over his passions:

> Though you may never be the kind of person you would like to be, you can certainly come a little closer to your goal with a bit of intelligent planning. Even if there be little or no visible growth through the years, at least you can offer Him a persevering daily effort as a sign of your genuine good will.
>
> Busy as your daily routine may be, you can fit your effort into the limited time available to you. You might follow this little plan: 1) Read a little, 2) Think a little, 3) Apply it to your daily routine, 4) Resolve a little, 5) Practice a little, and 6) Renew your intention when you fall, and begin again. Never count the failures, but rather count the renewed efforts. This positive attitude will help you maintain a firm determination to *keep trying* for the rest of your life. If you accomplish no more than to avoid the extremes of 1) discouragement, 2) complacency, or 3) rigid attitudes, your effort will be acknowledged by the Lord. In other

[17] Ibid.

words, your effort was the best proof of your sincerity and
love of God.[18]

This has brought me tremendous peace of soul. Regardless of how many times I fail, I can keep trying the rest
of my life. Brother Lawrence is a good example for us.
We are told that Brother Lawrence of the Resurrection
knew his "great need for a confessor to receive absolution
for the sins he committed. He acknowledged his sins and
was not surprised by them. He confessed them to God
and did not plead before him to excuse them; after that
he returned to his ordinary exercises of love and adoration in peace."[19] This shows a firm faith in the words of
Saint Paul that because of the Cross, "There is therefore
now no condemnation for those who are in Christ Jesus"
(Rom 8:1).

And Brother Lawrence understood the truth that God's
grace is the only means by which we stand or fall. It was
said of him when he sinned that

> when he failed he did nothing other than acknowledge his
> failure, telling God, "I will never do anything right if you
> leave me alone; it's up to you to stop me from falling and
> correct what is wrong." After that he no longer worried
> about his failure.[20]

How much peace of soul this view of our sins can bring
us. When we have a calm and realistic view of ourselves,
we can be gentle with ourselves, and then, even in the face

[18] Ibid., p. 33.
[19] Brother Lawrence of the Resurrection, *The Practice of the Presence of God*,
ed. Conrad de Meester, trans. Salvatore Sciurba (Washington, D.C.: ICS Publications, 1994), p. 101.
[20] Ibid., p. 100.

of our weaknesses, persevere in peace, trusting that God will bring us victory in his time—like he did with many a lusty saint who went before us. We'll talk about them in the next chapter.

The Wisdom and Example
of the Saints

The best means towards the understanding of truth and the performance of the commandments is to follow those others who have already been through the test with flying colors.

— Saint Clement of Alexandria[*]

And so, if we wish in very deed and truth to attain to the crown of virtues, we ought to listen to those teachers and guides who, not dreaming with pompous declamations, but learning by act and experience, are able to teach us as well, and direct us likewise, and show us the road by which we may arrive at it by a most sure pathway; and who also testify that they have themselves reached it by faith rather than by any merits of their efforts.

— Saint John Cassian[†]

When I think of my battles for chastity, I'm reminded of a favorite bit of dialogue I underlined years ago in Graham

---

[*]Clement of Alexandria, *Stromateis, Books 1–31, The Fathers of the Church, Volume 85,* trans. John Ferguson (Washington, D.C.: Catholic University of America Press, 2005), p. 26. Reprinted with permission of Catholic University of America; permission conveyed through Copyright Clearance Center, Inc.

[†]St. John Cassian, *The Institutes of John Cassian, Book XII, On the Spirit of Pride,* vol. 11 of *A Select Library of Nicene and Post-Nicene Fathers of the Christian Church,* 2nd series, ed. Philip Schaff and Henry Wace (New York: Christian Literature, 1894), p. 284.

Greene's novel *The End of the Affair*. One of the characters, Father Crompton, says to Maurice Bendix, the protagonist of the novel, "You can't teach me about penitence, Mr. Bendrix. I've had twenty-five years in the confessional. There's nothing we can do some of the saints haven't done before us."[1] This truth is a relief to anyone, aware of his weakness. I'm grateful to God that there have been plenty of men just like me who've gone before me. Their conversion and redemption teaches that there's hope for a weak man like me.

Saint Augustine

Saint Augustine's *Confessions* are indispensable reading for a man like me who desires to live chastely. Writing of his time in university at Carthage, Augustine recalls

> the abominable things I did in those days, the sins of the flesh which defiled my soul. I do this, my God, not because I love those sins, but so that I may love you. For love of your love I shall retrace my wicked ways. The memory is bitter, but it will help me to savour your sweetness, the sweetness that does not deceive but brings real joy and never fails.... Foolhardy as I was, I ran wild with lust that was manifold and rank. In your eyes my beauty vanished and I was foul to the core, yet I was pleased with my own condition and anxious to be pleasing in the eyes of men.[2]

The following paragraph is something that I could have written about my own life:

---

[1] Graham Greene, *The End of the Affair* (New York: Penguin Books, 1999), p. 180.

[2] Augustine, *Confessions* II.1, trans. R. C. Pine-Coffin (Middlesex, England: Penguin Books, 1961), p. 43.

From my own experience I now understood what I had read—that the impulses of nature and *the impulses of the spirit are at war with one another.* (Gal. 5:17) In this warfare I was on both sides, but I took the part of that which I approved in myself rather than the part of that which I disapproved. For my true self was no longer on the side of which I disapproved, since to a great extent I was now its reluctant victim rather than its willing tool. Yet it was by my own doing that habit had become so potent an enemy, because it was by my own will that I had reached the state in which I no longer wished to stay.... I could no longer claim that I had no clear perception of the truth— the excuse which I used to make to myself for postponing my renunciation of the world and my entry in your service—for by now I was quite certain of it.[3]

At some point in our lives, we must become aware of the truth that the path we're on isn't leading us to fulfillment. We either wake up and see the truth, or we go deeper into the pit of self-deception and self-indulgence. This is one reason, for example, why men who have sex with men so often end up in nonmonogamous relationships:[4] what they're seeking in a relationship with a man

---

[3] Ibid., VII.5, pp. 164–65 (italics in original).

[4] The rarity of monogamy with men who have sex with men is widely written about within the gay community. Sex columnist Dan Savage has coined the term "monogamish" to describe the open relationship he has with Terry Miller. Quoted in Mark Oppenheimer, "Married, With Infidelities", *New York Times Magazine*, June 30, 2011, http://www.nytimes.com/2011/07/03/magazine/infidelity-will-keep-us-together.html). Likewise, Michael Shelton notes "the great strides that have been made in our understanding of human sexuality in the fields of psychology, sexology, and brain research illuminate just how inescapably challenging monogamy is for the majority of gay men". Michael Shelton, *Boy Crazy: Why Monogamy Is So Hard for Men and What You Can Do About It* (New York: Alyson Books, 2008), p. 6. Eric Anderson is even more blunt in his assessment: "Gay men are promiscuous. Most are very promiscuous ... my message to gay men is that we should

can never be found where they are looking for it. Or in the case of porn: what once satisfied the itch of our desires no longer does. It starts to feel tame, and the soul caught in its snare digs deeper and deeper into more perversions. But in these moments of lust-induced fog, there is always a beacon that Christ shines into our hearts to reveal the truth to us, like he did for Saint Augustine.

I recall a similar moment in my life, where I finally saw what I was doing for what it was. I wrote about my addiction to phone sex lines in my journal:

August 23, 1999

I sit here in bed this morning on the heels of calling a phone line. I knew exactly what I was doing but did it anyway. The problem for me now is that I can no longer even deceive myself when I call a line—I know full well why I call. In the past I might've said for fun, or excitement—the thrill factor—or curiosity. There still can be a minute amount of "fun"—as much fun as biology allows, a "fun" that is only and is purely physiological—but it's so transitory and unsatisfying. The excitement and thrill is minimal as well.

I felt drawn to call the line, but I COULDN'T. I can't explain it fully—I just could not do it. Not out of moral strength, but rather out of an overwhelming sense of the TRUTH of the situation. Tandem with the urge to call was a clear awareness of the motivation to call: to salve loneliness. I was in a time of heightened clarity and knew how weak and pathetic the drug I was seeking really was. I was depressed actually and saddened knowing that it was all just a fraud—that I couldn't use that anymore like I

---

embrace our carnal desires. Be proud to be a slut." Eric Anderson, *The Monogamy Gap: Men, Love, and the Reality of Cheating* (New York: Oxford University Press, 2012), p. 20.

once did. I was angry, actually! Because I wanted to do it, and I wanted it to work.

It only took a few days before I called the line again. Each time, however, I know the truth and it can't be silenced. I'm doing the wrong thing to fill a void within me and it always comes up empty.

I didn't stop calling phone sex lines until several years later, but this moment was the beginning of the end. When you finally see things as they really are, you have to work hard to "unsee" them.

Here too I see the beauty of God's grace. I didn't stop calling phone sex lines because of "moral strength". Rather, I finally saw phone sex lines for what they are: pitiful corners of the world where sad and lonely men gather together, pretending to be someone they're not, each trying to fill the empty spots in each other's souls. God gave me the grace to see it this way, and then supported my desires to be freed from my addiction.

An addict trying to get sober never knows that the hit he's about to take is the last and final one. I can't tell you when the last moment I called a sex line was. I know that immediately afterward I became very angry and disappointed in myself. But little did I know that I was finally free.

I think chastity works this way. It's not through our moral strength that we will ever achieve freedom. Freedom comes in God's time, as he sees fit. It comes through seeing things, as they really are—which is what the virtues (especially prudence and chastity) provide us. God is the one who opens our eyes, and when we see—when we really see through the eyes of our Heavenly Father—that's when we're free. It's easy to say no to phone sex now, as easy as saying no to jumping out of an airplane without a parachute. I still have other battles, but I realize that the reason they're so enticing to me still is that I don't see them for what they really are. I don't like the idea of never having sex again, for example, but I know that this is because I see sexuality "through a mirror dimly" (see 1 Cor 13:12). Chastity—thanks be to God—is the corrective lens that helps me see things clearly enough that I'm resolved never to have sex with a man again—even though I desperately want to, because of the pulls of my flesh.

We'll now turn to one of Saint Augustine's contemporaries, and another Doctor of the Church, Saint Jerome.

Saint Jerome

Most portraits of Saint Jerome show an old and frail man, attendant on his studies, looking as if he's just about to enter his eternal reward. There's inevitably a picture of a skull in the painting—a *memento mori*, a reminder of death, that adds to the impression that whatever life may once have coursed through Saint Jerome's veins is close to its end.

But these paintings don't do justice to the full life of Saint Jerome.

When he was a young man, he lived in the desert as a hermit, living a life of extreme fasting and discipline. Even so, in one of his letters, he writes,

> How often, when I was living in the desert, in the vast solitude which gives to hermits a savage dwelling-place, parched by a burning sun, how often did I fancy myself among the pleasures of Rome![5]

[5] Jerome to Eustochium, "Letter 22", in *St. Jerome: Letters and Select Works*, trans. W. H. Fremantle, vol. 6 of *A Select Library of Nicene and Post-Nicene Fathers of the Christian Church*, 2nd series, ed. Philip Schaff and Henry Wace (New York: Charles Scribner's Sons, 1912), pp. 24–25.

He writes that, though "I had no companions but scorpi-
ons and wild beasts, I often found myself amid bevies of
girls" in his imagination. "My face was pale and my frame
chilled with fasting; yet my mind was burning with desire,
and the fires of lust kept bubbling up before me when my
flesh was as good as dead."[6]

I suspect that the fire of sexual desire will fade away
about six weeks after I'm six feet under. In the meantime,
I need Jesus, and I need to follow the example of Saint
Jerome. When he felt the stirrings of the flesh, he followed
the example of the sinful woman recounted in the Gospel:
"Helpless I cast myself at the feet of Jesus, I watered them
with my tears, I wiped them with my hair: and then I
subdued my rebellious body with weeks of abstinence."[7]

Here Saint Jerome reveals to us that the pleasures of the
bed and of the table often go hand in hand. If we desire to
see chastity grow, we must discipline our other appetites
as well. Saint Jerome advises a young woman who desired
chastity to show restraint in food, saying, "Not that the
Creator and Lord of all takes pleasure in a rumbling and
empty stomach"; rather, it is "indispensable as means to
the preservation of chastity."[8]

Saint Jerome gives us more practical advice: at the first
moment of temptation, we need to turn to Christ, our
salvation:

> When lust tickles the sense and the soft fire of sensual
> pleasure sheds over us its pleasing glow, let us immediately
> break forth and cry: "The Lord is on my side: I will not
> fear what the flesh can do unto me." ... You must never
> let suggestions of evil grow on you, or a babel of disorder

[6] Ibid., p. 25.
[7] Ibid.
[8] Ibid., p. 424.

win strength in your breast. Slay the enemy while he is
small; and, that you may not have a crop of tares, nip the
evil in the bud.[9]

This is common sense. The times when I have fallen have
been the times when a thought comes into my mind, and
instead of nipping it in the bud, I water it and fertilize it.
The only sane choice is to listen to Saint Paul, who tells
us to "take every thought captive" to Christ (2 Cor 10:5).
Saint Jerome says the same thing, but with more vigor:

> Because natural heat inevitably kindles in a man sensual
> passion, he is praised and accounted happy who, when
> foul suggestions arise in his mind, gives them no quarter,
> but dashes them instantly against the rock. Now the Rock
> is Christ.[10]

It's crazy to me how often my thoughts can turn toward
sex. It can happen in the middle of Mass. It can be in the
Adoration chapel, when I'm trying to meditate on God's
goodness, and suddenly my mind is drifting toward some
lustful sort of thought. It can even happen immediately
following confession.

It doesn't happen all the time, thankfully, but when it
does, I realize I have to be honest with the Lord: "Dear
God, I can't even seem to stay focused on you. Please help
me out, Lord—these thoughts keep coming unbidden, and
without you, I'm sunk. I'm a weak man who likes sensual
pleasures a bit too much. I want to contemplate you, but
alas, my body's getting in the way again." That's what it
means to dash our thoughts "instantly against the rock".

[9] Ibid.
[10] Ibid.

I've found this to be the healthiest way to attack the problem when it arises. And then I trust that God will look on me with eyes filled with compassion, and transform my desires through his grace. The transformation of our desires is fundamental here. Saint Jerome writes, "It is hard for the human soul to avoid loving something, and our mind must of necessity give way to affection of one kind or another. The love of the flesh is overcome by the love of the spirit. Desire is quenched by desire. What is taken from the one increases the other."[11]

We can't just extinguish the desires of the flesh; we need to replace them with something else: the only thing that ever satisfies us, our Lord and Savior. When temptations come, of course we must fight with whatever strength we have. Yet our primary task is to trust God, and allow him to act. He'll transform the desires of our hearts, in his time. And if we're tempted to despair at how slow these changes might be taking place in our lives, we need to understand that even the desire to change our desires is the result of his grace! Just by desiring to be a better man, God is already acting within us.

Now let's turn to a swashbuckler turned saint, the founder of the Jesuits.

Saint Ignatius of Loyola

Saint Ignatius of Loyola was no saint in his youth. As one of his biographers writes,

> While there is no sound basis for believing him to have been sunk in vice or shameless excesses, it would seem that in the heat of youth and amid the fires of temptation

[11] Ibid., p. 28.

he was sometimes carried into sins of lust, pride and passion.... Polanco, a contemporary [of Ignatius] puts it thus:
"The life he then led was far from being spiritual. Like
other young men living at court or intent on a soldier's
career, he was distinctly free in making love to women,[12]
and was devoted to sports and sword-play over points
of honour."[13]

His biographer adds:

Such was Ignatius the sinner.... We cannot question that
Ignatius knew the world, its pleasures, its fascinations, its
glamour—everyone sees that he knew, even by bitter
experience, the dark mysteries of sin.[14]

The brilliant military career and life of fame and fortune
that Ignatius looked forward to was suddenly cut short
on the battlefield, when he was struck by a cannonball
that shattered his legs. He was taken to a nearby castle to
recuperate, and found that, instead of the stories of pirates,
knights, and damsels in distress that he preferred, the only
books to be found there were the Bible and some lives of
the saints. When boredom led him to read these books for
lack of other options, he discovered a principle for understanding himself and his feelings that would change his life.
A biographer explains:

[12]It's an important distinction to know that when Polanco was writing,
"making love" didn't have the connotations that it does today. "Making love"
as a euphemism for "having sex" only came into common meaning in the
twentieth century. In Polanco's time, "making love" would have been considered wooing and flirtatious behavior. Regardless, it is clear from the biography
that though St. Ignatius didn't fall into a vice of "excess", he knew by bitter
experience the pull of the temptations of the flesh.

[13]John Hungerford Pollen, S.J., *Saint Ignatius of Loyola: Imitator of Christ,
1494 to 1555* (New York: P.J. Kennedy and Sons, 1922), p. 6.

[14]Ibid., pp. 7–8.

By constantly reading these books he began to be attracted to what he found narrated there. Sometimes in the midst of his reading he would reflect on what he had read. Yet at other times he would dwell on many of the things which he had been accustomed to dwell on previously.…

While reading the life of Christ our Lord or the lives of the saints,… he let his mind dwell on many thoughts; they lasted a while until other things took their place. Then those vain and worldly images would come into his mind and remain a long time. This sequence of thoughts persisted with him for a long time.

But there was a difference. When Ignatius reflected on worldly thoughts, he felt intense pleasure; but when he gave them up out of weariness, he felt dry and depressed. Yet when he thought of living the rigorous sort of life he knew the saints had lived, he not only experienced pleasure when he actually thought about it, but even after he dismissed these thoughts, he still experienced great joy.… One day, in a moment of insight, he began to marvel at the difference. Then he understood his experience: thoughts of one kind left him sad, the others full of joy. And this was the first time he applied a process of reasoning to his religious experience. Later on, when he began to formulate his spiritual exercises, he used this experience as an illustration to explain the doctrine he taught his disciples on the discernment of spirits.[15]

I'm grateful God raises up saints who know like I do, from "bitter experience, the dark mysteries of sin," and who have learned as well the lasting joy that comes from dwelling on the things of God. If there's hope for the likes of Saint Ignatius of Loyola, there's hope for weak men like me, and for you as well. God will prevail, if we wait for him to act within us.

[15] *Acta Sanctorum*, Julii, 7 [1868], 647.

We turn now to a Doctor of the Church who isn't known for his sins of excess—rather, he is known for an unhealthy scrupulosity, which in its own way can become as much a prison as sexual excess.

Saint Alphonsus Liguori

Saint Alphonsus Liguori, the founder of the Redemptorists, was not known for sins of excess. Rather, he struggled with an excessive fear of failing, often called scrupulosity. By his own experience he can help us to keep balance and perspective in the battle for chastity. In particular, I find him to be a great intercessor for someone trying to break the habit of masturbation, as a story from his life illustrates:

> The fear of committing sin at night filled him with anxiety; scruples about whether he had consented to sexual pleasure tormented him. We have it on the explicit testimony of his brother, Cajetan, that Alphonsus adopted the expedient of tying his hands together in a canvas bag before retiring to rest, lest he should touch himself immodestly, as he feared, during the night.... Apparently the very sight of women—even his own in-laws—disturbed him sexually and troubled his scrupulous conscience. It took him years of what must have been agony to come to terms with himself in this matter; he poured out his worries to his confessors and directors, recorded their instructions in a personal note-book which he consulted from time to time, vowing blind obedience to their directions, as we shall see later. One sentence recorded in his note-book reveals everything: "Speaking with women is not an occasion of sin *per se* even though it causes some sexual arousal."[16]

[16] Frederick M. Jones, C.Ss.R., *Alphonsus de Liguori: Saint of Bourbon Naples, 1696–1787, Founder of the Redemptorists* (Liguori, Mo.: Liguori Publications, 1999), p. 30.

Saint Alphonsus shows us that extremes of license and extremes of scrupulosity can both be dangerous. Neither are *reasonable*, in the sense that we desire to be guided in our lives by reason and rational judgment. We can't say, "It's no good—I'm helpless, I'm going to give in anyway to temptation, so why put up a fight?" On the other hand, we must avoid the trap of falling into a rigid puritanism and scrupulosity. Tying one's hands with a canvas bag out of fear of "immodestly touching" oneself isn't the freedom for which Christ came! Nor can we be so fearful of violating purity that we refuse to look at anyone we might find sexually attractive. "What is injurious to us," says Saint Francis de Sales, "is not so much the casual glance, but rather the intentional gaze."[17] In his adolescent strivings for chastity, Saint Alphonsus shows us what not to do. He engaged in what Father John Harvey, the founder of the Courage Apostolate, would often call "white knuckled chastity", an attempt to maintain purity by sheer force of will.[18] This isn't the way forward, but thanks to the grace of God, Saint Alphonsus Liguori can guide the overscrupulous to the path to freedom.

For example, he writes comforting words for those who feel guilty over every stray sexual thought that crosses their minds:

And, for the consolation of timid and scrupulous souls, I will here state that, according to the common opinion

[17] Quoted in St. Alphonsus Liguori, *The Twelve Steps to Holiness and Salvation from the Works of St. Alphonsus Liguori*, adapted from the German of Rev. Paul Leick by Cornelius J. Warren, C.Ss.R. (Charlotte, N.C.: TAN Books, 2010), p. 98, Location 1281.

[18] John F. Harvey, interview by Connie Pilsner, "Homosexuality and the Courage to Be Chaste", *National Catholic Register*, April 27, 2003, http://www.ncregister.com/site/article/homosexuality_and_the_courage_to_be_chaste/.U.

of theologians, when a soul that fears God and hates sin is in doubt whether she gave consent to a bad thought, she is not bound, as long as she is not certain of having given consent, to confess it: for it is then morally certain that she has not consented to it. Had she really fallen into grevious [sic] sin she would have no doubt about it; for mortal sin is so horrible a monster, that it is impossible for him who fears God to admit it into the soul without his knowledge.[19]

A person plagued with scruples can be tempted to rely primarily on his own efforts to be chaste. Here Saint Alphonsus reiterates the important lesson that "Jesus is our holiness":

To escape defeat, and to conquer the devil, there is no other defense than prayer. St. Paul says that we have to contend, not with men of flesh and blood like ourselves, but with the princes of hell. "Our wrestling is not against flesh and blood, but against principalities and powers"— *Eph.*, vi. 12. By these words the Apostle wished to admonish us that we have not strength to resist such powerful enemies, and that we stand in need of aid from God. With his aid we shall be able to do all things.... But this divine aid is given only to those who pray for it. "*Ask and you shall receive.*" Let us, then not trust in our purposes; if we trust in them, we shall be lost. Whenever the devil tempts us, let us place our entire confidence in the divine assistance, and let us recommend ourselves to Jesus Christ, and to the most holy Mary. We ought to do this particularly as often as we are tempted against chastity. For this is the most terrible of all temptations, and is the one by which the devil gains most victories. We have not strength to

[19] St. Alphonsus Liguori, *Sermons for All the Sundays in the Year*, trans. Nicholas Callan, D.D. (Dublin: James Duffy and Sons, 1882) p. 357.

preserve chastity; this strength must come from God.... In such temptations, then, we must instantly have recourse to Jesus Christ, and to his holy mother, frequently invoking the most holy names of Jesus and Mary. He who does this, will conquer; he who neglects it, will be lost.[20]

Here then, too, is another gem of wisdom from Saint Alphonsus: we need to appeal for Mary's help in conquering our vices.

When I was Protestant, I didn't understand the intercession of the saints, nor the beautiful reality that Jesus, from the Cross, gave Mary to all of us as our Mother (see Jn 19:26–27). She is the New Eve, the new "Mother of the Living" whose mantle of maternal love becomes a great protector for those of us who struggle with chastity.

In 1904, Saint Pope Pius X wrote of the value of Mary in aiding us in conquering our passions—and tells us how her example in chastity shines forth, as a bright light in the darkness of our sin:

"Such was Mary," very pertinently points out St. Ambrose, "that her life is an example for all." And, therefore, he rightly concludes: "Have then before your eyes, as an image, the virginity and life of Mary from whom as from a mirror shines forth the brightness of chastity and the form of virtue" (*De Virginib.* L. ii., c. ii.).[21]

From the overly scrupulous, I'll turn now to a man who fancied himself a sorcerer and was a student of the dark

[20] St. Alphonsus Liguori, *Preparation for Death; or Considerations on the Eternal Maxims* (Dublin: James Duffy, 1843), pp. 377–78.

[21] Pius X, Encyclical Letter on the Immaculate Conception *Ad Diem illum Laetissimum* (February 2, 1904), no. 20, http://w2.vatican.va/content/pius-x/en/encyclicals/documents/hf_p-x_enc_02021904_ad-diem-illum-laetissimum.html.

arts—and tried to use spells and incantations to get a beautiful woman into bed with him. He was a despicable character, but as proof that there is no evil we can ever do that can't be overcome and transformed by the Blood of Jesus, there stands Saint Cyprian of Antioch.

Saint Cyprian of Antioch

Throughout my ministry, I have met men ashamed of their sexual desires and deeds. The more disordered and horrible our deeds, the more we must cling to the mercy of God. Some people find themselves going down a circle of great evil in regard to sexual sins and compulsions. Saint Cyprian is the saint for the man who thinks he has sunk lower than anyone else. His story of conversion can give hope to anyone.

Saint Gregory of Nazianzen told the story of Saint Cyprian's life in a homily following his death. Before his conversion, Cyprian had been a "worshipper of demons" who engaged in sorcery and had a "voracious appetite for carnal pleasure". His eyes fell on a young woman, a Christian, who "was very beautiful".[22]

Saint Gregory tells us,

> Cyprian was not merely taken with her, but he actually made an attempt on her virtue.... For a go-between, he selects not an old hag from among those who practice the trade, but one of the demonic devotees of carnal delights, for the spiteful hosts of apostasy, constantly on the lookout for large numbers of recruits to share in their fall, are quick

[22]St. Gregory of Nazianzus, Oratory 24, "In Praise of Cyprian", in *The Fathers of the Church: St. Gregory of Nazianzus, Select Orations*, trans. Martha Vinson (Washington, D.C.: Catholic University of America Press, 2003), pp. 146–47.

to offer their services in such affairs. The price of procurement consisted of sacrifices and libations, and the kinship that is born of bloodshed and smoke: exactly the kinds of payment that those who bestow such benefits require.[23]

But the young woman, Saint Juliana, rebuffed his intentions by seeking refuge with God and taking Christ as her champion. Saint Cyprian realized how weak evil was compared to the power of Christ, as expressed in the virtue of Saint Juliana. Having found greater power in Christ than in evil, he immediately left his former ways to follow Christ. His life was transformed—he became a priest, then a bishop, and is now venerated as a saint. Saint Gregory says of Saint Cyprian's conversion, "The divine wisdom knows how to lay the foundations of great events far in advance and to use opposites to produce opposites in order to rouse even greater wonderment."[24]

If God can bring such a soul as Saint Cyprian from the brink of such grave sin, all of us have hope. The more horrific our deeds have been, the more glorious will be our redemption.

In closing, I turn to words of Saint Basil the Great. His words are a balm for any man or woman who stumbles into sexual sins.

Saint Basil the Great

These are the closing words of a letter Saint Basil the Great wrote to a woman who had consecrated herself and her virginity to God, written after she stumbled and fell into a sin of unchastity. These words ring through the ages and bring hope and inspiration for any of us who fall:

[23] Ibid., pp. 147–48.
[24] Ibid., p. 150.

We can escape now. While we can, let us lift ourselves from the fall: let us never despair of ourselves, if only we depart from evil. Jesus Christ came into the world to save sinners. "O come, let us worship and fall down; let us weep before Him." (Psalm 1:3) The Word Who invited us to repentance calls aloud, "Come unto me all you that labour and are heavy laden, and I will give you rest." (Matthew 11:28) ... He does not lie when He says, "Though your sins be scarlet they shall be as white as snow. Though they be red like crimson they shall be as wool." (Isaiah 1:18) The great Physician of souls, Who is the ready liberator, not of you alone, but of all who are enslaved by sin, is ready to heal your sickness. From Him come the words, it was His sweet and saving lips that said, "They that be whole need not a physician but they that are sick.... I am not come to call the righteous but sinners to repentance." (Matthew 9:12–13) What excuse have you, what excuse has any one, when He speaks thus? The Lord wishes to cleanse you from the trouble of your sickness and to show you light after darkness.

The good Shepherd, Who left them that had not wandered away, is seeking after you.... He, in His love, will not disdain even to carry you on His own shoulders, rejoicing that He has found His sheep which was lost. The Father stands and awaits your return from your wandering. Only come back, and while you are yet afar off, He will run and fall upon your neck, and, now that you are cleansed by repentance, will enwrap you in embraces of love.... He will announce the day of joy and gladness to them that are His own, both angels and men, and will celebrate your salvation far and wide. For "verily I say unto you," says He, "there is joy in heaven before God over one sinner that repents."[25]

---

[25] *St. Basil: Letters and Select Works*, vol. 8 of *A Select Library of Nicene and Post-Nicene Fathers of the Christian Church*, 2nd series, ed. Philip Schaff and Henry Wace (New York: Christian Literature, 1895), pp. 151–52.

How to Run the Race

But let us all by God's grace run the race of chastity, young men and maidens, old men and children; not going after wantonness, but praising the name of Christ. Let us not be ignorant of the glory of chastity: for its crown is angelic, and its excellence above man.

—Saint Cyril of Jerusalem[*]

Chastity is self-restraint, and the mastering pleasures which fight, just as in war the trophies are most honorable when the contest is violent, not when no one raises a hand against us. Many are by their very nature passionless; shall we call these good tempered? Not at all.

—Saint John Chrysostom[†]

Having seen the example of the saints, and since we've discussed the importance of relying on Jesus as our holiness, we now need to discuss the importance of *trying*. There's a

[*]St. Cyril of Jerusalem, Lecture XII, in *S. Cyril of Jerusalem. S. Gregory Nazianzen*, vol. 7 of *A Select Library of Nicene and Post-Nicene Fathers of the Christian Church*, 2nd series, ed. Philip Schaff and Henry Wace (New York: Christian Literature, 1894), p. 81.

[†]St. John Chrysostom, Homily 36 on the Gospel of John, in *St. Chrysostom: Homilies on the Gospel of St. John and the Epistle to the Hebrews*, vol. 14 of *A Select Library of the Nicene and Post-Nicene Fathers of the Christian Church*, ed. Philip Schaff and Henry Wace (New York: Charles Scribner's Sons, 1906), p. 127.

temptation when we talk about grace, or when we humble ourselves enough to say that "Jesus is our all in all", that we just sit back and relax and don't do anything to bring about change in our lives.

Saint John Cassian warns us against too much complacency in trusting in God's grace alone to bring about the virtue of chastity. Though he writes "that no one can be altogether cleansed from carnal sins, unless he has realized that all his labours and efforts are insufficient for so great and perfect an end", he tells us that we must still apply ourselves to the task:

> I do not say this in order to nullify human effort or in an attempt to turn anyone away from diligence and intense toil. Rather, I declare clearly and most firmly—not by my own say-so but by that of the elders—that without these things perfection cannot be grasped at all, yet that no one can attain it with these things alone and without God's grace. For in saying that human effort by itself cannot seize it, apart from God's help, we thus assert that God's mercy and grace are bestowed only on those who toil and labor and that, to use the Apostle's words, they are given to those who will and those who run.[1]

We can't distill this teaching of Saint John Cassian to the mistaken aphorism "God helps those who help themselves." God delights in reaching down in his tenderness and fatherly care to those who seem completely unable "to help themselves". But in order to live chaste lives, we must try, with our free will, to exercise our muscles of resistance. Saint Ambrose of Milan wrote that "chastity is

[1] St. John Cassian, *The Institutes*, in vol. 58 of *Ancient Christian Writers: The Works of the Fathers in Translation*, trans. Boniface Ramsey, O.P. (New York: Newman Press, 2000), pp. 261–62.

increased by its own sacrifices."[2] If your goal is to run a marathon, the first step is to buy some sensible shoes. Then you've got to open the door, and at least walk around the block. So too with chastity. We have to *try*.

This chapter, then, is about the sorts of things we can and should do if we want to see the virtue of chastity realized in our lives.

Don't Go It Alone

I remember the first time I told someone about my struggles for chastity, particularly as they related to my attractions to the same sex. I was twenty-eight when I finally told the therapist I had been seeing at the time. It was terrifying. I was so nervous about it that I wrote him a letter instead of telling him face-to-face. Yet this step led me to great freedom. He suggested I join a Protestant group in the area associated with Exodus International. I was nervous when I called the leader of the program, but after speaking with him, I wrote in my journal, "Talk about a burden being lifted! To finally talk with someone with the same struggles as me! I have reached a point where I am weary of fighting alone, silently—it really is impossible—and silence has proven a weak weapon for me.... I feel emboldened, ready to fight the battle.... I no longer feel alone! Praise be to God!"[3] It was soon after this that I told my parents about my attractions, as well as a few select friends.

Going it alone is very hard and makes living chastely all but impossible. We need help on the journey. But we

[2]St. Ambrose to Emperor Valentinian, *Epistle XVIII*, in *St. Ambrose: Select Works and Letters*, trans. H.D. Romestin, in vol. 10 of *A Select Library of Nicene and Post-Nicene Fathers of the Christian Church*, 2nd series, ed. Philip Schaff and Henry Wace (New York: Christian Literature, 1896), p. 419.

[3]Journal, August 2, 1999.

need to be cautious and prudent as well, as we considered in our earlier discussion of coming out.

I suggest you share your attractions to the same sex (as well as any challenges you have toward chastity) with a close and trusted person in your life. If you are a young person, ideally this will be your parents, though you may determine that the best person to share this with first is your priest. He might be able to help you tell your parents, if the idea of doing it yourself makes you feel uncomfortable. Be judicious in telling friends and classmates or colleagues. Information such as this tends to spread like wildfire—at least it was the case in my experience. I have found it more challenging to live my life of chastity now that so many people know about my attractions to men. I can't stress enough the need to be judicious and prudent in sharing this information, and to err on the side of discretion rather than revelation.

Another person I suggest contacting is your local Courage chaplain. Meeting with him will be of great assistance. Your local Courage chaplain can also help you find a kind and loving spiritual director, who will be knowledgeable and sensitive to issues surrounding same-sex attractions. I have found having a spiritual director vital in my pursuit of chastity.

Joining a Courage group and going to the annual conference will be one of the best things you can do to "not go it alone". There you will find men and women who exude great joy, and who will lovingly journey with you as you work to make sense of this part of your life. One of the five goals of Courage is "to foster a spirit of fellowship in which we may share with one another our thoughts and experiences, and so ensure that no one will have to face the problems of homosexuality alone." One of the best things I've ever done in my life is to join Courage.

In some dioceses, there still isn't a Courage chapter. If there isn't one where you live, I suggest you write your local bishop and ask him to consider bringing Courage to your diocese. Until that happens, Courage has online resources available as well for connecting with other men and women striving for chastity. Another good resource for living a chaste life is the Living Waters program, run by Andrew Comiskey. This in-depth program isn't geared specifically for those with same-sex attractions—rather, it is for anyone who lives with sexual or relational broken-ness. I took part in the program in the late 1990s and found it to be a tremendous help.

Common Sense: Give the Internet the Boot

We seem to think that our lives can't be lived unless we have the Internet, but here is where the words of Christ should come to bear on our lives: "If your right eye causes you to sin, pluck it out and throw it away; it is better that you lose one of your members than that your whole body be thrown into hell" (Mt 5:29). I remember a moment in 1999 when I surfed the net for more than twenty-four hours straight—I only became free when I cut the cord that brought the Internet into my house. The admonition of cutting out your right eye is symbolic, but sometimes, the smartest thing we can do is to eliminate the Internet from our lives. You also need to ask yourself if having a smartphone is worth it. I know a saintly man in his mid-fifties who has lived a chaste life for many years. He attri-butes that in part to his refusal to have the Internet in his house, or to have a smartphone.

Sometimes it may be impossible, because of work or school, not to have the Internet at home. At the very least, there are many affordable filters available for you if you are serious about living out the virtue of chastity. Some of the filters can be set up with an accountability partner. This becomes a powerful disincentive to look at pornography: your accountability partner will always see what you take a peek at. This is healthy and holy shame, which is a gift from God that helps us stay on the right path.

Fasting and Other Disciplines

Regarding homosexuality and chastity, the *Catechism* says, "By the virtues of self-mastery that teach them inner freedom, at times by the support of disinterested friendship, by prayer and sacramental grace, they can and should gradually and resolutely approach Christian perfection."[4]

The "virtues of self-mastery that teach them inner freedom" aren't just relegated to chastity. The virtue of chastity falls under the larger virtue of temperance, defined by the *Catechism* this way:

> *Temperance* is the moral virtue that moderates the attraction of pleasures and provides balance in the use of created goods. It ensures the will's mastery over instincts and keeps desires within the limits of what is honorable. The temperate person directs the sensitive appetites toward what is good and maintains a healthy discretion: "Do not follow your inclination and strength, walking according to the desires of your heart" (Sir 5:2; cf. 37:27–31). Temperance is often praised in the Old Testament: "Do not follow your base desires, but restrain your appetites" (Sir 18:30). In the New Testament it is called "moderation" or "sobriety." We ought "to live sober, upright, and godly lives in this world" (Titus 2:12).[5]

[4] *CCC* 2359.
[5] *CCC* 1809 (italics in original).

Thus the self-mastery that helps us live chaste lives can be built up in other areas besides sexuality. Saint Jerome says, "Fasting is not a complete virtue in itself but only a foundation on which other virtues may be built."[6]

Exercise in self-control and restraint, especially with food, has always been viewed by the Church Fathers as essential to growth in chastity. They made a very common-sense argument: If you can't control your appetite for food with moderation, how can you control an appetite that is so much stronger? I have to be honest: this is another of my great battles—I like food just a little too much.

Extremes aren't necessary here and should be avoided, as Saint Jerome advises in a letter to a young woman who consecrated her virginity to God:

> I do not, however, lay on you as an obligation any extreme fasting or abnormal abstinence from food. Such practices soon break down weak constitutions and cause bodily sickness before they lay the foundations of a holy life.[7]

But these disciplines mustn't merely be about meaning-less denial. Denial of our passions must lead to fulfillment through more noble means. We need to cultivate positive elements into our lives too. Where lust once resided, we must install a new habit

While he was Secretary of the Congregation for Catholic Education, Cardinal José Saraiva Martins wrote wise words on how to grow and nurture chastity in our lives, and how chastity doesn't grow on its own:

---

[6] St. Jerome to Demetrius, A.D. 414, in *St. Jerome: Letters and Select Works*, trans. W. H. Fremantle, vol. 6 of *A Select Library of Nicene and Post-Nicene Fathers of the Christian Church*, 2nd series, ed. Philip Schaff and Henry Wace (New York: Christian Literature, 1893), p. 267.

[7] St. Jerome to Demetrius, A.D. 414, in *Letters and Select Works*, p. 267.

Chastity is not a gospel flower enclosed within some greenhouse, but growing alongside all the other blooms in the garden of evangelical life. It needs a positive, orderly, clean, outdoor environment; chastity harmonizes with the demands of work and study, grows stronger in the commitment of a genuine personal and community piety, expands in the fellowship of human relations. *It needs to be balanced to be healthy, it needs regular times set aside for rest and recreation, the activity of some kind of sport, and some kind of artistic or intellectual hobby*; it matures with the initial experiences of apostolate and service to others. The celibate life takes shape and draws strength in the joy of open fellowship, where deeds, words and duties are steeped in truth and cordiality.[8]

There's a lot of wisdom here. If we're going to cultivate chastity, we need to understand the importance of rest and recreation, as well as cultivating other interests. Finding an activity where we experience a joyful and healthy self-forgetfulness is essential to living the virtue of chastity. For me, photography is a hobby where I can lose track of time and forget all the cares of the world. The pursuit of the perfect photograph becomes an obsession for me. When I'm trying to get it "just right", lustful thoughts don't have a chance. Creative endeavors can bring me more joy and substantive pleasures than sins of unchastity ever have. I realize now that this is because I've always used sex the wrong way: to bring me pleasure, rather than to use it knowing its inherent purpose is to *create*. Which is why I've never felt satisfaction afterward. Not so with creative endeavors: I often leave a great day of photography

[8]José Saraiva Martins, *Training for Priestly Celibacy* (January 1, 1993), http://www.vatican.va/roman_curia/congregations/cclergy/documents/rc_con_cclergy_doc_01011993_train_en.html (italics added).

hungering for more because of the pure delight it brought to my heart. I think this is because sexuality is so intimately connected with our deepest creative potential: becoming fathers and mothers. Though I am single, I have found that all creative endeavors echo the creative mind of God. I recall the line of G. K. Chesterton that "art is the signature of man."[9] I feel alive when I'm engaged in artistic pursuits. These creative endeavors have helped me in filling up the gap left where unchaste behaviors once existed. Physical exercise, volunteering our time helping others, and spending time in community with good friends are all necessary in our pursuit of the virtue of chastity.

Prayers and Spiritual Reading

The Church Fathers all prescribed prayer and spiritual reading in the battle for chastity. This calls to mind the wise words of Saint Paul, who said, "Finally, brethren, whatever is true, whatever is honorable, whatever is just, whatever is pure, whatever is lovely, whatever is gracious, if there is any excellence, if there is anything worthy of praise, think about these things" (Phil 4:8).

I've often thought about how many images must be stored in my mind after years and years of addiction to pornography. Where pornography once fed the fuel of lust, I realize now I need to feed virtue by filling my mind with good and noble thoughts. This transforming and renewal of our minds won't happen overnight, but I am always amazed at how peaceful I feel after reading something by one of the saints. Naturally, prayer is good and necessary—but at certain times it's not quite enough. A human being is a unity of both body and soul, and sometimes I find that the

[9] G. K. Chesterton, *The Everlasting Man* (San Francisco: Ignatius Press, 2008), p. 166.

pull of the body is so strong and powerful that in order to overcome a temptation to unchastity, I have to go and do something *else* with my body. Prayer should always be the first answer—we need to dash our thoughts on the Rock—but then I think we need to go dash someplace else, away from wherever it is we can be alone with our thoughts.

Time in the Adoration chapel, in front of the Blessed Sacrament, is invaluable in the battle of chastity. There's a calming peace that always fills me when I go to the Adoration chapel. I don't, however, believe that running to the Adoration chapel in times of grave temptations is the most beneficial thing for me to do. My desires for sex stem most often from loneliness, isolation, stress, or even boredom. If temptations come from loneliness, I call a friend and see if he's free to do something. Getting out of the house is more important than prayer. Saint Alphonsus Liguori wrote, "In temptations against chastity, the spiritual masters advise us, not so much to contend with the bad thought, as to turn the mind to some spiritual, or, at least, indifferent object. It is useful to combat other bad thoughts face to face, but not thoughts of impurity."[10] I find more often than not—since I'm not a saint like Saint Alphonsus—turning to "an indifferent object" is sometimes a more effective first step than turning immediately to prayer. When temptations stem from boredom, the wise counsel of Saint Jerome to the same virgin referenced above helps here. Though she is wealthy, and has no need of doing any work, he advises her to do some work daily with her hands. For the Scripture says: "the soul of every idler is filled with desires" (Prov. 13:4).[11]

If temptations come because of an overwhelming sense of despair, or in moments of self-loathing, that's when a

[10] St. Alphonsus Liguori, *Sermons for All the Sundays in the Year*, trans. Nicholas Callan, D.D. (Dublin: James Duffy and Sons, 1882), p. 359.

[11] St. Jerome to Demetrius, A.D. 414, in *Letters and Select Works*, p. 269.

trip to the Adoration chapel is in order for me. Sometimes temptations to look at pornography can come
from envy—I want to see the sort of men I am tempted
to wish I was. These are moments when I need to be in
front of the Blessed Sacrament and rest in the truth that
I am a beloved child of God, fearfully and wonderfully
made, knit in my mother's womb by the hand of God (see
Ps 139:13–14).

As to daily prayers, a good place to start is to begin and
end each day with the Liturgy of the Hours.[12] As we start
our day, we can commend our hopes and efforts to the
good graces of God, and as we close the day, it's good to
recall the events of the day, seeing where we could do
better, and then asking God's grace to help us do better
the next day. Naturally, the Rosary has been a great aid
for many men and women battling for chastity. My prayers
throughout the day are usually rather informal. I often find
myself saying, "Dear Jesus, please help me." Sometimes it
gets shortened to just, "Dear Jesus, please." I think sometimes I say that a hundred times a day. And then I go on
my way, trusting that he will come to aid me in his time
and in his way.[13]

The Sacrament of Reconciliation

I love going to confession. When I was a child growing up
in the Church, it terrified me. Now it's one of the most
precious things in the world to me.

---

[12] The Liturgy of the Hours is a daily devotional in the Church that uses Scripture and prayer. See the website of the United States Conference of Catholic
Bishops at http://www.usccb.org/prayer-and-worship/liturgy-of-the-hours/.

[13] A more specific program of prayers especially suited for chastity can
be found at the website of the Angelic Warfare Confraternity (http://www
.angelicwarfareconfraternity.org/).

Thomas Merton, who himself understood the temptations of the flesh, wrote that

the beginning of wisdom is the confession of sin. This confession gains for us the mercy of God. It makes the light of His truth shine in our conscience, without which we cannot avoid sin. It brings the strength of His grace into our souls, binding the action of our wills to the truth in our intelligence.[14]

The *Letter to the Bishops of the Catholic Church on the Pastoral Care of Homosexual Persons* says that authentic pastoral programs for people like me "will assist homosexual persons at all levels of the spiritual life: through the sacraments, and in particular through the frequent and sincere use of the sacrament of Reconciliation, through prayer, witness, counsel and individual care. In such a way, the entire Christian community can come to recognize its own call to assist its brothers and sisters, without deluding them or isolating them."[15] The frequent use of the Sacrament of Reconciliation has been instrumental in combatting my temptations to unchastity.

In particularly challenging times of temptation, I have sometimes had to confess the same sins several times over a short period. There is an insidious temptation of the devil that says we should be ashamed of our failings, and that only a pathetic fool would go to confession so frequently. Or perhaps you're embarrassed because the priest might

[14] Thomas Merton, *Thoughts in Solitude* (New York: Farrar, Straus and Giroux, 1999), p. 73.
[15] Congregation for the Doctrine of the Faith, *Letter to the Bishops of the Catholic Church on the Pastoral Care of Homosexual Persons* (October 1, 1986), no. 15, http://www.vatican.va/roman_curia/congregations/cfaith/documents/rc_con_cfaith_doc_19861001_homosexual-persons_en.html.

recognize your voice, remember how little time has passed since you last confessed the same things, and think you're a total wreck. We must banish these thoughts from our minds! We need to remember that priests are called to see us with the eyes of Christ, who always looked with great compassion on men and women caught in the snares of sexual sin. Does a one-year-old get embarrassed when he's learning to walk and stumbles? God views us that way: he's pleased with our efforts to stand and walk in the path he's set before us. Our sins of unchastity are the sins of our spiritual childhood—Reconciliation is when we get to reach our hands up to our Heavenly Father to steady our feet again. He always smiles at us with loving-kindness when we run to him.

The words of Psalm 103 can be a great comfort to us:

> As a father pities his children,
>   so the LORD pities those who fear him.
> For he knows our frame;
>   he remembers that we are dust. (vv. 13–14)

That's a priest's job, to see us the way God does. Confession cleans the slate, and it's as if our sins never happened. I often reflect on the mercy of God expressed in the inconceivable idea that our transgressions are removed as far from his mind as the east is from the west.

It doesn't matter how many times we might have fallen into the same sin—God always picks us up, and tomorrow is a new day. We should never be embarrassed about going to confession again and again. Only a fool is embarrassed to seek healing where it can be found! If we feel ashamed for having committed the same thing again and again, Saint Paul must be our example. He writes that there is one thing he is sure to do: "forgetting what lies behind and straining

forward to what lies ahead" (Phil 3:13). My advice to anyone striving for chastity is simple: Go to confession—and
go there often!

The Eucharist

This brings us to the most important sacramental grace we
can receive. Nothing helps conquer sins of the flesh more
than the Body and Blood of the Lamb of God.

Saint Aelred of Rievaulx, a man who had succumbed
to pleasures of the flesh before he became a monk, knows
what he's talking about when he says "that a person may
love himself, let him not corrupt himself by any delight
of the flesh. That he may not succumb to the concupis-
cence of the flesh, let him extend his full attachment to the
attractiveness of the Lord's flesh.... Let him gaze with the
eyes of his mind on the tranquil patience of his beloved
Lord and Saviour."[16]

Saint Francis de Sales writes similarly when he says,
"Keep yourself always near to Jesus Christ crucified, both
spiritually by meditation and really by the holy communion. For as they who lie on the herb called *agnus castus*, become chaste and modest, so you, laying down your
heart to rest upon our Lord, who is the true, chaste [*castus*],
and immaculate Lamb [*agnus*], will see that your soul and
your heart will soon be cleansed from all the defilements
of impurity."[17]

In his beautiful book called *This Tremendous Lover*, Dom
Eugene Boylan, O.C.R., writes of the Eucharist:

---

[16] St. Aelred, *The Mirror of Charity*, trans. Elizabeth Connor, O.C.S.O.
(Kalamazoo, Mich.; Cistercian Publications, 1990), p. 232.

[17] St. Francis de Sales, *Introduction to the Devout Life*, ed. W.H. Hutchings
(London: Rivingtons, 1882), p. 127.

Just as the two torn pieces of a sheet of paper fit perfectly together, so Christ fits perfectly into our life and fills it completely. It does not matter how small is the part of the page which represents our life—or if you prefer it, our lack of life—He can and will supply all the rest of the page. He is our full complement; He is our perfect supplement.... In one Holy Communion we can receive the perfect complement of all our wasted past and our damaged self....

We should be convinced not only of the completeness of God's work for our salvation, but also of His readiness to bestow its superabundant fruits on us at any time we approach Him with suitable disposition. There is no moment in our life in which we cannot turn to Him and find in Him not only the perfect complement of our self, no matter how much we have lost, but also the perfect restoration of all our past. For He is God, and He is our Savior.[18]

For the man or woman striving to live the virtue of chastity, Pope Saint John Paul II points us to the Eucharist. He says, "Every commitment to holiness ... must draw the strength it needs from the Eucharistic mystery and in turn be directed to that mystery as its culmination. In the Eucharist we have Jesus, we have his redemptive sacrifice, we have his resurrection, we have the gift of the Holy Spirit, we have adoration, obedience and love of the Father. Were we to disregard the Eucharist, how could we overcome our own deficiency?"[19]

---

[18] M. Eugene Boylan, O.C.R., *This Tremendous Lover* (Notre Dame, Ind.: Christian Classics, 2009), pp. 49–50.

[19] John Paul II, Encyclical Letter on the Eucharist in Its Relationship to the Church *Ecclesia de Eucharistia* (April 17, 2003), no. 60, http://www.vatican.va/holy_father/special_features/encyclicals/documents/hf_jp-ii_enc_20030417_ecclesia_eucharistia_en.html.

PART FOUR

A MISCELLANY: REFLECTIONS ON THE *CATECHISM*, FRIENDSHIP, AND LONELINESS

What Does the Word "Disordered" Mean Anyway?

> We are sometimes obliged to use hard words in books, for the sake of greater accuracy or exactness. By dressing soldiers in a different style from that in which citizens are dressed, we can easily distinguish them from citizens. So every science has generally, in its words, a dress of its own.
>
> —*A Common-School Grammar of the English Language*, 1866[1]

Groucho Marx apparently always used to joke that he wouldn't belong to a club that would have him as a member. Well, I wouldn't belong to a church who said that I was disordered simply because I find men sexually attractive. But some people seem to believe that's what the Catholic Church teaches about a man like me, who is sexually attracted to other men. It's true that the Church describes homosexual *acts* as being "intrinsically disordered", and says that the homosexual *inclination* is "objectively disordered", and from this language, some people conclude that the Church teaches that people attracted to the same sex, or who have engaged in sexual acts with members of the same sex, are themselves disordered people. This is

[1] Simon Kerl, *A Common-School Grammar of the English Language* (New York: Ivison, Phinney, and Blakeman, 1866), p. 5.

simply not true—I wouldn't be Catholic if that's what the Church taught about a man like me.

There's a lot packed into the *Catechism*—nearly three thousand paragraphs' worth—and there are only three paragraphs about homosexuality in the whole document. The *Catechism* has to cover a lot of ground, and to accomplish this task, it uses the language of anthropology and theology, where words have specific and precise meanings. Most people associate the word "disorder" with mental illness, but this is not the way the Church uses the term.

> Homosexuality refers to relations between men or between women who experience an exclusive or predominant sexual attraction toward persons of the same sex. It has taken a great variety of forms through the centuries and in different cultures. Its psychological genesis remains largely unexplained. Basing itself on Sacred Scripture, which presents homosexual acts as acts of grave depravity (cf. Gen 19:1–29; Rom 1:24–27; 1 Cor 6:10; 1 Tim 1:10), tradition has always declared that "homosexual acts are intrinsically disordered".[2] They are contrary to the natural law. They close the sexual act to the gift of life. They do not proceed from a genuine affective and sexual complementarity. Under no circumstances can they be approved. (no. 2357)

> The number of men and women who have deep-seated homosexual tendencies is not negligible. This inclination, which is objectively disordered, constitutes for most of them a trial. They must be accepted with respect, compassion, and sensitivity. Every sign of unjust discrimination in their regard should be avoided. These persons are called to fulfill God's will in their lives and, if they are Christians,

[2] CDF (Congregation for the Doctrine of the Faith), *Persona humana* 8 (Declaration on Certain Questions concerning Sexual Ethics, December 29, 1975).

to unite to the sacrifice of the Lord's Cross the difficulties
they may encounter from their condition. (no. 2358)

Homosexual persons are called to chastity. By the virtues
of self-mastery that teach them inner freedom, at times
by the support of disinterested friendship, by prayer and
sacramental grace, they can and should gradually and resolutely approach Christian perfection. (no. 2359)

Understandably, some of these phrases fall hard on the
ear and could easily be misconstrued by those who don't
understand how the Church speaks about moral issues.
Taken out of context, the phrases "intrinsically disordered"
and "objectively disordered" are hard to understand and
can seem harsh to people and hurtful to those who are not
familiar with the way the Church speaks about such issues.

For example, Stuart Edser, in his book, *Being Gay, Being
Christian: You Can Be Both*, writes, "So here we have it.
The Catholic church says that I am an intrinsically disordered person and worse, if that is possible, that I am
intrinsically inclined toward moral evil. And this because,
when my partner and I make love, there is no possibility
of pregnancy."[3] Edser, like many others, reads the words
"intrinsically disordered" as a condemnation of himself, as
a person, rather than as a moral evaluation of sexual actions
or inclinations. Edser's analysis of the *Catechism*'s language
misses the fact that the Church's judgment of homosexual acts is about more than just procreation; it also makes
reference to the physical and spiritual complementarity inherent to being male and female that puts sexual intimacy
in its appropriate context. He hears the Church's teaching,

---

[3] Stuart Edser, *Being Gay, Being Christian: You Can Be Both* (Wollombi, Aus-
tralia: Exisle Press, 2012), p. 175.

not as an invitation to authentic human fulfillment, but as
a rejection of himself and the person he cares about.

Clearly, Catholics need to be aware of the way in which
the Church's teaching comes across to people, and to
make every effort to present that teaching in a positive,
life-giving way, as a plan and a challenge that leads to freedom and authenticity. Pope Benedict XVI gives us a good
template for how to speak about the virtue of chastity in
an address he gave to bishops of the United States making
a visit to the Vatican:

> In this great pastoral effort there is an urgent need for the
> entire Christian community to recover an appreciation
> of the virtue of chastity. The integrating and liberating
> function of this virtue (cf. *Catechism of the Catholic Church*,
> 2338–43) should be emphasized by a formation of the heart,
> which presents the Christian understanding of sexuality as
> a source of genuine freedom, happiness and the fulfilment
> of our fundamental and innate human vocation to love. It
> is not merely a question of presenting arguments, but of
> appealing to an integrated, consistent and uplifting vision
> of human sexuality. The richness of this vision is more
> sound and appealing than the permissive ideologies exalted
> in some quarters; these in fact constitute a powerful and
> destructive form of counter-catechesis for the young.[4]

Plans to Prosper Us and Not to Harm Us

When a man or a woman who experiences same-sex
attractions asks about the teaching of the Church, the best
place to begin is with the formation of the heart, which

---

[4]Address of His Holiness Benedict XVI to the Bishops of the United
States of America from Region VIII on Their "Ad Limina" Visit (March 9,
2012), https://w2.vatican.va/content/benedict-xvi/en/speeches/2012/march
/documents/hf_ben-xvi_spe_20120309_us-bishops.html.

involves sharing with him the love of God, and God's plan for humanity. The *Catechism* proclaims God's goodness and loving plan for humanity in its very first paragraph:

> God, infinitely perfect and blessed in himself, in a plan of sheer goodness freely created man to make him share in his own blessed life. For this reason, at every time and in every place, God draws close to man. He calls man to seek him, to know him, to love him with all his strength. He calls together all men, scattered and divided by sin, into the unity of his family, the Church. To accomplish this, when the fullness of time had come, God sent his Son as Redeemer and Savior. In his Son and through him, he invites men to become, in the Holy Spirit, his adopted children and thus heirs of his blessed life.

The profound truth that we as Christians have to share with the world is that God's commands and counsels about chastity are part of this "plan of sheer goodness" that help us "share in his own blessed life", and that pursuing chastity and authentic relationships with others is necessary to grow in relationship with God, who "calls together all men".

As I was coming to know who God is, and who I am as his son, this was the most important lesson for me to learn: that God loves me, that it is good that I exist, and that God has a plan for my life to bring me happiness and blessings. When I understood this divine plan of God, and finally believed that God's plans truly were to prosper me and not to harm me (cf. Jer 29:11), I could finally begin to see the moral claims proposed to me by the Church, not as an onerous demand, but instead as an invitation to reclaim the dignity that was given to me in the Creation, and redeemed by the Passion, death, and Resurrection of Jesus Christ.

In this context, the phrases "objectively disordered" and "intrinsically disordered" become helpful signposts on the journey of life, urging me to seek and follow the path, the order, that God has established for my life and my relationships. The Church understands that human beings are wounded creatures: the natural unity of body and soul, and the natural harmony of the mind, will, and emotions, are damaged by the Original Sin of Adam and by our own personal sins. Natural feelings and desires, which were created to guide us to choose good and avoid evil, can become distorted, sometimes pulling us in the opposite direction, toward choices that are truly not good for us. Though Christ has saved us from sin, its effects remain in us, which means that we all can be led astray by disordered appetites—urges and desires for things that are not part of God's plan for human life and relationships.

I need this teaching in order to understand who I am, why I am here, and where I am going. Unless I am honest about the effects of sin—Original and personal—on my mind and heart, I am tempted to assume that everything I feel is "good" and "natural". With the knowledge that the Church's moral teaching provides, I know how to evaluate and respond to my attractions in ways that will lead me to human fulfillment; I can govern them rather than being governed by them. The Church's teaching on homosexuality has thus become words of life for me. To reach this understanding wasn't easy, however. It took a lot of time, and a good deal of patient accompaniment by my friends, family, and spiritual leaders.

An Order to Human Relationships

Governing our passions, instead of being governed by them, is hard work. At least I've found that to be the case, in many areas of my life besides sexuality. There are other things besides sexuality where we can leave God's plan for human fulfillment. Homosexuality isn't the only area of the moral life where the Church speaks of things being disordered. The *Catechism* quotes Pope Pius XII, who teaches us that man's emotions and appetites can be disordered and thus deviate from God's plan, in many areas of our lives. All of us, as inheritors of the effects of Original Sin, must be on guard:

> Though human reason is, strictly speaking, truly capable by its own natural power and light of attaining to a true and certain knowledge of the one personal God, who watches over and controls the world by his providence, and of the natural law written in our hearts by the Creator; yet there are many obstacles which prevent reason from the effective and fruitful use of this inborn faculty.... The human mind, in its turn, is hampered in the attaining of such truths, not only by the impact of the senses and the imagination, but also by disordered appetites which are the consequences of original sin.[5] (no. 37)

The *Catechism* uses the term "disordered" to describe, not just homosexuality, not even just sexual sins, but other immoral choices that involve a departure from God's plan for human relationships. Lying, for example, is "intrinsically disordered", which means that no set of circumstances or good intentions can make a lie right and just.[6] The *Catechism*'s discussion of the evil of lying helps to illustrate what the Church is getting at when she chooses the term "disordered" to describe it:

> "Men could not live with one another if there were not mutual confidence that they were being truthful to

[5] Pope Pius XII, *Humani generis* 561: DS 3875.
[6] *CCC* 1753.

one another."[7] The virtue of truth gives another his just
due. Truthfulness keeps to the just mean between what
ought to be expressed and what ought to be kept secret:
it entails honesty and discretion. In justice, "as a matter of
honor, one man owes it to another to manifest the truth."[8]
(no. 2469)

Truthfulness in dealings honors the dignity both of ourselves and of others. It helps bring order to our lives and
to society; it is important in fair dealings, economically
and politically. A world filled with lies would be a world
gravely harmed by disorder. Other things that the *Catechism* says are disordered include an excessive desire for
money[9] and calumny,[10] which harms another's reputation
through spreading lies. In the use of the natural world, the
Catechism teaches that we must "avoid any disordered use
of things which would be in contempt of the Creator and
would bring disastrous consequences for human beings
and their environment."[11] Foundational to the Church's
moral teaching is that

> *Each creature possesses its own particular goodness and perfection*
> [italics in original]. For each one of the works of the "six
> days" it is said: "And God saw that it was good." "By the
> very nature of creation, material being is endowed with
> its own stability, truth, and excellence, its own order and
> laws." (*GS* 36 §1). Each of the various creatures, willed
> in its own being, reflects in its own way a ray of God's infi-
> nite wisdom and goodness. Man must therefore respect
> the particular goodness of every creature. (no. 339)

[7] St. Thomas Aquinas, *STh* [*Summa Theologica*] II–II, 109, 3 ad 1.
[8] *STh* II–II, 109, 3, corp. art.
[9] *CCC* 2424.
[10] *CCC* 1753.
[11] *CCC* 339.

Inherent Order and Purpose

The "particular goodness" of each creature "with its own stability, truth, and excellence, its own order and laws", is the foundation for what the Church calls the *natural law*. Specifically, it is from the "particular goodness" of man, who is the pinnacle of creation, that the Church's teaching on sexuality comes.

The natural law is what Saint Paul said is "the law written on our hearts" (cf. Rom 2:15); it is also written into the shape of our bodies. The bodily complementarity of men and women enables them to share that intimate union that both Old and New Testaments acknowledge with the proclamation that the two "become one flesh" (Gen 2:24; cf. Mt 19:5–6; Eph 5:28–31; 1 Cor 6:16). This one-flesh union is not just a part of the enjoyment of sexual intimacy; it is the characteristic that makes it what it is, the purpose that explains human bodies and human attractions. I don't intend here to do an in-depth explanation of natural law—anyone interested in a full treatment of natural law and human sexuality should read J. Budziszewski's excellent book *On the Meaning of Sex*.[12] I bring up natural law here in order to help us understand why the Church speaks of things being "disordered".

Pope Benedict XVI acknowledged that the concept of a natural moral law "for many today is almost incomprehensible due to a concept of nature that is no longer metaphysical, but only empirical. The fact that nature, being itself, is no longer a transparent moral message creates a sense of disorientation that renders the choices of

---

[12] J. Budziszewski, *On the Meaning of Sex* (Wilmington, Del.: ISI Books, 2014).

daily life precarious and uncertain."[13] We live in a world today guided by the philosophies of materialism: the only acceptable measure of truth is that which can be empirically measured, weighed, catalogued, or numbered, based on a metric devised by a scientist in a lab. Man has been distilled to statistics, raw matter, with so much carbon, so much water, so many cells, so many neurons firing in the brain, with no innate meaning or purpose in life other than to exist merely as a random by-product of the universe. Man as raw material, to be shaped into whatever he wants or decides himself to be, is the claim of existentialism. Questions of "innate meaning" and "ultimate purpose" are judged to be irrelevant.

Yet man has always wondered who he is, why he is here, and if there is any meaning in life, and what it means to live a good and moral life. These questions can't be answered by science, just like the beauty someone finds in a painting by Claude Monet can't be reduced to a chemical analysis of the paint that he used. These are questions for philosophers, artists, poets, and priests:

> What a piece of work is a man! How noble in reason, how infinite in faculty! In form and moving how express and admirable! In action how like an angel, in apprehension how like a god![14]

So says Hamlet, in those words of Shakespeare that have stirred men's hearts to contemplate their own nobility

---

[13] Address of His Holiness Benedict XVI to the Participants in the International Congress on Natural Moral Law (February 12, 2007), https://w2.vatican.va/content/benedict-xvi/en/speeches/2007/february/documents/hf_ben-xvi_spe_20070212_pul.html.

[14] William Shakespeare, *Hamlet*, act 2, scene 2.

since they were first uttered four centuries ago. These are the questions that the Church considers: What is the form of man—that is, what are his inner qualities? What makes a man noble, admirable, or courageous? Why do we admire some men and hold others in disregard? What helps man fulfill his true nature? What hinders him in becoming a good and noble man? In the eyes of the Church, virtues and vices, good and bad, are knowable, based on the form and nature of man. The Church believes, in continuity with philosophers since the time of Aristotle, that *what something is* points to *how that thing itself can find fulfillment*. The ear is for hearing, the eye for seeing. A good ear is one that hears well; a good eye is one that sees well. Man has feet and legs for walking about, upright. For man to live his life, crawling about on all fours, like an animal, would be man living in opposition to his true nature, which is revealed to him in his body. In other words, there is a "human" way of doing things, like eating: humans bring food to the mouth, not the mouth down to the food, like my dog does. The lungs give us another good example. The lungs are for breathing—yet we can use lungs to bring us pleasures, such as the high some people derive from sniffing glue. Sniffing glue, though it may be pleasurable for some, leads away from true human fulfillment and is a misuse of the body. The Church's position is that in order for man to enjoy things in a way suitable to man's dignity, man must use things in accordance with the purpose and design of a thing. This holds especially true of man's body, whose nature and "being itself" provides man with a "transparent moral message".

In his encyclical *Veritatis Splendor*, Pope Saint John Paul II gives a good description of the Church's view of the natural law:

It refers to man's proper and primordial nature, the "nature of the human person",[15] which *is the person himself in the unity of soul and body* [italics in original], in the unity of his spiritual and biological inclinations and of all the other specific characteristics necessary for the pursuit of his end. "The natural moral law expresses and lays down the purposes, rights and duties which are based upon the bodily and spiritual nature of the human person. Therefore this law cannot be thought of as simply a set of norms on the biological level; rather it must be defined as the rational order whereby man is called by the Creator to direct and regulate his life and actions and in particular to make use of his own body".[16]

In this light, we can begin to understand the Church's teaching on human sexuality more clearly. The Church recognizes that the one system of the human body that requires two people to be complete is the procreative system. As a man, I don't, in any real sense, *have* a "reproductive system", despite what I learned in my middle school biology class. Yes, I have a system that produces sperm—it's a complete system in that it fulfills its function of producing sperm, but sperm does not achieve its goal of reproduction without its complement, eggs. We can say further that the sexual organs of men and women make no sense without reference to the other. This is the one area of the corporeal human person that requires union

[15]Second Vatican Council, Pastoral Constitution on the Church in the Modern World *Gaudium et Spes* (December 7, 1965), no. 51.

[16]John Paul II, encyclical *Veritatis Splendor* (August 6, 1993), no. 50, quoting the Congregation for the Doctrine of the Faith, Instruction on Respect for Human Life in Its Origin and on the Dignity of Procreation *Donum Vitae* (February 22, 1987), Introduction, 3: *AAS* 80 (1988), 74. http://w2.vatican .va/content/john-paul-ii/en/encyclicals/documents/hf_jp-ii_enc_06081993 _veritatis-splendor.html

with another to be complete. There is only a complete reproductive and procreative system when a man and a woman unite together in sexual union, where the fertility of the couple is not deliberately thwarted. Combined with divine revelation and the teaching of Scripture, this bodily reality is a foundational source of the Church's teaching on human sexuality.[17]

From *Is* to *Ought*

Now, plenty of people argue that this should have no bearing on what we ought to do with our sexual organs. "An 'is' doesn't mean an 'ought'," they would argue. Yet in so many areas of life, we all live with an awareness that man has a certain nature, and when he leaves the path of his nature, he needs help. That explains things like Weight Watchers, or Gamblers Anonymous, or Alcoholics Anonymous. Why do those organizations exist, unless we recognize that man's happiness is impeded when he has no control over his palate, wallet, or alcohol? Indeed, every "self-help" book reveals to us that man innately knows he *should* (and *wants* to) be a certain sort of person—but may be stymied in his desires for achieving the goal. Why do we have standards of behavior or normalcy in human relations? Normalcy in behavior is connected with our human nature. It would be strange to see a man relieve himself in public, but we have no problem when a dog does it on a fire hydrant. This is because we know that man is innately a certain sort of creature who should act in a certain way based on rightly ordered choices. And of course, when it comes to the body, we all live with an understanding of the

[17] For this insight, and the example above regarding the misuse use of the lungs to bring us pleasure, I am indebted to Dr. J. Budziszewski.

natural law all the time. We instinctively know that if you don't eat, you will die; if you don't hydrate, you will die. If you eat too much, you will die; if you drink too much, you will die. If you are addicted to the pleasures of heroin, there is a high chance you will overdose and die. Why do we accept "*is* means *ought*" as self-evident when we talk about every other system of the body, yet reject this principle when it is applied to the reproductive system?

Unlike the world's view of sexuality, the Church does not reject the natural law but rather looks to the *is* of our bodily nature as an important source of the *oughts* of sexual morality. This teaching is more than just about the design of the human body, however. The Church recognizes that in the design of the body, everyone carries within himself or herself an ordering toward sexual love to another, the "other" who is the opposite sex. This difference is what the Church calls the "complementarity" of the sexes. The *Catechism* states, "Physical, moral, and spiritual *difference* and *complementarity* are oriented to the goods of marriage and the flourishing of family life."[18] This complementarity is not merely a clinical awareness of physiological difference, but a joyous encounter with another "I", who is both the same as I am, yet profoundly different. The complementarity of the sexes means that each has distinct gifts to offer, which—in the well-ordered person—are welcomed by the other, including the gift of fertility and the particular ways of loving that are distinctly connected with being male or female, and with fatherhood and motherhood. These differences are not merely physical—they are emotional, psychological, and relational differences as well. At an ecumenical and interfaith colloquium convened to discuss the importance of sexual complementarity, Pope

[18] *CCC* 2333 (italics in original).

Francis noted that "complementarity assumes many forms, since every man and every woman brings their personal contribution—personal richness, their own charisma—to the marriage and to the upbringing of their children." The importance of this personal contribution is not to be underestimated, the Pope insisted. In the intimate union of marriage, "complementarity becomes a great treasure. It is not only an asset but is also a thing of beauty."[19]

Why It All Makes Sense to Me

The foundation of all of the Church's teaching on human sexuality is God's good and beautiful plan for creation, when he created man and woman in his "image" and "likeness" (Gen 1:26–27), gave them to each other to be "one flesh" (Gen 2:24), and gave them the charge to be "fruitful and multiply" (Gen 1:28). The Church teaches that sexual intimacy is not simply a means for obtaining pleasure; its inherent purpose is fulfilled only when it is shared by a man and a woman joined to one another in a lifelong marriage whose intimate acts are open to the procreation of children. Then—and only then—will acting on our sexual desires actually lead to fulfillment according to our nature.

With this foundational understanding of the Church's teaching, we can better consider what the Church means when she says certain things are *intrinsically disordered*. When the Church says that certain choices around sexual intimacy are *intrinsically disordered*, it means that something about the choice, by the nature of what is being chosen,

[19] Pope Francis, Address to the Participants in the International Colloquium on the Complementarity between Man and Woman, Sponsored by the Congregation for the Doctrine of the Faith, Rome (November 17, 2014), https://w2.vatican.va/content/francesco/en/speeches/2014/november/documents/papa-francesco_20141117_congregazione-dottrina-fede.html.

is lacking or deviating from the beautiful plan of God for sexuality. With regards to homosexuality, the phrase is used to refer to homosexual acts themselves, which means that there is something inherent within the actions themselves that make them disordered. To use Saint Thomas Aquinas' phrase for such things, he would say that sexual activities between two members of the same sex are *contra naturum*—that is, gravely contrary to the nature of human sexuality itself.[20] Thomas also includes contraception and masturbation under the same category, for the same reasons: both masturbation and contraception distort the meaning of human intimacy and love revealed to us by human nature and confirmed by divine revelation. In the case of masturbation, two do not become one flesh and there is no procreative potential. Likewise, contraception impedes the two fully becoming one flesh by the deliberate withholding of fertility, which in turn excludes the possibility of a new life. Likewise, homosexual acts are considered *contra naturum* because they radically depart from the design, the end, the order, and the purpose of human sexuality: the husband and wife who form "one flesh" (Gen 2:24; cf. Mt 19:5), and the procreative potential of the sexual faculty (cf. Gen 1:28). No amount of good will on the part of those engaging in homosexual acts, contraception, or masturbation can change the fact that these actions are opposed to the true ends and meaning of human sexuality. In man, sexual organs are by design ordered toward procreation. To ignore this end and to seek sexual pleasures for their own sake, through a use of our sexual organs that prevents the fulfillment of the design of human sexuality, would be to live in opposition to man's true nature, and thus lead away from man's fulfillment and happiness.

[20] *STh* II–II, 154, a. 11.

To help us better understand the Church's teaching on homosexuality, let's consider more closely the Church's teaching on masturbation, which she also considers to be intrinsically disordered.

Quoting the Congregation for the Doctrine of the Faith (CDF), the *Catechism* says this about masturbation: "Both the Magisterium of the Church, in the course of a constant tradition, and the moral sense of the faithful have been in no doubt and have firmly maintained that masturbation is an intrinsically and gravely disordered action."[21]

Now, I recognize that a lot of people think the Catholic Church is crazy for suggesting that masturbation is an "intrinsically and gravely disordered action". It seemed crazy to me too for much of my life. But for me now, the Church's teaching on masturbation makes sense, for masturbation is ultimately an inwardly selfish, self-focused, and indeed narcissistic activity, which closes man in on himself. Complementarity and openness to procreativity are essential to sexual intimacy, because they draw a person out of himself and toward the other, unlike masturbation. Over my life, I always have noticed how angry and impatient I have been with others when I indulged in masturbation—no wonder. Unlike the fantasies of masturbation, the real world doesn't cater to my every whim. Real relationships take work, but gratification is easy to obtain. The effect this has on a person—the effect it has had on me—is to stunt emotional maturity, to keep a man thinking and acting like a child, focused on his own desires and needs.

C. S. Lewis writes of masturbation in one of his letters, saying:

For me the real evil of masturbation would be that it takes an appetite which, in lawful use, leads the individual out

---

[21] *CCC* 2352, quoting CDF, *Persona humana* 9.

of himself to complete (and correct) his own personality in that of another (and finally in children and even grandchildren) and turns it back; sends the man back into the prison of himself, there to keep a harem of imaginary brides.... In the end, they become merely the medium through which he increasingly adores himself.... After all, almost the *main* work of life is to *come out* of our selves, out of the little dark prison we are all born in. Masturbation is to be avoided as *all* things are to be avoided which retard this process. The danger is that of coming to *love* the prison.[22]

I wholeheartedly agree, and I'm grateful the Church teaches that masturbation is intrinsically disordered. Masturbation is ultimately self-focused, a constant peering at one's own sexual desires and proclivities in a mirror, indulging and taking delight in the selfish love of self. The Church, through clearly teaching that masturbation is intrinsically disordered, pulls the mirror from before our eyes, and in so doing, helps us peer out from the cave of our own selfishness. Yes, it's a difficult phrase, a hard phrase, but I'm glad it's worded in such a strong way—it gets my attention (like something a physician might say, to an unhealthy patient he cares about, to try to wake him up from his complacency).

Here's a good case in point from my own life: I like to eat food a bit too much. My doctor has said that I'm "clinically obese". Well, that falls hard on my ears too, and to be honest, I prefer "big-boned" or "portly", or better yet, "barrel-chested", as one friend of mine once described me. But I recognize that in his diagnosis of my medical condition, there is a precise language he must use

---

[22]Lewis to Keith Masson, March 6, 1956, in *The Collected Letters of C. S. Lewis, Volume 3: Narnia, Cambridge, and Joy, 1950–1963*, ed. Walter Hooper (New York: Harper Collins, 2004), p. 758.

so that other doctors who've never seen me before might understand my condition, as well as to stir me from my apathy. And alas, for me and my pride, I fall under the rubric of "clinically obese". That, of course, is a result of eating more food than I need. I succumb sometimes to what the Church says is gluttony, which at its core means that my appetites for food are out of whack. My appetite outweighs my needs, thus my eating habits are out of alignment with what is good and healthy for me, and in this sense, my appetites are "out of order". That, of course, is what "disordered" means.

It's easy to see this with food: eat too much, you're going to get unhealthy. There is a purpose and design in the human body for food and digestion. All of us recognize the need for balance and moderation in food in order for us to remain healthy. The Church views everything this way: man has an inherent design, and the rightly ordered man will live in accordance with the reality of what is revealed to him by the very design of his body. He will rule his passions by his reason.

When people question these difficult phrases and why the Church uses them—or find them hurtful, like Stuart Edser did—I believe it is important to walk with them gently through the *Catechism*'s teaching on chastity, emphasizing the continuity and inner logic of her teaching so that people can better understand that she is not singling out those with same-sex attractions or even those who engage in homosexual behavior. When she uses the word "disordered", or the phrase *contra naturum*, she is consistent and coherent in her teaching by reminding us of what we know through self-reflection and nature about the twofold purpose of sexual intimacy: physical union of husband and wife as an expression of the union of their hearts, and the unimpeded procreative potential of the sexual faculty.

It is only from understanding that the Church's teaching on human sexuality is derived from man's nature itself that it will ever make sense to anyone. From the point of view of the Church, the Church's teaching about human sexuality isn't true because she teaches it; rather, she teaches it because it is true.

What about "Objectively Disordered"?

A word on the *Catechism*'s use of the phrase "objectively disordered" is necessary here, which refers in this case not to sexual behavior, but rather to the "homosexual inclination" itself. It too is one of the phrases some people dislike when they hear it, but I find it necessary and helpful in understanding the truth of my attractions. Simply put, the phrase means that something good—in this case, the gift of sexuality—is being directed toward something that is opposed to our human flourishing, as revealed to us by the design of our body. The CDF puts it in more precise theological language: "It is a more or less strong tendency ordered toward an intrinsic moral evil."[23] Naturally, this falls hard on the ears too, but here we see in the Church's teaching that the reason the attraction is disordered is because it's an attraction toward intrinsically disordered acts.

In speaking about the phrase "objectively disordered", the United States Conference of Catholic Bishops explains that "any tendency toward sexual pleasure that is not subordinated to the greater goods of love and marriage is

---

[23] Congregation for the Doctrine of the Faith, *Letter to the Bishops of the Catholic Church on the Pastoral Care of Homosexual Persons* (October 1, 1986), no. 3, http://www.vatican.va/roman_curia/congregations/cfaith/documents/rc_con_cfaith_doc_19861001_homosexual-persons_en.html.

disordered, in that it inclines a person towards a use of sexuality that does not accord with the divine plan for creation."[24] The bishops don't single out men and women with same-sex attractions for special treatment; they acknowledge that people attracted to the opposite sex "not uncommonly have disordered sexual inclinations as well" and remind us that "it is not enough for a sexual inclination to be heterosexual for it to be properly ordered."[25] As I stated at the outset of this chapter, this does not imply a complete disordering of the person; rather, as the bishops explain:

> It is crucially important to understand that saying a person has a particular inclination that is disordered is not to say that the person as a whole is disordered. Nor does it mean that one has been rejected by God or the Church. Sometimes the Church is misinterpreted or misrepresented as teaching that *persons* with homosexual inclinations are objectively disordered, as if everything about them were disordered or rendered morally defective by this inclination. Rather, the disorder is in that particular *inclination*, which is not ordered toward the fulfillment of the natural ends of human sexuality. Because of this, acting in accord with such an inclination simply cannot contribute to the true good of the human person. Nevertheless, while the particular inclination to homosexual acts is disordered, the person retains his or her intrinsic human dignity and value.[26]

---

[24] United States Conference of Catholic Bishops, "Ministry to Persons with a Homosexual Inclination: Guidelines for Pastoral Care", under "Homosexual Inclination Is Not Itself a Sin" (November 14, 2006), http://www.usccb .org/about/doctrine/publications/homosexual-inclination-guidelines-general -principles.cfm.

[25] Ibid.

[26] Ibid. (italics in original).

Critics of the Catholic Church think this is just backwards thinking—so be it, but it would be refreshing if her critics would actually take her arguments seriously enough to at least not misrepresent them. Many gay activists like to argue that the Church singles out people with SSA for particularly onerous treatment in the *Catechism*, even going so far are as to argue that the Church's teaching is discriminatory, even hateful. But as we've seen, this is not the case. The demands and teachings of Christianity are difficult for everyone, particularly in the realm of human sexuality. Though difficult, they are burdensome only when we see the demands upside down. In truth, the Church's teaching on human sexuality is difficult and challenging because the gift of human sexuality is so great a gift from God to man that man can easily misuse and abuse the gift, hurting himself and others in the process. The Church says no to certain things—never to persons, but choices— because she loves us and desires our happiness and fulfillment. The Church's no to disordered sexual inclinations and choices is always in service of a great yes to man's true nature and fundamental dignity. This is why I've come to value the *Catechism*'s three paragraphs (nos. 2357–59; see pp. 210–11 above) on homosexuality so much—including the parts that fall hard on the ear.

Some people think the phrases "intrinsically disordered" and "objectively disordered" are problematic or should be expunged from the Church's language. Yet for me, there is much value I see in the word "disordered" to describe my attractions to men. These words point me toward the "order" of creation, and thus to reality. As a man who desires to live his life in accordance with the truth of the way things really are, I find that the Church's teaching that my inclinations toward men are "objectively disordered" safeguards me from living in a state of unreality, by protecting me from following the path where my disordered inclinations lead: to chaos and unhappiness. I value the phrase in the same way I value the vivid warning signs of a man falling to his death that line the edge of the Grand Canyon. I know the phrase exists because the Church loves me enough to tell me the truth, and that in her maternal care, she knows and teaches that it is the divine design and ordering of creation that gives the person his intrinsic human dignity and value. This, then, is the key point for me in valuing the Church's use of the word "disordered" so much: by declaring the inclination that I have as being "objectively disordered", and acts I might be tempted to commit with another man as "intrinsically disordered", the Church protects and honors my intrinsic human dignity and value as a child of God—and protects me from using another person in a way that does injury to his dignity as a child of God too. The preamble to the *Catechism*'s discussion of morality—of which homosexuality is just one small part—begins with the exhortation of Saint Leo the Great: "Christian, recognize your dignity."[27] All of the moral teachings of the Church proceed from reclaiming the fundamental truth of man's dignity. These two phrases, "objectively disordered" and "intrinsically disordered", have thus become precious to me, for they help secure my dignity before God. They help me understand that my inclination toward men is a sign of a privation within me—that I don't see things clearly, as I ought. The virtue of chastity, and the teachings of the Church, such as the phrase "objectively disordered", are corrective lenses that help me to see myself for who I really am and others for who they truly are, and thus to see the only path that will lead me to happiness in the realm of

[27] *CCC* 1691; quotation in *Sermo 21 in nat. Dom.*, 3: PL 54, 192C.

human sexuality: refraining from following those inclinations, guided by the virtue of chastity.

Having considered what "disordered" means, let's consider another phrase that sometimes falls hard on the ears. What exactly does the Church mean when she talks about "disinterested friendship"?

Disinterested Friendship

What qualities must the love of our neighbor have?

It must be, 1. Sincere; 2. Disinterested; 3. General

—A Catechism of the Catholic Religion, 1862[*]

A love that is not conditioned on reciprocity or recognition; a love that is unselfish, uncraving, ever out-going and ever on-going; a love that consists in loving rather than being loved, and that is based on what the loved one is in himself, not on what he is to the one who loves,—cannot be brought to an end by any act, or by any lack, of another than the one whose best personality it represents and exhibits; nor by him while he is still himself. A true friendship is changeless in all changes.

—Henry Clay Trumbull[†]

Besides the phrases "objectively disordered" and "intrinsically disordered", I think the most misunderstood phrase in the *Catechism*'s treatment of homosexuality is the phrase "disinterested friendship".

---

[*]Joseph DeHarbe, S.J., *A Full Catechism of the Catholic Religion*, trans. John Fander, ed. P.N. Lynch (New York: Catholic Publishing and Bookselling, 1863), p. 162.

[†]Henry Clay Trumbull, *Friendship: The Master Passion* (Philadelphia: John D. Wattles, 1894), p. 59.

Here is the phrase again, in context:

> Homosexual persons are called to chastity. By the virtues
> of self-mastery that teach them inner freedom, at times
> by the support of disinterested friendship, by prayer and
> sacramental grace, they can and should gradually and reso-
> lutely approach Christian perfection. (no. 2359)

I think most people immediately imagine it must be
synonymous with "uninterested", in the sense of apathetic
or bored. With the prefix "dis", it sounds like a negative condition, as if it means a lack of *interest* in someone.
Or worse: perhaps a disinterested friendship is one where
a person is *disregarded*. Or perhaps what the *Catechism* is
talking about is a merely perfunctory, obligatory sort of
friendship that comes from God's call that we just love
everyone in a blanket sort of way.

This is where the rich history of the Church's thinking
on love can help make sense of what the *Catechism* says.
Disinterested love isn't a detached love—far from it. Disinterested love is the sort of love that God has for us all.

The French theologian Jacques Maritain described it
this way:

> In God there is absolutely no love of covetousness,
> because God has absolutely no need of anything. There is
> only disinterested love: friendship certainly, and infinitely
> generous, but also mad, boundless love, in which He
> gives Himself to a whole (the created person) other than
> Himself.
>
> And if God requests our love in return for His love, it
> is purely by virtue of disinterested love itself: not because
> He had need of being loved by us, but because He loves
> us. It is for us, not for Himself, says St. Thomas Aquinas,
> that God seeks His glory. It is for us, not for Himself, that

He asks that we give Him our heart. *Praebe mihi cor tuum* [Give me your heart].[1]

It's important here to see that disinterested love isn't a stoic form of love that doesn't care if the love we give is returned or not. Christ, who is our model for how to love, showed us in his sacred humanity his own human desires to be loved. I see it most poignantly in the Garden of Gethsemane when he asked the Apostles, "Could you not watch with me one hour?" (Mt 26:40). In Luke 19:41, Jesus sees Jerusalem and weeps, out of love for those he came to save. "Jesus wept" at the tomb of Lazarus (Jn 11:35). And then there's the moment when Judas betrayed him. I think the most painful words in the Gospels are when Jesus said to Judas, "Would you betray the Son of man with a kiss?" (Lk 22:48).

But here, we see the remarkable magnanimity of Jesus: though he was betrayed, he didn't love Judas any less. He didn't love Peter any less for his three betrayals either. This is the essence of disinterested love: it is the most free of loves, because it gives, as an *act of the will*, unconditionally, and without requirement of return. Disinterested love is never transactional; it doesn't require some sort of quid pro quo in order to be given to another—though, like the love of Christ for us, disinterested love always desires that the love given will be returned.

Pope Saint John Paul II provided helpful insights for me as I wrestled with what the Church meant by disinterested love:

The fact is that a person who desires another as a good desires above all that person's love in return for his or

---

[1]Jacques Maritain, *Notebooks*, trans. Joseph W. Edwards (Albany, N.Y.: Magi Books, 1984), p. 227.

her own love, desires that is to say another person above all as co-creator of love, and not merely as the object of appetite.... Since reciprocity is in the very nature of love, since the interpersonal character of love depends on it, we can hardly speak of "selfishness" in this context. The desire for reciprocity does not cancel out the disinterested character of love.[2]

Disinterested love then is not about *not receiving love*, or being above the desire to be loved. No, because receiving love is part of what love is all about. Disinterested friendship is a love that gives boundlessly as an act of the will. It's not a love that keeps tally or score. Nor is it the sort of love that borders on the romantic—at least not between members of the same sex, since romance is meant just for those who have the possibility of marriage. Most importantly, disinterested love is not a needy, demanding, clingy sort of love, the sort of love that filled my life for many, many years.

So now, to understand disinterested love, let's look at it from the other way around, by observing what the opposite sort of love looks like.

An example from my own life is a good case in point.

When I realized that I wasn't really all that attracted to women, I started to dream of having a friendship like Jonathan and King David—and envisioned in my own mind what their friendship was like. If God wasn't going to make me attracted enough to women to be married, I didn't want to be *alone* for the rest of my life. So I created a dream world, where I imagined a life shared with a man who was my best friend and soul mate. My vision didn't have all that much to do with reality—I know that now—but the words used in the Bible to describe David and

[2] Karol Wojtyła, *Love and Responsibility* (San Francisco: Ignatius Press, 1993), pp. 85–86.

Jonathan's friendship inspired hope in me that I could find something similar.

The passage in the Old Testament describing friendship says that "the soul of Jonathan was knit to the soul of David, and Jonathan loved him as his own soul", and that because of this, "Jonathan made a covenant with David." He loved David so much that he "stripped himself of the robe that was upon him, and gave it to David, and his armor, and even his sword and his bow and his belt" (1 Sam 18:1, 3–4). I wanted to find a friend who could be the David to my Jonathan. I thought I had found the answer in my friendship with a fellow I'll call Jake.

A mutual friend had connected us. Both of us had shared with her how often we felt lonely and unworthy of friendship. He didn't experience attractions to men, but we both suffered from a terrible sense of isolation. We became friends quickly—and I quickly became addicted to his friendship.

I wrote a short history of our friendship in my journal on November 1, 1998, about half a year after we first became friends:

> So, as the first tentative communication began between us with a letter sent to him by me and a letter in return from him, our friendship took root in the fertile ground which C.S. Lewis describes [in *The Four Loves*] as the awe and wonder two people feel when they meet and say, "What? You too?" Jake said that until I wrote him, he thought he was the only one who felt that sort of isolation and loneliness. As I reflect upon that moment, I remember how much joy it brought to be able to let him know that he was not alone!

Yet as I thought back that day on how the friendship had progressed, I saw how I became more and more focused on the good feelings I received from investing in his life:

Have I not thought more and more of the joy this friendship brings me? Have I not begun to think of the satisfaction his friendship brings me? Have I not hoped beyond hope that Jake is the friend who will be my companion, my kindred spirit—my best friend? Yes, and yes again! And I must confess, that though I do long to be a blessing to him, my desires to have my needs met by this friendship supersede my selfless magnanimous intentions.

As I wrote, I started to take scattered notes of my thoughts. Reading them now, I see now that this was the day I began to understand how unhealthy and distorted my desire for close friendships with men was:

I desire to minister to Jake—Though that is the case, I realize Jake has become a way for me to fulfill needs I have as well—I am focused on *my* needs. Yet I shouldn't beat myself up—but I hate the self-focus, since I realize it inhibits my ability to give love [to him].

I had a sobering awareness of the real situation of our friendship when I wrote, "Jake and 'the friendship' have become far too important to me: idolatrous."

I had always dreamed of having a close friend, a "buddy", which was what guys called their close friends when I was in high school. My desires for Jake had nothing to do with *sex*—I was relieved when I first met him that I wasn't sexually attracted to him. Jake was the "buddy" I had hoped for all my life—or so I thought. But I was realizing I was very unbalanced in my view of what friendship between men looks like, in reality. Men don't *dream* or *fantasize* about the next time they're going to see their friends—this awareness made me realize something was amiss within my understanding of a good, healthy friendship. And it made me wonder what to do about it:

Do I put to death my hopes and dreams? Do I "take what I can get"? I must give my hopes and dreams to God. If I am ever hurt, I close off—but are dashed unrealistic dreams cause to be hurt? I dream and dream and dream again about spending time with Jake. I dream until I get the warm-fuzzies, and when my dream world fantasies aren't realized in the real world of life, why should I be sad at all?

It's OK to thrill at the thought of being with a friend though, isn't it? Where is the balance? I don't want to shut that off—I feel I "dream" too much, but the solution to that can't be to turn off all thoughts—that just leads to being closed-off.... At what point do thoughts that spring up from time to time become too much and detrimental to the actualization of a relationship?

As I wrote, I began to realize that my obsession with this friendship was similar to why I had turned to pornography: it had become a drug for me.

I have attempted to satisfy my desire for intimacy in my life with pornography. I am in "complete control" of a "relationship" which satisfies my "needs" exactly as I want them. I desire for lust in my life to be conquered. I recognize that lust is a substitute for true intimacy. I have viewed the gift of Jake's friendship as a gift from God to find out what true intimacy is all about. With lust, I have fantasized about sexual intimacy completely under my control: a substitute for the real thing. Yet now I find myself fantasizing about how time with my friend Jake would be spent—*to make me happiest*. I have fantasized about camping trips, or reading together, or just how I would like to spend an afternoon at Rose Lake, and even what we might talk about. I have fantasized about how wonderful it could be to finally have "the friend I've always wanted". If I expect the reality of my friendship to fulfill all of my hopes, or fantasies, then I will always be disappointed, and will always feel that in order for the friendship to be fulfilling, I will need to work to capture even the slightest hint of my "dream world" friendship, and I will ultimately fail and be disappointed. I HATE THAT THIS I BELIEVE IS THE TRUTH!!! Lust is a substitute for sexual love under God's control, and is a drug to sate my need for intimacy. A dream world friendship is a substitute for real world friendship. I spend time in the hopes of my dream world because it is a drug to sate my need for intimacy. FACT: My only source of INTI-MACY is with Jesus Christ. Everything else is a poor, impotent substitute. Lust and pornography and any dream world friendships are sinful, but understandable, though inexcusable, reactions to legitimate needs—my need for the love of Christ.

Even so, I saw hope that somehow my views about friendship with men—including with Jake—could some-how be transformed. I realized that though our deepest form of intimacy is with Christ, Christ himself had inti-mate friendships of his own:

Here is a beautiful realization! As I sit here questioning how my view of my friendship with Jake can be refined, I realize that the love of Christ, which is my deepest need, is something my Father in Heaven desires to see flourish in my friendship with Jake! A dream world friendship simply glorifies love of self—it is poisoned by my selfish desires and a focus on my needs, but a friendship which is rooted in the love of Christ, sees a death to self, and all that is left is LOVE, and there, one can begin to see the realization of the admonition to place the interests of others above our own.

Realizing I didn't know how to do this, I wrote a quick prayer to Jesus to help me make this a reality in my life.

The balance I needed would come many years later. What I see now so clearly is how much I invested in this friendship because of my needs and wounds. The corrective I needed was to understand how important disinterested love is in friendship. By the grace of God, I don't have moments like this now, and I don't view friendships like this. I had bizarre views of what friendship was about back then—I wanted something that was more than what friendship really is all about. In the middle of all of the wounds I lived with, I thought the only answer for me was to have a deep, godly friendship with my friend Jake. But my ideas of what a godly friendship was between two men placed unrealistic and inordinate demands on our friendship. I learned that what I wanted wasn't really friendship at all. My view of this godly, spiritual friendship was a sad distortion of the beauty of true friendship. Which leads us to a reflection on the particular temptations of friendship that are unique to those of us who live with same-sex attractions. We'll tackle that in the next chapter.

The Temptations of Friendship

Friendship, at its very best and purest, has limits.

—Hugh Black[*]

Our friendships hurry to short and poor conclusions, because we have made them a texture of wine and dreams, instead of the tough fibre of the human heart. The laws of friendship are austere and eternal, of one web with the laws of nature and of morals. But we have aimed at a swift and petty benefit, to suck a sudden sweetness. We snatch at the lowest fruit in the whole garden of God, which many summers and many winters must ripen. We seek our friend not sacredly, but with an adulterate passion which would appropriate him to ourselves. In vain.

—Ralph Waldo Emerson[†]

O madness, which knowest not how to love men, like men!

—Saint Augustine, *Confessions*[‡]

Jake seemed like an answer from God to me, to show me what true friendship between men was all about. But I fell into a potentially fateful trap for men like me: I began to

[*]Hugh Black, *Friendship* (New York: Fleming H. Revell, 1904), p. 191.

[†]Ralph Waldo Emerson, *The Works of Ralph Waldo Emerson* (New York: George Routledge, 1883), p. 45.

[‡]St. Augustine, *The Confessions of St. Augustine*, ed. Temple Scott, trans. E. B. Pusey (New York: E. P. Dutton, 1900), p. 69.

view his friendship as a substitution for the sort of fulfillment that exists only in marriage. This pushes friendship to the breaking point, because that's not what friendship is for. This view of friendship must be avoided at all costs if a man like me who lives with same-sex attractions truly wants to live a fulfilling life.

As my friendship with Jake developed, I started to wonder how healthy it was. On July 3, 1999, I wrote about it in my journal:

> I look through shattered glass, desperately trying to see and experience love. I filter everything through a grid of my own selfishness, pride, fear, inadequacies and pain. I have sought for the solution in the wrong places. The answer, of course, is Jesus Christ, yet our experience of loving and being loved by others is so much a part of our human existence.
>
> One thing I know: I want to experience love to the fullest! Is this idolatry? The question to be asked is whether or not the desire to experience love supersedes my desire to experience and know God. The sobering answer must be "yes." "Thou shalt have no other gods before me." But what do I do with the exhilaration I feel at the thought of sharing my love with others? Especially with my friend Jake?

Those were confusing times for me. I succumbed to a temptation common among men with same-sex attractions: we can easily turn friendship into something that friendship is not.

Making Friendship in Our Own Image

Hugh Black provides valuable insights about the need for having an appropriate understanding of the legitimate boundaries that support and protect friendship:

The influence of a friend or near relative is bound to be great.... There is a spiritual affinity, which is the closest and most powerful thing in the world, and yet, in the realm of morals, it has definite limits set to it. At best, it can go only a certain length and ought not to be allowed to go further than its legitimate bounds.[1]

The beacon that has guided me in navigating the legitimate bounds of friendship between other men is the classic distinction of C. S. Lewis describing friendship in *The Four Loves*:

Those who cannot conceive Friendship as a substantive love but only as a disguise or elaboration of Eros betray the fact that they have never had a Friend. The rest of us know that though we can have erotic love and friendship for the same person yet in some ways nothing is less like a Friendship than a love-affair. Lovers are always talking to one another about their love; Friends hardly ever about their Friendship. Lovers are normally face to face, absorbed in each other; Friends, side by side, absorbed in some common interest. Above all, Eros (while it lasts) is necessarily between two only. But two, far from being the necessary number for Friendship, is not even the best.[2]

This last part is vital to friendship. In my friendship with Jake, I found myself wanting it to be a friendship that was about "us". The intrusion of another person was often an irritation to me. I've since learned that this is opposed to the good of friendship.

C. S. Lewis writes,

Friendship is the least jealous of loves. Two friends delight to be joined by a third, and three by a fourth, if only the newcomer is qualified to become a real friend.[3]

[1] Black, *Friendship*, p. 198.
[2] C. S. Lewis, *The Four Loves* (New York: Harcourt, 1988), p. 61.
[3] Ibid.

This seems to be a near universal understanding of friendship. A fellow named Ray Stannard Baker wrote in 1910,

> It is not short of miraculous how, with cultivation, one's capacity for friendship increases. Once I myself had scarcely room in my heart for a single friend who am now so wealthy in friendships.... [W]hen a man's heart really opens to a friend he finds there room for two. And when he takes in the second behold the skies lift and the earth grows wider and he finds there room for two more![4]

C. S. Lewis writes that the "typical expression of opening Friendship would be something like, 'What? You too? I thought I was the only one.' "[5] But lest we think this is the view of Lewis only, let us turn to one of the bright lights of Catholic philosophy of the twentieth century, Josef Pieper:

> There are, of course, several aspects of the phenomenon known as "love". One such, for example, is friendship, or more exactly, the love of friends. That is in fact a special form of love, though one that nowadays, oddly enough, comes in for little praise, whereas Aristotle devoted to it one entire book of the ten books that make up his *Nicomachean Ethics*. Friendship takes time, he says there; it is normally not kindled just by the sight of the other, but by the surprise at discovering that here is someone else who "sees things exactly" the way one sees them oneself, someone of whom one can say happily, "It's good that you exist!" Friends do not gaze at each other, and totally unlike erotic lovers they are not apt to talk about their friendship. Their gaze is fixed upon the things in which they take a common interest. That is why, it has been

---

[4] Ray Stannard Baker, *Adventures of David Grayson* (New York: Book League of America, 1910), p. 264.

[5] Lewis, *Four Loves*, p. 65.

said, people who simply wish for "a friend" will with fair certainty not find any. To find a friend you first have to be interested in something.[6]

I was always talking about my friendship with Jake. I wrote in my journal effusive entries on how much his friendship meant to me. Yet it wasn't really a friendship at all. What I was looking for—I now realize—was a form of spousal love, within the confines of a friendship. To quote Hugh Black again, I pushed friendship past its legitimate bounds.

There is a temptation among those of us who live with same-sex attractions to reject this vision of friendship. I find it stems from a deep desire to have some semblance of the love spouses have for each other, but we do not have the right—or the power—to reinvent what love is meant to be between friends. There is a love that is proper between spouses and a love that is proper between friends: the love of the latter certainly must exist in the former, but the sort of love that is particularly ordered toward spousal love threatens and undermines friendship.

The Catholic thinker and philosopher Dietrich von Hildebrand helped me to understand this more deeply:

There are two fundamental dimensions of communion: the I-thou communion, where two persons stand face to face, and the we-communion, where persons stand side by side and turn together towards a third object.... I would say that, in general, friendship is a we-communion where persons stand side by side and together turn toward common goods and values and share mutual interests.

[6] Josef Pieper, *An Anthology* (San Francisco: Ignatius Press, 1989), pp. 42–43. Excerpt from *About Love*, trans. Richard and Clara Winston (Chicago: Franciscan Herald Press, 1974).

In spousal love, on the contrary, love itself is specifically the theme. Here, an explicit I-thou situation predominates, always with the longing for the attainment of the ultimate union in the mutual interpenetration of souls in love.[7]

Romantic and spousal love is the domain of an exclusivity of "two". Hildebrand writes,

Spousal love alone constitutes the organic link to the sensual sphere, a sphere essentially foreign to every other love, such as friendship, the love of a mother, or the love of a child. This does not exclude that sexual instincts in fact oftentimes creep into other types of love. But in such cases it is always more or less a perversion or at least some foreign body that has been added, and not something which is in its very quality and nature ordered to be an organic fulfillment and expression of that love.[8]

I realize now that my desire for close friendships when I was younger came wrapped in this "sensual" sphere. How I wish I had understood then what I know now! Perhaps then I would have avoided the counterfeit of friendship that I had tried to find in my friendship with Jake. I thought my friendship with Jake was a great and grand experiment, an attempt to recover what true friendship was all about. But what I was trying to engage in with him was really a distortion of what true friendship is. Though it felt like a spiritual form of friendship, at its roots it was a worldly and carnal version of friendship, rooted

[7]Dietrich von Hildebrand, *Love, Marriage, and the Catholic Conscience: Understanding the Church's Teaching on Birth Control* (Manchester, N.H.: Sophia Institute Press, 1998), pp. 25–26.

[8]Ibid., p. 31.

more in the good feeling of having a friend, rather than in loving him as a friend, disinterestedly. Because of the unrealistic expectations I had for the friendship, and the undue burdens I placed on him to meet my needs, our friendship sadly dwindled away.

Commenting on Augustine's well-known prayer "You have formed us for Yourself, our hearts are restless until they find rest in You",[9] Henry Nouwen wrote,

> You can say that much of what we are doing is to find some solution for our loneliness. On a very deep level we know that if we want human beings or human structures to solve our loneliness, we can quickly become extremely demanding and obsessive. If you use your relationship to solve your loneliness, you can quickly find yourself being very clinging and oppressive. This is why loneliness often leads to so much violence. You want somebody else to take that loneliness away and it doesn't work.[10]

This points out one of the most important lessons I've needed to learn: on this side of heaven, we all, in reality, live alone.

Failing to Recognize the Distance between Us

On July 5, 1999, I wrote an effusive outpouring of my gratitude to God for the friendship with Jake, saying, "I find myself overwhelmed with joy! Oh, what amazing, wonderful, remarkable joy can come from merely the thought of a friend! Dear God, you are so good to me! Thank you for Jake! I'm overwhelmed at the joy his friendship brings to me!"

---

[9] Saint Augustine, *Confessions*, bk. 1, chap. 1, http://www.newadvent.org/fathers/110101.htm.

[10] Henri Nouwen and Philip Roderick, *Beloved: Henri Nouwen in Conversation* (London: Canterbury Press Norwich, 2007), pp. 6–7.

And yet, just a week later, after a very traumatic weekend with Jake, involving a horrific debacle in a sailboat on Lake Michigan, I wrote the following:

July 12, 1999

Last night, I got together with Jake, and after he left, I went around the room, turning off the lights. I stopped in the dark and said, "Ultimately, we live alone." It was a resignation in my mind of the inability for us to truly know anyone or share ourselves fully with another. Towards the end of the evening, in which we gathered to discuss sailing the previous week, I said to Jake, "I'll be glad when none of this stuff gets in the way of relating one to another."

He laughed, smiled, and said, "We'll be dead!"

And I said, "Exactly!"

That is undoubtedly one of the greatest desires for heaven for me.

Perhaps the most valuable lesson I needed to learn about relationships with other people—whether it be with my family, with friends, or even, if in Divine Providence, with a potential future wife—is that God has ordained our human loves on this earth so that we are never so close to another person that we fail to understand how alone we are without God.

"Even the closest friendship cannot reach a person's innermost self," writes Hugh Black. "In spite of the community of human life," he says, "there is the other fact of the singleness of human life. We have a life that we must live alone."[11]

Paul D. O'Callaghan, an Orthodox priest, shares the same insight in his excellent book *The Feast of Friendship*: "If perfect intimacy is to be attained and preserved in a friendship ... certain basic principles must be honored.

[11] Black, *Friendship*, p. 202.

The first is the absolute necessity of maintaining distance in the relationship."[12]

The mature person must come to this awareness at some point in his life, if he truly desires to live a life of freedom in his relationships. Until we know the gap that always must exist between us and the deepest recesses of another person's soul, we will never be able to view friendship—or any relationship—through the lens of reality. We will place undue burdens on our friend to "know us" more than is actually possible within the confines of our temporal existence on earth.

Hugh Black says, "We may be leaves from the same tree of life, but no two leaves are alike. We may be wrapped up in the same bundle, but one bundle can contain very different things.... So, while it is true that we stand or fall together, it is also true—and it is a deeper truth—that we stand or fall alone."[13]

Fundamental then to true friendship is a deep respect for the autonomy of the other person. Any relationship that fails to recognize the inherent "aloneness" of the other is doomed to fall into neediness, selfishness, and unreal expectations.

This was a hard, but necessary, lesson for me to learn.

Falling in Loving with Loving

There is another temptation in friendship that often masquerades as benevolence and self-love, but really, at its core, is selfishness. That is the temptation to fall in love with the feeling of loving itself.

---

[12] Paul D. O'Callaghan, *The Feast of Friendship* (Wichita, Kans.: Eighth Day Press, 2007), p. 99.

[13] Black, *Friendship*, p. 203.

Saint Augustine wrote of this in his *Confessions*:

> To love and be loved was sweet to me, and all the more
> when I gained the enjoyment of the body of the person
> I loved. Thus I polluted the spring of friendship with
> the filth of concupiscence and I dimmed its luster with the
> slime of lust.[14]

As I look back on so many of my past yearnings for friendship, I realize that I was like Saint Augustine. I was in love
with "loving". "To love and be loved was sweet to me."

An email I wrote in July of 2000 to a friend of mine (who
also experiences same-sex attractions) is a case in point:

> I feel for me, however, the temptation is to make a "com-
> forting" friendship unhealthy by gaining so much joy out
> of the comforting—joy that in a way can become idola-
> trous, rather than the healthy satisfaction one can take in
> the knowledge that you're helping someone else through
> a particular struggle.... I still struggle, and believe I always
> will, with the fine line between comforting others, as
> Christ calls us to do, and comforting others for the emo-
> tional high it gives me. I think for me it's an issue of Christ
> purifying my desires. The desire is healthy and good, but
> it's tainted by my weakness and brokenness.... Hopefully,
> over time, my desires will be ordered rightly so that being
> a vessel of God's love excites me all the time more than
> the idea of becoming [a] guy's best friend. The first one is
> selfless, the other is selfish.[15]

The German philosopher Robert Spaemann writes, "He
who only wants to be the giver does not give enough."

---

[14]Saint Augustine, *Confessions*, ed. Albert Cook Outler (Peabody, Mass.:
Hendrickson Publishers, 2011), pp. 37–38.

[15]Personal email, July 7, 2000.

He adds, "He who truly wishes another well with all his heart will let him feel that he, the lover, also needs him, the beloved." It's an insight derived from Christianity itself, which, he says, "teaches that the ultimate gift of God is that he makes himself into a receiver with regard to us".[16]

"He who gives someone to understand that he is ready to be everything for him, but that he is not interested in being loved himself," Spaemann says, "humiliates the other."[17]

The perversity of this is that this can be represented as a noble form of love: "I give all of myself to you—that is reward enough. I have no need of anything from you." Thankfully, I don't really ever experience this any longer. It's taken a lot of work to get there, but I have great freedom in my friendships now, for I now recognize the distance between us, and enjoy them for who they *are* rather than how being their friend makes me feel. This has been liberating for me.

Temptations That Arise from Neediness

I placed unrealistic demands on my friendship with Jake, but didn't have enough self-awareness to realize what I was doing. It stemmed from the gaping wound of loneliness within me, desperate for closure and healing. I thought what we were doing was healthy and good.

But I entered the friendship broken and wounded. In my woundedness, I was a very demanding friend, though at the time I thought I was being magnanimous. I took offense easily—if we were scheduled to meet at a certain time, I became horribly annoyed, out of all proportion to

---

[16]Robert Spaemann, *Love and The Dignity of Human Life: On Nature and Natural Law* (Grand Rapids: William B. Eerdmans, 2012), p. 21.
[17]Ibid.

the natural grace and benefit of the doubt that I've learned
is a characteristic of true friends. I see this now as a defect
within me that needed time—and God's grace—to heal.

Hugh Black again provides words of wisdom:

> Some of the limits of friendship are ... due to a defect in
> the relationship, perhaps an idiosyncrasy of character or a
> peculiarity of temper.... A friend may be too exacting and
> may make excessive demands that strain the bond to the
> breaking point. There is often a good deal of selfishness
> in the affection, which asks for absorption, and is jealous
> of other interests. Jealousy is usually the fruit, not of love,
> but of self-love.[18]

The demands I placed on my friendship with Jake
strained the bond to the breaking point. Psychologically,
I wasn't fully capable of loving him, as he deserved to be
loved. Indeed, as the pressure I placed on the friendship
caused it to begin to unravel, Jake wrote an email to me
saying that my enjoyment in his friendship seemed at times
a "pathological exuberance".

I can see some of the problems with my friendship with
Jake in a passage from *The Feast of Friendship*:

> We have seen how solid friendship requires two per-
> sons that are fundamentally psychologically sound. The
> element of neediness on the part of one or the other is
> an inherently destabilizing force that seeks to obliterate
> the distance between the two. The needy person seeks
> to make the other perform a desired function within his
> own unhealthy psychic system. He thus must subjugate
> the friend and mold him into the role his needs demand.
> The other then is not encountered as a true person and is

[18] Black, *Friendship*, pp. 192–93.

not allowed his full humanity. He exists as a role player in the inner world of the needy friend. The distance that must exist between two real people cannot abide because the needy one must wholly encompass the other to gain his required psychological fix.[19]

Here is where I find the Church's wise understanding of the homosexual condition helpful. The Church understands that deep-seated homosexual tendencies that remain unresolved can have a negative impact on relating with others in a healthy and mature fashion. The Church has spoken frequently about "affective maturity" that is often not fully developed in people who experience same-sex attractions. "Such persons," one Vatican document asserts, "find themselves in a situation that gravely hinders them from relating correctly to men and women."[20]

Those of us with deep-seated homosexual tendencies need help in order to learn how to love others properly. I have seen this in my own life. It is with much time and help that I have learned what true friendship looks like. This has been aided by many loving people in my life, including counselors, priests, and spiritual directors, as well as friends and family, and from authors who understand what true friendship is. In a way, I realize that I needed help to "grow up" in love before I could love others well. This is what affective maturity is all about.

Pope Saint John Paul II wrote, "Affective maturity presupposes an awareness that love has a central role in human life" and that this "love involves the entire person,

[19] O'Callaghan, *Feast of Friendship*, p. 100.

[20] Congregation for Catholic Education, *Instruction concerning the Criteria for the Discernment of Vocations with Regard to Persons with Homosexual Tendencies in View of Their Admission to the Seminary and to Holy Orders* (November 4, 2005), no. 2, http://www.vatican.va/roman_curia/congregations/ccatheduc/documents/rc_con_ccatheduc_doc_20051104_istruzione_en.html.

in all his or her aspects—physical, psychic and spiritual—and which is expressed in the 'nuptial meaning' of the human body, thanks to which a person gives oneself to another and takes the other to oneself."[21] Here the psychological wounds that often accompany deep-seated homosexual tendencies can wreak havoc with friendships. The "nuptial meaning" of the human body—the giving and receiving that is beautifully written into the complementarity of the two sexes—is negatively impacted when men like me have deep-seated homosexual tendencies: we don't see the two sexes as we should, and as they really are. But here also the virtue of chastity can help and aid men like me. As the Holy Father says, chastity is the "virtue that develops a person's authentic maturity".[22]

He adds helpful words for someone like me, with a confused and disordered sexual inclination:

Human maturity, and in particular affective maturity, requires a clear and strong training in freedom, which expresses itself in convinced and heartfelt obedience to the "truth["] of one's own being, to the "meaning" of one's own existence, that is to the "sincere gift of self" as the way and fundamental content of the authentic realization of self (Cf. *Gaudium et Spes*, 24). Thus understood, freedom requires the person to be truly master of oneself, determined to fight and overcome the different forms of selfishness and individualism which threaten the life of each one, ready to open out to others, generous in dedication and service to one's neighbor.[23]

---

[21] John Paul II, Post-Synodal Apostolic Exhortation on the Formation of Priests in the Circumstances of the Present Day *Pastores Dabo Vobis* (March 25, 1992), no. 44, http://w2.vatican.va/content/john-paul-ii/en/apost_exhortations/documents/hf_jp-ii_exh_25031992_pastores-dabo-vobis.html.

[22] Ibid.

[23] Ibid.

Fundamental, then, to reaching affective maturity is "heartfelt obedience to the truth of one's own being". Here is one more reason why I refuse to consider myself a gay man. Embracing my true sexual identity is vital in developing affective maturity: if I don't see myself as I truly am, I cannot relate with people in an honest and mature manner. Growth in the virtue of chastity is the only way forward.

Seeing myself as I truly am—and seeing others as they truly are, which is what chastity allows—helps me navigate another temptation of friendship: placing other men on a pedestal.

The Pedestal—Idealizing Other Men

There have been men in my past whom I placed on an unhealthy pedestal. They became the idealization of what I wished I could be myself. Reflecting back on these moments, I realize how much envy was involved in the way I looked at them: "If I was only more like him, then surely I'd be happy." Of course, such thinking leads to the opposite of happiness.

This idealization, however, had its own reward. Placing someone on a pedestal can often be akin to lust, even if there is no sexual attraction involved. It indulges in contemplating and desiring what the other has. Certainly admiration has always been an aspect of friendship, and indeed often is a motivation for friendship. But what I am talking about here is a kind of fascination that sees the other not as an equal, but as a superior whom I am tempted to honor—even to adore—because he represents what I wish were different about myself. This shows the problem with the pedestal: it's usually not an honest vision of the other person, but an image projected onto him.

Pope Saint John Paul II writes of this sort of relationship in his book *Love and Responsibility*. Though he is talking here about love between men and women, the same principle applies to those who live with same-sex attractions:

> Here, the ideal is more powerful than the real, living human being, and the latter often becomes merely the occasion for an eruption in the subject's emotional consciousness of the values which he or she longs with all his heart to find in another person.... Sentimentality is subjective and feeds, sometimes to excess, above all on values which the subject bears within himself or herself, and for which he or she consciously or unconsciously yearns.[24]

He writes that the "salient feature" of this "human sentiment ... seems to be the main source of the weakness of affection. That form of love shows a characteristic ambivalence; it seeks to be near the beloved person, seeks proximity and expressions of tenderness, yet it is remote from the beloved in that it does not depend for its life on that person's true value, but on those values to which the subject clings as to its ideal. This is why sentimental love is very often a form of disillusionment."[25]

Ralph Waldo Emerson writes that "the higher the style we demand of friendship, of course the less easy to establish it with flesh and blood. We walk alone in the world. Friends such as we desire are dreams and fables."[26]

I have found freedom in friendship in allowing my friends to be themselves—as they really are. I have no interest in living in the realm of fables and dreams any longer. It is the

[24] Karol Wojtyła, *Love and Responsibility* (San Francisco: Ignatius Press, 1993), pp. 112–13.

[25] Ibid., p. 113.

[26] Emerson, *Works of Ralph Waldo Emerson*, p. 48.

virtue of chastity that helps me see—and love—my friends as they really are, not in an idealized way.

The Temptation of Attraction

Naturally, there is a rather obvious temptation of friendship for people who experience same-sex attractions: What do you do when you find a friend attractive?

I can't go around life trying to pretend that I don't find certain men handsome. Ignoring the reality of an attractive man would be like trying to ignore the color red every time I saw it. Good-looking men just "are" in the same way that stop signs are red. If I tried to ignore the beauty in the people around me, I think I'd go insane.

What I do have is the choice of what I do with that awareness. In this way, I'm no different than a man who sees a beautiful woman and has a choice with what to do with her beauty.

Some men I see haunt my memory, and I have to figure out what to do with my thoughts of them.

Not long ago I was at a coffee shop. I went there to read and write in my journal. As I sat down, I looked and saw a man who captured my imagination. He was studying; perhaps he was a student in graduate school.

He was handsome, but my instant feeling seeing him wasn't sexual; rather, it was a deep longing to connect with him. It was far more than his looks. I wanted to know what he was reading; I wanted to know what he was studying. I desired to know what he dreamed about in his life, what motivated him to pursue whatever it was that he was studying.

This feeling stunned me in its intensity. It wasn't a feeling of lust, or of sexual desire, though he was sexually attractive to me. It was far more visceral than mere sexual desire.

We tend to think that sexual desire and longing is our most primal desire. But I would say even deeper than this is to know and be known, to love and be loved.

I longed to be known by him, and to know him as intimately as I could ever know another human person. I wanted to be united with him somehow, to know everything about him, and to share everything I had to share with him.

My rational mind observed these emotions with surprise. He was a stranger—why did these deep feelings of longing enter into my mind?

I saw some attractive women enter the store, the sort of pretty girls who always make men turn their heads. He looked up at the sound, but his eyes didn't linger. I wondered if he had no interest in them either. I tried to focus on my book, but my mind kept wandering through the longing that arose in me as soon as I saw him.

He got up to go to the bathroom, and for a moment I thought of somehow writing him a note, a scribble of—I don't know what—that might lead to a connection. I thought that when he returned I might find a way to throw my cup away in the trash bin behind him, lean in toward him in a friendly way, and with a lame attempt at a conversation say: "So, it looks like you're really hard at work studying."

He came back, and I did none of those things, wishing I had. I looked at him again, wanting more than I've ever wanted anything in my life to know him and be known by him. I suppose I whispered a quiet prayer of desperation to God: Where did this come from, and what am I supposed to do with this, dear Lord?

The answer came quickly.

"Not here, not now, not yet. Keep going. One day, yes. But not today."

It reminded me from a line in Thomas Howard's essay on the British author Charles Williams: "All creation whispers 'Not yet. Not here. Keep going.' Idolatry stops in its tracks, and thus loses both Beatrice and Beatific Vision."[27]

My longing for that man wasn't lust. It wasn't a desire for sex, though sex with him would be a powerfully addictive substitute used to sate the deep longing I felt when I saw him. Nor was my longing for him precisely for *him*. The longing I felt was too strong to be explained by a random man sitting in a random coffee shop. He distilled in that moment a longing we all have, a longing rooted in what it means to be human: we are made for union with others. Put another way, we are made to be united in love with everyone else who has ever walked the planet.

It was easy for me to see this clearly, since it was such a strange and powerful emotion to experience toward a stranger.

My desire for men—no, my desire for everything!—points me to the one place where my desires can actually be fulfilled. My desire for joy, for love, for beauty, all those desires that are never fully satisfied in the way I think they should be satisfied, all point to the reality that there must be a place that finally satisfies us. Saint Augustine said it all so long ago: my heart is restless until it rests in God.

The union that I most desire will only be found in heaven. Not here. Not now. Not yet. Keep going.

My longings that remain unsatisfied here on earth point me toward heaven, toward God, toward what the poets have called the "Beatific Vision".

[27] Thomas Howard, *The Night Is Far Spent: A Treasury of Thomas Howard* (San Francisco: Ignatius Press, 2007), p. 130.

Nothing on earth ever fully satisfies me, but I'm constantly trying to fill what I've often heard described as the God-shaped void that exists in all men's hearts.

I have tried to fill that void with men, with porn, with sex, with food, with pleasures, and indeed with a distorted version of friendship. But the longing remains. Every attractive man I see reminds me that I'm made for a better place than this.

Lewis writes often of this longing as "the far-off country", the one place where, we believe, true happiness can exist. The Buddha found his answer to the suffering of this world in the extinguishing of all desire. Christianity, in contrast, embraces desire, for the very fact that desires that are not satisfied in this world point us to the next, where we will find ultimate happiness.

That unmet desire, that unscratched itch that motivates us so often to try to find happiness in pleasure, ambition, wealth, or power, is something that we can't articulate, because, as Lewis says, "It is a desire for something that has never actually appeared in our experience. We cannot hide it because our experience is constantly suggesting it, and we betray ourselves like lovers at the mention of a name. Our commonest expedient is to call it beauty and behave as if that had settled the matter."[28]

He says that the things where we thought "beauty was located will betray us if we trust to them; it was not *in* them, it only came *through* them, and what came through them was longing."[29]

This, then, is how I have learned to respond to the aching beauty of a handsome man: his attractiveness, and my

[28] C. S. Lewis, *The Weight of Glory and Other Addresses* (New York: Harper Collins, 1980), p. 30.
[29] Ibid.

longing for him, reveals to me, more clearly than any other means possible, that my deepest desires and my deepest longings will never be fulfilled or realized here on this earth. I can thank God for the beauty I see, but through the grace of God, I realize that the beauty I see on earth—everywhere—is nothing in comparison to the beauty of seeing the face of God. And that's what we all truly long for, whether we know it or not.

Now, of course, choosing to find my happiness in God, rather than in sexual connections with men, means that I'm most likely going to live a single life. And that's going to mean that there are times of great loneliness. I have learned the art of friendship—for that I'm grateful—but even though I have a wealth of friends, there are still moments of bone-crushing loneliness in my life.

And for that, I thank God.

The Gift of Loneliness

Thou wentest forth in the Spirit of power, fresh from the baptismal wave, into the desert, that a pattern of the solitary life also might not be wanting in Thy Person. Loneliness, forty days' fast, the sharp tooth of hunger, temptations from the deceiver-spirit,—all were borne by Thee with even mind, that thus all might by Thy working be made bearable to us.

—Saint Anselm[*]

And we shall take everything for good; even though the exercises that meet us, which Your arrangement brings to us for the discipline of our steadfastness, appear to be evil.

—Saint Clement of Alexandria[†]

When I think of loneliness today, I see it through the eyes of Henri Nouwen. In his book *The Wounded Healer*, he said that "the wound of loneliness is like the Grand Canyon—a deep incision in the surface of our existence which has become an inexhaustible source of beauty and self-understanding."[1] When I first read those words fifteen

[*]St. Anselm, *St. Anselm's Book of Meditations and Prayers*, trans. M. R. (London: Burns and Oates, 1872), p. 107.

[†]St. Clement of Alexandria, *Stromata* 7.12, trans. William Wilson, *Ante-Nicene Fathers*, vol. 2, ed. Alexander Roberts, James Donaldson, and A. Cleveland Coxe (Buffalo, N.Y.: Christian Literature Publishing, 1885), rev. and ed. by Kevin Knight, NewAdvent.org, http://www.newadvent.org/fathers/02107.htm.

[1]Henri Nouwen, *The Wounded Healer* (New York: Image Books, 1979), p. 84.

years ago, I hadn't seen the Grand Canyon, except in pictures. Nor could I understand then why he found loneliness so beautiful. But time and many years with moments of loneliness have carved an incision in the surface of my soul—and now I see the beauty he saw too, and agree with what he said:

> The Christian way of life does not take away our loneliness; it protects and cherishes it as a precious gift. Sometimes it seems as if we do everything possible to avoid the painful confrontation with our basic human loneliness, and allow ourselves to be trapped by false gods promising immediate satisfaction and quick relief.... When we want to give up our loneliness and try to overcome the separation and incompleteness we feel, too soon, we easily relate to our human world with devastating expectations. We ignore what we already know with a deep-seated, intuitive knowledge—that no love or friendship, no intimate embrace or tender kiss, no community, commune or collective, no man or woman, will ever be able to satisfy our desire to be released from our lonely condition. This truth is so disconcerting and painful that we are more prone to play games with our fantasies than to face the truth of our existence. Thus we keep hoping that one day we will find the man who really understands our experiences, the woman who will bring peace to our restless life. Such false hope leads us to make exhausting demands and prepares us for bitterness and dangerous hostility when we start discovering that nobody, and nothing, can live up to our absolutistic expectations.
>
> Many marriages are ruined because neither partner was able to fulfill the often hidden hope that the other would take his or her loneliness away. And many celibates live with the naive dream that in the intimacy of marriage their loneliness will be taken away.[2]

[2] Ibid., pp. 84–85.

When I first read those words, they didn't make sense to me. Loneliness chafed against me. I'm like any man. There's nothing about loneliness I particularly like. Nonetheless, loneliness has become precious to me, for I realize now that loneliness is an invitation to joy, peace, and fulfillment, for now I know that loneliness is an invitation to love.

The journey to reach that awareness has been arduous. I remember moments where I lay in the middle of my living room, curled up on the floor in a fetal position, weeping and wailing in agony, feeling loneliness creep over me like a shroud. Loneliness causes me physical pain sometimes, like a vise gripping my chest. The loneliness I have felt in my life has been the greatest source of doubt about God's love and faithfulness in my life. So often in moments of loneliness I wondered when I would experience the "peace" that "passes all understanding", as Saint Paul promised (Phil 4:7).

I was a man in search of an answer. Viktor Frankl, a survivor of Auschwitz, helped me to find one. His book *Man's Search for Meaning* tells of how he survived the horrors of the Holocaust, and it convinced me that there is always meaning in suffering. "If there is a meaning in life at all," he wrote, "then there must be a meaning in suffering. Suffering is an ineradicable part of life, even as fate and death. Without suffering and death human life cannot be complete."[3]

I was greatly moved by a passage from Frankl's book recalling the story of a young woman whose death he observed in Auschwitz. "It is a simple story," he says. "There is little to tell and it may sound as if I had invented it; but to me it seems like a poem."

[3] Viktor E. Frankl, *Man's Search for Meaning* (New York: Simon and Schuster, 1985), p. 88.

He writes:

> This young woman knew that she would die in the next
> few days. But when I talked to her she was cheerful in
> spite of this knowledge. "I am grateful that fate has hit me
> so hard," she told me. "In my former life I was spoiled and
> did not take spiritual accomplishments seriously." Pointing
> through the window of the hut, she said, "This tree here
> is the only friend I have in my loneliness." Through that
> window she could see just one branch of a chestnut tree,
> and on the branch were two blossoms. "I often talk to this
> tree," she said to me. I was startled and didn't quite know
> how to take her words. Was she delirious? Did she have
> occasional hallucinations? Anxiously I asked her if the tree
> replied. "Yes." What did it say to her? She answered, "It
> said to me, 'I am here-I am here-I am life, eternal life.' "[4]

The words of this young woman cleaved my heart. "I
am grateful that fate has hit me so hard." Who could ever
say *that* in a concentration camp? There was something
that called to me in her story—I wanted to be like her. If
this woman could find such dignity and nobility in the face
of the horrors of a concentration camp, surely I could find
a way to be like her in my own sufferings.

I read this at a time of profound loneliness, and it seemed
that she spoke through the pages of Frankl's book and said
to me, "Loneliness is the path set before you right now. In
your former life, you were spoiled. Just like me, you didn't
take spiritual accomplishments seriously. But God, in his
grace, has allowed you to be afflicted. Pain has cut you to
the core. In your loneliness, in your pain, the Tree is the
only friend you have. Look through the window at it—
see, it blossoms with life in the midst of the pain around
you. It is life, eternal life. The path before you today is this

[4] Ibid., p. 90.

loneliness. Accept it, and follow Him. Be grateful that fate has hit you so hard, for it is a sign of God's love for you."

I thought of the many lonely nights I had endured, so many filled with tears, where I asked questions rooted in despair: "Will I be single forever?" "Is the only path before me to come home to an empty bed every night?" "Will anyone ever care if I make it home from the airport after a trip?" "Will I die alone, forgotten in some retirement home somewhere?" These fears haunted me for years—life on my own felt like a prison sentence to me. How could I respond to this pain, like that young woman in the concentration camp?

I learned how to respond to loneliness from another woman who suffered tremendous loneliness in her own life. Elisabeth Elliot and her husband Jim were Protestant missionaries who went to serve in Ecuador in 1953. Jim, along with four other men, was speared to death in an attempt to share the Gospel with the Auca tribe, a primitive people living deep in the jungle. Left with a ten-month-old daughter to care for on her own, Elisabeth pressed on, eventually helping to bring the Gospel to the tribe who killed her husband. She lived as a single mother until she married again in 1969—only to lose her new husband from cancer just four years later. Reading her reflections on loneliness, I realized that Elisabeth had asked the same sorts of questions I asked: Why does loneliness exist? Why won't God take it away? Can anything good come from my loneliness?

"Our loneliness cannot always be fixed," Elliot says, "but it can always be accepted as the very will of God for now, and that turns it into something beautiful."[5] In her own painful journey through loneliness, she began to view

[5] Elisabeth Elliot, *The Path of Loneliness: Finding Your Way through the Wilderness to God* (Grand Rapids: Revell, 2007), p. 109.

loneliness as the field with the hidden treasure, the field
a man sells everything to buy (cf. Mt 13:44). "We must
buy the field. It is a bleak and empty place, but once we
know it contains a jewel the whole picture changes." For
Elliot, selling everything "meant giving up the self-pity
and the bitter questions". This has been tremendously
helpful for me in my own journey through loneliness. So
too Elliot's wise counsel to accept loneliness when it is
inevitable: "When, through a willed act we receive this
thing we did not want, then Loneliness, the name of the
field nobody wants, is transformed into a place of hidden treasure."[6]

The "hidden treasure" of loneliness, when accepted
and embraced, becomes a beautiful gift of love, offered on
behalf of others. In "the field no one wants", Elliot sees the
transformative power of the cross:

> When a man or woman, a boy or girl, accepts the way
> of loneliness for Christ's sake, there are cosmic ramifica-
> tions. That person, in a secret transaction with God, actu-
> ally does something for the life of the world. This seems
> almost inconceivable, yet it is true, for it is one part of the
> mystery of suffering which has been revealed to us.[7]

As a Protestant at the time, unfamiliar with the concept
of redemptive suffering, this was a surprising idea. Before
this, all I ever heard about suffering was that it was a test of
man's faith, or of his perseverance, or a time of trial. But
here, in the words of Elisabeth Elliot, I started to glimpse
an idea that suffering could be far more than merely a test.
For many years she believed "suffering for Christ" could
only refer to the sort of suffering that martyrs endured

---

[6] Ibid.
[7] Ibid., p. 128.

for their public witness to the faith, or the sufferings that come from being in full-time ministry. Her view of suffering was transformed, however, when she began reflecting more deeply on the words of Saint Paul in his Letter to the Colossians. Saint Paul, she said:

> saw the great truth of "exchange"—that out of his suffering would come good for others, meaning not only the Church in Colosse. He goes on to say, "This is my way of helping to complete, in my poor human flesh, the full tale of Christ's afflictions still to be endured, for the sake of his body which is the church. I became its servant by virtue of the task assigned to me by God for your benefit" (Col. 1:24–25, NEB). While it is not difficult to see the task of an apostle as a divine assignment, it is often difficult to see our own as in any sense divinely assigned.[8]

This completely turned my understanding of suffering upside down. The idea that suffering could somehow be united with the suffering of Christ on behalf of another person, united with Christ's suffering on the Cross, was revolutionary to me. It was especially strange to my Protestant ears, and yet I kept running into this idea of what I had heard Catholics call "redemptive suffering". Even C. S. Lewis, so beloved by Protestants, seemed to believe that our suffering could actually help others, if we only chose to offer it up on their behalf:

> I have not a word to say against the doctrine that Our Lord suffers in all the sufferings of His people (see Acts IX.6) or that when we willingly accept what we suffer for others and offer it to God on their behalf, then it may be

[8] Ibid., p. 129.

united with His sufferings and, in Him, may help to their redemption or even that of others whom we do not dream of. So that it is not in vain: though of course we must not count on seeing it work out exactly as we, in our present ignorance, might think best. The key text for this view is *Colossians* I.24.[9]

I tentatively began embracing the idea of offering up my suffering on behalf of others—and the change in my experience of suffering was remarkable. In moments of intense pain, I wasn't just enduring it, waiting for it to abate like I waited for an illness to pass. Now I began to accept it, and the more I accepted loneliness into my life, the more I began to embrace it when it came. Everything changed when I realized my suffering became an opportunity through which I could love and care for others.

I began to understand something more about suffering too. One's suffering is his own, and his alone; just as each person is unique, so too is the suffering he endures. That means in our suffering, we're the only ones in the history of the world who have been given the unique opportunity to suffer in the particular way that we suffer, and then invited to offer our particular suffering to God, on behalf of the world. As Elisabeth Elliot said, reflecting on Saint Paul's suffering, "While it is not difficult to see the task of an apostle as a divine assignment, it is often difficult to see our own as in any sense divinely assigned." I began to understand that when suffering is unavoidable, God hasn't left us—the situation we are experiencing has been permitted by God, for a reason and purpose that he knows very well, and a wise man will embrace it as

[9]Lewis to Mary Van Deusen, September 12, 1951, in *Yours, Jack: Spiritual Direction from C. S. Lewis*, ed. Paul F. Ford (New York: HarperOne, 2008), p. 170.

his unique task to endure it and to unite it with the Cross of Christ.

This lesson, so valuable for maintaining peace of mind, and a positive outlook in the face of unchosen suffering, came from Frankl, in words I underlined when I first read them. I have returned to these words again and again when I have been tempted to question if there is any meaning or purpose in suffering at all. Frankl wrote:

> When a man finds that it is his destiny to suffer, he will have to accept his suffering as his task; his single and unique task. He will have to acknowledge the fact that even in suffering he is unique and alone in the universe. No one can relieve him of his suffering or suffer in his place. His unique opportunity lies in the way in which he bears his burden.[10]

Frankl understood the concept of redemptive suffering too. He recalls in his book a moment when he tried to bring hope to his fellow prisoners, racked in despair:

> And finally I spoke of our sacrifice, which had meaning in every case. It was in the nature of this sacrifice that it should appear to be pointless in the normal world, the world of material success. But in reality our sacrifice did have a meaning. Those of us who had any religious faith, I said frankly, could understand without difficulty. I told them of a comrade who on his arrival in camp had tried to make a pact with Heaven that his suffering and death should save the human being he loved from a painful end. For this man, suffering and death were meaningful; his was a sacrifice of the deepest significance. He did not want to die for nothing. None of us wanted that.[11]

[10] Frankl, *Man's Search for Meaning*, pp. 98–99.
[11] Ibid., pp. 104–5.

When we start to see suffering not as something random, but as the source of rich meaning and a source of life and joy, then everything changes. We start to see with the eyes of Christ—suffering not only has meaning, but it becomes the source of life and joy for us and others, just so long as we choose to unite it with the suffering of Christ.

Thomas Merton said something that changed my life when I read it:

> Suffering, therefore, must make sense to us not as a vague universal necessity, but as something demanded by our own personal destiny. When I see my trials not as the collision of my life with a blind machine called fate, but as the sacramental gift of Christ's love, given to me by God the Father along with my identity and my very name, then I can consecrate them and myself with them to God. For then I realize that my suffering is not my own. It is the Passion of Christ, stretching out its tendrils into my life in order to bear rich clusters of grapes, making my soul dizzy with the wine of Christ's love, and pouring that wine as strong as fire upon the whole world.[12]

Here, at last, was the answer I had been looking for all my life. This brought meaning to all the tears and sorrows of my life, meaning to those moments when I wondered when my life would end, meaning to all those times of self-doubt and pain, all the rejection I felt from women, all those moments when I lay in the middle of my living room floor, rocked with sobbing, wondering if there was any joy in life at all. It all finally made sense! It all had a purpose—and the purpose was love. I finally understood the words of Saint Paul to the Romans: "I appeal to you therefore,

---

[12] Thomas Merton, *No Man Is an Island* (New York: Harcourt, 2002), p. 83.

brethren, by the mercies of God, to present your bodies as a living sacrifice, holy and acceptable to God, which is your spiritual worship. Do not be conformed to this world but be transformed by the renewal of your mind, that you may prove what is the will of God, what is good and acceptable and perfect" (Rom 12:1–2). To lay down our lives for our friends—that's what is "good and acceptable and perfect". This is what Saint Paul meant when he said, "To live is Christ" (Phil 1:21). That means putting ourselves gladly and willingly on the Cross, for the sake of the world. The *Catechism* exhorts those who live with attractions to the same sex "to unite to the sacrifice of the Lord's Cross the difficulties they may encounter from their condition".[13] This is a great invitation to love others, the way Christ loved us, and for me, this has become the most important gift the Church has given to me in her teaching on homosexuality.

That's why I choose to embrace loneliness when it comes; I don't merely accept or consent to it—I choose it, no matter how excruciating and painful it can be at times.

In his book *Interior Freedom*, Father Jacques Philippe wrote,

We should not limit ourselves to accepting things grudgingly, but should truly consent to them—not endure them, but in a sense "choose" them (even if in fact we have no choice, and that's what most annoys us). Choosing here means making a free act by which we not only resign ourselves but also welcome the situation. That isn't easy, especially in the case of really painful trials, but it is the right approach, and we should follow as much as possible in faith and hope. If we have enough faith in God to believe him capable of drawing good out of whatever

[13] *CCC* 2358.

befalls us, he will do so. "As you have believed, so let it be done to you," he says repeatedly in the Gospel.[14]

There's another benefit I've learned about embracing loneliness: the wilderness, the dry wasteland, is where God delights to care for us, just as he did for the Israelites for forty years during the Exodus. For most of my life, I grumbled like the Israelites did, but now I know that the desert is the place I will learn best how much I am cherished by God. Thomas Merton taught me this lesson.

The desert was the region in which the Chosen People had wandered for forty years, cared for by God alone. They could have reached the Promised Land in a few months if they had travelled directly to it. God's plan was that they should learn to love Him in the wilderness and that they should always look back upon the time in the desert as the idyllic time of their life with Him alone.[15]

Loneliness touches everyone's life on earth. Marriage doesn't take away loneliness; a large family doesn't ensure that we will never be lonely, nor do friends—certainly not a thousand "friends" on social media. The most devastating moments of loneliness in my life have been when I've been surrounded by people who love me, and yet I felt desperately alone, as if no one truly knew me. Yet we know that Christ felt alone many times, and thus the way of the Cross must necessarily include times of loneliness. When they come, though they may chafe against us, the

[14] Jacques Philippe, *Interior Freedom*, trans. Helena Scott (New York: Scepter Press, 2007), pp. 44–45. Here I must thank my friend Mark Maier, who was led by God to send me the book. The book changed my life, and for that, I will be eternally grateful to Mark for heeding the urging of God to send it to me.

[15] Thomas Merton, *Thoughts in Solitude* (New York: Farar, Straus and Giroux, 2011), p. 5.

answer is to embrace them as Christ embraced the Cross, and offer them for the salvation of those whom we love.

Russians have a great understanding of the beauty of the desert. In Russian Orthodoxy there is a tradition of men and women purposely going into "the desert", to live a life in a little hut called a "poustinia", a word that literally means desert. They are called "poustiniks", and they dedicate their lives to prayer, penance, and service to others. They have become my model and inspiration in my own journey through the desert and wilderness of the single life.

The founder of the Madonna House Apostolate, Catherine Doherty, was originally from Russia and wrote about poustiniks in a beautiful book about prayer and solitude she called *Poustinia: Encountering God in Silence, Solitude and Prayer.*

She recalls the poustiniks from her childhood. They weren't like hermits, closed off from the world. "There was some kind of difference," she said.

> The poustinik seemed to be more available. There was a gracious hospitality about him, as if he were never disturbed by anyone who came to visit him. On the contrary, his was a welcoming face. His eyes seemed to sparkle with joy at receiving a guest. He seemed to be a listening person. A person of few words, but his listening was deep, and there was a feeling that he understood. In him Saint Francis' prayer seemed to become incarnate: he consoled, he understood, and he loved—and he didn't demand anything from anyone for himself.[16]

This attitude of the poustinik seems a good model for me to adopt—I want to be a welcoming face, a listening

---

[16] Catherine Doherty, *Poustinia: Encountering God in Silence, Solitude and Prayer* (Combermere, Ontario: Madonna House Publications, 2012), pp. 16–17.

ear, to have a sparkle of joy when someone sees me. I want to be available for others when they need help. The key for me to a happy life is to *embrace* my singleness, as an act of the will, daily accepting it as God's will for my life, *at this particular moment in time*, and then through embracing it, find outlets by which I can pour myself out in love toward others. It seems a good and noble life if I try to emulate Saint Francis of Assisi and worry about others more than about myself—and by the grace of God, and with the passage of time, I believe that's the sort of person I can become.

But the most important thing the poustinik did was to become a living sacrifice. Doherty says, "They were people who craved in their hearts to be alone with God and his immense silence. Why did they crave that silence, that solitude? For themselves? No. A hermit of this type, according to the Eastern spirituality, went into the poustinia *for others*. He offered himself as a holocaust, a victim for others."[17]

And when they made the conscious choice to embrace loneliness, they found an unexpected blessing:

> It was for all mankind that the poustinik was to pray, to weep, and to endure all the temptations that come to him who lives in the desert. It was for *them* that he was to mortify his flesh, for *them* that he accepted the loneliness that transcends our understanding, and which at the same time, once accepted, is no real loneliness at all.[18]

It's the paradox of the Cross: "If any man would come after me, let him deny himself and take up his cross daily

[17] Ibid., p. 21 (italics in original).
[18] Ibid., p. 23.

and follow me. For whoever would save his life will lose it; and whoever loses his life for my sake, he will save it" (Lk 9:23–24). This is the only answer that has ever made any sense to me. Once loneliness is accepted—and consciously chosen as a vehicle of Christ's love for others—well, then it's no real loneliness at all. Instead, it's love.

PART FIVE

THE MOST IMPORTANT THINGS

Humility and Magnanimity

Humility presents in specifically sharp relief that general aspect of all Christian morality—the unreserved recognition of the metaphysical situation of man, the attitude of throwing all illusions overboard and granting to the whole of reality the response that is due to it. Thus, it has been said justly: "Humility is Truth."

—Dietrich von Hildebrand*

But they reached such a pitch of magnanimity, that not one of them let a sigh or a groan escape them; thus proving to us all that those holy martyrs of Christ, at the very time when they suffered such torments, were absent from the body, or rather, that the Lord then stood by them, and communed with them.

—Epistle on the Martyrdom of Polycarp†

In the battle for chastity, I've learned that the most important virtues I need to acquire are humility and magnanimity. Though I need all of the virtues, these two are the bedrock on which I have learned I must build a life of chastity.

---

*Dietrich von Hildebrand, *Transformation in Christ* (San Francisco: Ignatius Press, 2001), p. 157.

† *The Encyclical Epistle of the Church at Smyrna Concerning the Martyrdom of the Holy Polycarp*, in *The Apostolic Fathers with Justin Martyr and Irenaeus*, vol. 1 of *The Ante-Nicene Fathers: The Writings of the Fathers down to A.D. 325*, ed. Alexander Roberts, James Donaldson, and Arthur Cleveland Coxe (New York: Charles Scribner's Sons, 1903), p. 39.

Humility is the most important of the two. A man who lives with same-sex attractions won't ever be free to live chastely until he has the humility to accept that he is not his own master, and that he has no say in the matter of "who he is". "Humility," Josef Pieper says, "is the knowledge and acceptance of the inexpressible distance between Creator and creature. It is, in a very precise sense, as Gertrud von le Fort once said, 'man's true and proper worth before God'. Man's worth, as that of a being possessed with a soul, consists solely in this: that by his own free decision, he knows and acts in accordance with the reality of his nature—that is, in truth."[1] The humble man accepts the truth that God "is closer and more intimate to us than we are to ourselves".[2] Humility recognizes the truth that man does not have the freedom to rename or redefine what has already been named and defined by God. Here the humble man is guided by the teaching of the Church: "Everyone, man and woman, should acknowledge and accept his sexual *identity*."[3] The humble man recognizes and accepts the truth of the sexual identity given him by God.

The model of humility is our Master, Christ himself. "Have this mind among yourselves," Saint Paul says, "which was in Christ Jesus, who, though he was in the form of God, did not count equality with God a thing to be grasped, but emptied himself, taking the form of a servant, being born in the likeness of men" (Phil 2:5–7). The greatest challenge for every man, everywhere, and at every time is accepting that he is not God—we grasp at "equality with God", wanting to be our own masters, especially today in the realm of human sexuality. Pope Benedict XVI used the occasion of his Christmas address to the Curia

[1] Josef Pieper, *On Hope*, trans. Mary Frances McCarthy, S.N.D. (San Francisco: Ignatius Press, 1986), p. 29.

[2] Ibid., p. 42.

[3] *CCC* 2333 (italics in original).

in 2012—that moment when Christ humbled himself, to become a man, like us—to decry man's denial of the reality of God's design and plan for human sexuality. "People dispute the idea that they have a nature," he said, "given by their bodily identity, that serves as a defining element of the human being. They deny their nature and decide that it is not something previously given to them, but that they make it for themselves."[4] He said it is the promotion of "'gender' as a new philosophy of sexuality" that has resulted in a rejection of the truth that "being created by God as male and female pertains to the essence of the human creature". Instead of humbly accepting the dual expression of human sexuality, "now we decide for ourselves. Man and woman as created realities, as the nature of the human being, no longer exist. Man calls his nature into question." Man has embraced a new form of the ancient heresy of Gnosticism—"reality" has now become what an individual's mind or will wish it to be, without reference to the physical fact of the body. "From now on he is merely spirit and will. The manipulation of nature, which we deplore today where our environment is concerned, now becomes man's fundamental choice where he himself is concerned. From now on there is only the abstract human being, who chooses for himself what his nature is to be."[5] This is the sin of pride, and the sin of our first father.

By striving for humility, I have the hope of accepting my true nature, as a man, and not mislabeling myself. If I embrace a false identity as a gay man, then I deny the bodily reality of my created nature, and I reject and

4 Address of His Holiness Benedict XVI on the Occasion of Christmas Greetings to the Roman Curia (December 21, 2012), http://w2.vatican.va /content/benedict-xvi/en/speeches/2012/december/documents/hf_ben-xvi _spe_20121221_auguri-curia.html.
5 Ibid.

rebel against the sexual orientation revealed by my body. That authentic identity is ordered toward fatherhood, directed toward creating new life. I have no choice in the matter of defining my own sexual identity. "When the freedom to be creative becomes the freedom to create oneself," Benedict said, "then necessarily the Maker himself is denied and ultimately man too is stripped of his dignity as a creature of God, as the image of God at the core of his being.... And it becomes clear that when God is denied, human dignity also disappears. Whoever defends God is defending man."[6] Here then, I see the importance of the Church's admonition that all men and women accept and acknowledge their God-given sexual identity. Accepting the truth of our sexual nature honors and defends man's dignity. Humility opens us to discover and find contentment in reality, and live with a daily acknowledgment that we are not our own masters. For me, humility leads me to the truth that I am not my own. It teaches me to be docile to God's will in my life. As Jesus consoles us, "my yoke is easy, and my burden is light" (Mt 11:30). If my path is the single life, humility gives me peace and tranquility that comes from saying, "Thy will be done, not mine." Humility reveals to me the truth that this world is not my home. It is a novi-tiate for heaven; it is a place of "becoming", a pilgrimage where God shapes us into who we are meant to be. C. S. Lewis said it best for me: "If you think of this world as a place intended simply for our happiness, you find it quite intolerable: think of it as a place of training and correction and it's not so bad."[7]

[6] Ibid.

[7] C. S. Lewis, "Answers to Questions on Christianity", quoted in *A Mind Awake: An Anthology of C. S. Lewis*, ed. Clide S. Kilby (New York: Harcourt, 1968), p. 176.

And when I stumble and fall in this novitiate for heaven, it's humility that leads me to seek repentance; I run to confession, accept God's forgiveness, dust myself off, and forget what has passed, trusting even more for God to strengthen the weakness of my humanity with the power of his divinity.

It's magnanimity that sets me on my feet again. Magnanimity is that virtue that desires to do great things. Pieper tells us:

> Magnanimity, a much-forgotten virtue, is the aspiration of the spirit to great things, *extensio anima ad magna*. A person is magnanimous if he has the courage to seek what is great and becomes worthy of it. This virtue has its roots in a firm confidence in the highest possibilities of that human nature that God did "marvelously ennoble and has still more marvelously renewed" (Roman Missal). Thus magnanimity incorporates into itself the aspiration of natural hope and stamps it according to the truth of man's own nature.[8]

My battles for chastity are borne on the current of magnanimity. Magnanimity is why I want to try and fight for chastity.

The pursuit of chastity isn't for the faint of heart. There's nothing *easy* about it at all. It goes against every fiber of my bodily being. Magnanimity is what causes me to embrace the challenge.

I've been confronted with a choice of how I'm going to live my life. I'm not interested in the *easy* path any longer. It's far less interesting to consider a relationship with a man than it is to battle against my passions, or to be able to offer up any loneliness I suffer on behalf of those I love. What the world offers is, well, just so *boring*. It's bland and

[8] Pieper, *On Hope*, p. 28.

humdrum in comparison with the invitation Christ offers to me. I like that it's hard—it's magnanimity that gives me the excitement to at least try my darndest.

I think battling for chastity is sort of like running along in a bramble-filled ditch next to a perfectly smooth highway. The folks up on the highway look down at the crazy Christians for not jumping up onto the smooth path, but they don't understand that the brambles are where the real action is—it's the tough stuff of life that makes us truly human. We're not made for a life of ease here on this earth, nor is this place our true home. People don't run marathons because they're easy—they run them because they're challenging. That's the fruit of magnanimity, and it's the reason I've chosen the path of chastity.

Magnanimity is the reason I'm determined never to have sex with a man again. Pope Saint John Paul II speaks of magnanimity when he writes, *"Jesus brings God's commandments to fulfilment,* particularly the commandment of love of neighbour, *by interiorizing their demands and by bringing out their fullest meaning.* Love of neighbour springs from *a loving heart* which, precisely because it loves, is ready to live out *the loftiest challenges.* Jesus shows that the commandments must not be understood as a minimum limit not to be gone beyond, but rather as a path involving a moral and spiritual journey towards perfection, at the heart of which is love."[9]

When loneliness hits, I get inspired by Saint Teresa of Calcutta, who willingly accepted suffering for the sake of others. As relayed in the book *Come Be My Light,* "she had insisted that it would be 'worth going through every

[9]John Paul II, encyclical *Veritatis Splendor* (August 6, 1993), no. 15, http://w2.vatican.va/content/john-paul-ii/en/encyclicals/documents/hf_jp-ii_enc_06081993_veritatis-splendor.html (italics in original).

possible suffering just for one single soul' and 'offering everything—for just that one—because that one would bring great joy to the Heart of Jesus.'"[10]

This is the sort of thing that gets me fired up about being a follower of Christ. It's not namby-pamby stuff. I've always longed to do great things—I think that desire is within us all, since we are made in the image and likeness of the King of Kings. We tend to be drawn to stories of superhuman strength in the face of adversity. But what does a Marvel superhero have on Saint Teresa of Calcutta, really?

I want to help people. I want to help people see the face of Jesus. It's not my *strength*, or wisdom, or ability with words that gets them there—it's humbly embracing the suffering I receive, and then uniting that suffering with the Cross of Christ on their behalf, out of love for them. That's a noble calling, and it's good for a man to be faced with a challenge.

I never liked sports, but I like Vince Lombardi; two other trombone players in my orchestra love the Green Bay Packers, and their love has rubbed off on me. When I think of magnanimity in the battle for chastity, I think Coach Lombardi's words sum it up best:

In truth, I've never known a man worth his salt who in the long run, deep down in his heart, didn't appreciate the grind, the discipline. There is something in good men that really yearns for discipline and the harsh reality of head to head combat.

I don't say these things because I believe in the "brute" nature of men or that men must be brutalized to be

[10]Mother Teresa, *Come Be My Light: The Private Writings of the Saint of Calcutta*, ed. Brian Kolodiejchuk (New York: Doubleday, 2007), p. 173.

combative. I believe in God, and I believe in human decency. But I firmly believe that any man's finest hour—his greatest fulfillment to all he holds dear—is that moment when he has worked his heart out in a good cause and lies exhausted on the field of battle—victorious.[11]

That's what magnanimity is all about.

[11] Vince Lombardi, "What It Takes to Be Number One", VinceLombardi.com, accessed November 4, 2016, http://www.vincelombardi.com/number-one.html.

Claiming Our Belovedness

I, too, wish to say this to you all: in your daily difficulties, in moments of trials and discouragement, when it seems that every commitment is almost emptied of interest and value, remember that God knows our troubles! God loves you, one by one, he is close to you, he understands you! Trust in him and in this certainty find the courage and the joy to carry out your duty lovingly and joyfully.

—Pope Saint John Paul II[*]

Do not fear, my child, God loves you; he loves you personally; he thought of you before you came into the world and called you into being to fill you with love and with life; and for this reason he came to meet you, he made himself like you, he became Jesus, God-man, like you in all things but without sin; he gave himself for your sake to the point of dying on the Cross, and thus he gave you a new life, free, holy and immaculate.

—Pope Benedict XVI[†]

God likes you.

—Pope Francis[‡]

---

[*] Address of His Holiness John Paul II to the Congregation of St. Joseph (December 1, 1978), no. 1, https://w2.vatican.va/content/john-paul-ii/en/speeches/1978/documents/hf_jp-ii_spe_19781201_giuseppini-murialdo.html.

[†] Address of His Holiness Benedict XVI on the Solemnity of the Immaculate of the Blessed Virgin Mary (December 8, 2010), http://w2.vatican.va/content/benedict-xvi/en/speeches/2010/december/documents/hf_ben-xvi_spe_20101208_immacolata.html.

[‡] Pope Francis, General Audience (May 8, 2013), http://w2.vatican.va/content/francesco/en/audiences/2013/documents/papa-francesco_20130508_udienza-generale.html.

I think the greatest battle of my life has been accepting that it is good that I exist, and that it's good that I exist in the way God made me. It's always been hard for me to believe the words of King David apply to me when he spoke of mankind being "fearfully and wonderfully" made (Ps 139:14, NIV).

I always accepted that God loved me—but it seemed to me that it was something he sort of *had* to do, because it was his job. Back in 2008, when I was still reeling from the loss of Kelly in my life, and just a year before I became reconciled with the Catholic Church, I had an epiphany of sorts about God's love for me. I was thirty-eight years old; it had taken me nearly forty years to discover that God loves me because he *likes me*.

Thursday, July 17, 2008

I was thinking about Kelly, and wishing that there was some way that I could relate to her and communicate the love that God has for her. As I reflected on the concept of God's love, I envisioned Christ's sacrifice on the Cross for us. And suddenly it hit me: I've always viewed the Cross completely wrong. Tonight it seemed like the verse that we all know by heart, John 3:16, came to life for me, sur- prisingly in my thinking about Kelly. The thought came to me that I'd do anything to know that Kelly could know the love of God. And that thought brought the love of God for me to life in new ways.

Since I'm not a father, it's hard to know what it must be like to have such love for your child that you would do anything for them, so the impact of imagining what Our Father's love for us must be like doesn't resonate with me as strongly as does my love for Kelly. Tonight I realized that I've always viewed Christ's death and sacrifice on the Cross as something that "just had to be done," as if Christ was duty bound to die for us, and God the Father was duty bound to offer his only begotten Son on our behalf because it was what the rules required....

Tonight, a glimmer of God's overwhelming love wedged its way into my thinking. I realize that I have absolutely no concept of how much God loves me. None. I know rationally that He does, I accept the truth that He does, and indeed I see evidence of His love in my friends, family and life but it all feels rather intellectual. The magnitude of His love for me, a love that exists as more than a faith-based reality, is something I don't believe I have ever come remotely close to grasping. Tonight, I saw clearly that God WANTED to offer His Son on behalf of us, because of His love.... Here's what I saw tonight: He offered Himself up for me because He delights in me, and everyone else who's ever walked the face of the planet. His love for one person is more immense than the purest love of all of humanity. And here's the most remarkable part for me: it's not a love that's motivated out of obligation from the Maker to the made, but rather it's motivated out of love that stems from a God who genuinely LIKES us.

I guess tonight was a good night not to sleep, since I began to see a glimmer of the fact that indeed God happens to like me.

For me, learning and understanding that God "likes me" has been far more important than accepting that God loves me. I can love someone I don't particularly *like*, and much of my life I always wondered why anyone could actually *like* me—I believed lies about myself for so long. I didn't think that I was loveable or likeable, and for most of my life I lived behind a mask, feeling like the Wizard of Oz, always pulling levers behind a curtain, projecting a made-up image of the sort of Dan I thought people might like. Yet behind the curtains was a scared kid who feared and expected rejection.

Of course, that's because of how I viewed myself. Thanks be to God, I'm starting to see myself and others with the eyes of Christ. I'm finally learning to accept my true identity: I'm a beloved son of God, thought into being, created out of love, made in God's image, unique, and unrepeatable. He made me, and he delighted in making me, more than Michelangelo delighted in carving David from stone.

Pope Francis said,

> The Holy Spirit teaches us to see with the eyes of Christ, to live life as Christ lived, to understand life as Christ understood it.... He tells us that we are loved by God as children, that we can love God as his children and that by his grace we can live as children of God, like Jesus.... God loves you, *God likes you*.... God is love, God is waiting for us, God is Father, he loves us as a true father loves, he loves us truly and only the Holy Spirit can tell us this in our hearts.[1]

How good it is to hear from the Pope the simple yet powerful phrase that God likes us! He likes every little quirky thing about me, including all the things I've always worried would make other people think I'm weird. He understands me—he's closer to me than I am to myself. That boggles my mind, but it's true. All he wants to do is to shower down his love on me, and make me understand how good it is that I exist. And then he invites me to love him in return.

That's what Henri Nouwen said conversion means:

> Conversion is claiming again and again and again the truth of myself. And what is the truth of myself? That I am

[1] Pope Francis, General Audience (May 8, 2013), http://w2.vatican.va/content/francesco/en/audiences/2013/documents/papa-francesco_20130508_udienza-generale.html (italics added).

God's beloved child, long before I was born, and [before] my father and my mother and my teachers and my church got involved, and I will be God's beloved child long after I have died. I go from God's intimate embrace into God's intimate embrace. God says, "I have loved you with an everlasting love, I've loved you before you were born.... I love you and I've written your name in my hand—you're safe in the palm of my hand.... And I'm sending you into this world for a little time ... so that you'll have the chance to say, 'I love you too.' "[2]

We don't really understand what will make us happy. Being loved by God and being able to love him in return is where true joy resides. That's what the Blessed Trinity is all about—perpetual, life-giving, and eternal love, given and received. Heaven is when we'll finally be consumed and absorbed by love—overflowing and boundless love, cascading with joy and delight back to God and our fellow man. Thomas Merton writes that this invitation of loving God is our destiny

because my own individual destiny is a meeting, an encounter with God that He has destined for me alone. His glory in me will be to receive from me something He can never receive from anyone else—because it is a gift of His to me which He has never given to anyone else & never will. My whole life is only that—to establish that particular constant with God which is the one He has planned for my eternity![3]

[2] *Journey of the Heart: The Life of Henri Nouwen* directed by Karen Pascal, written with William Finlay, narrated by Susan Sarandon (Markham, Ontario: Gateway Films, 2003).

[3] Thomas Merton to Mark Van Doren, March 30, 1948, in *Echoing Silence: Thomas Merton on the Vocation of Writing*, ed. Robert Inchausti (Boston: New Seeds Books, 2007), p. 12.

That's remarkable to me. All of my life I have been searching for what would bring me peace. I've learned it's true what Saint Augustine said so long ago, that our hearts are restless until they rest in God. That's where our joy is—abiding in him, as Christ abides in the Father, perpetually in love. That's why Christ came. He wanted our joy to be complete.

All of the sex, all of the porn, all of my hopes and dreams of loves and earthly happiness, were a two-dimensional caricature of happiness. Happiness comes when we finally know who we are, why we're here, and where we're headed.

There's not a day that goes by when I don't think about heaven. I long to get out of here, to finally be able to say, "I've put in my time—I've had enough of this world. I'm ready to go Home." There's not much here in this life that makes me think this is better than what God has in store for us. For that, I'm grateful.

My longing for heaven isn't macabre, or a desire to die. No—it's a longing that stems from my deep desires for fulfillment and happiness, and a desire for what we're always reaching for, but never finding here on earth.

When I was younger, I never really understood Saint Paul when he said that "to live is Christ, and to die is gain" (Phil 1:21). I get it now. To die is to escape this world, with its heartbreak, pain, sorrow, and tears, and to go home to my Father's house, to go to the place where all the joy is, where all my longings have always pointed me. To live, I've come to realize now, is to accept and embrace all of the unavoidable and unchangeable sufferings that come into our lives, and to view them as our daily crosses. "To live is Christ" means that we must take up our crosses and follow him (see Mt 16:24). There's a certain sort of joy to be found in that: when we accept the little miseries that come our way, whether it be the pain of loneliness, or of sickness, or of unfulfilled desires, these little sorrows can be united with his sorrow, with his pain, for the salvation of the world, and for those we love most.

And of course, in the midst of the pains and travails of this earth, there is happiness. When you realize that the earth is not our home, and that our time here is a place of "becoming what we are made to be", which necessarily means hardships and difficulty, then you can have peace and enjoy the good things that come your way, and have perspective when the bad things happen. The good things always come as a nice surprise.

The greatest lesson I've learned living with same-sex attractions is knowing what's *true*. This place ain't home, but as a stomping ground for a lifetime, it's not too bad. There are friends to laugh with, nieces and nephews to love, music to be made, songs to be sung, beer to be drunk. There's the beauty of the Grand Canyon, the wonder of Lake Michigan, the mysteries of the ocean, and the beauty of moon-fall behind Half Dome at Yosemite. There's Shakespeare and Sinatra, Mozart and Mahler, good food, good wine, Traverse City cherries, and my mom's apple pie. There's poetry and bacon, Tolkien and Lewis, winter and spring, summer and fall, an old man's laugh, the giggle of a baby, and the joy of watching my dog dream.

I don't need to have sex to have joy, or to find happiness. Indeed, I finally know that to have sex with a man really leads me away from true happiness. Thanks be to God, I know that now. That was a hard lesson to learn, but I'm glad I learned it. For I know who I am, why I'm here, and where I'm headed. There isn't much more one could ask for than that. Life makes sense now. Once I didn't believe those words of Jeremiah, that God had plans to prosper me and not to harm me, plans to give me a hope and a future, but now I know those words are true.

I see it. I see it all so clearly now, how God guided me, every step of the way. I see that he has been with me the whole time, always leading me home, always guiding me to the truth, always leading me to the place where all the happiness is: to him.

And for that, I will sing praises forever to him, for he is my Lord, God, Savior, and Redeemer—my all in all, my joy, my hope, my safe harbor, my compass. He is my Father, and my teacher, who has told me the secret of everything: everything's about love.

Coda

It was Lent 2010, in the year after my reconciliation with the Church. Easter would soon be here when I would finally receive the Sacrament of Confirmation and complete the Sacraments of Initiation in the Catholic Church. Those were joyous times.

During that year, I often drove by the Basilica of St. Adalbert, but my view of it had changed. Once I flipped it off in anger, but now it was the loveliest sight in all of Grand Rapids. Once it represented what I believed was the unfaithfulness and cruelness of God, but now it represented his all-encompassing love. Those three green-tinted copper domes became a sign of God's goodness and kindness, a safe haven and harbor against the travails and temptations of the world.

As Lent marched on toward Easter, winter turned to the new life of spring, and with the coming of spring I saw changes take place at the basilica.

Scaffolding slowly rose, surrounding the perimeter of the building. When it reached the height of the highest dome, I understood why: the old dome was being stripped off and replaced. Day by day, row by row, the old and weathered green-tinted copper was peeled off.

Then I saw the restoration take place. Layer by layer, shingle by shingle, glistening copper was put in place of the old, until the sky shimmered with sunlight, reflected from those three copper domes. They shined as brightly as a freshly minted penny.

As I saw those domes being clothed with the sun, I thought of the words of Isaiah:

> Come now, let us reason together,
>   says the LORD:
> though your sins are like scarlet,
>   they shall be as white as snow;
> though they are red like crimson,
>   they shall become like wool. (1:18)

In the blinding beauty of the domes of the basilica, I saw the mercy of God. He was the loving Father, ever watchful for the prodigal son who had left him. From afar, he had run to greet me, his son who had done such shameful things. I came to him, broken and tattered, worn down like the century-old dome of the basilica. "Father," I said to him, "I have sinned against heaven and before you; I am no longer worthy to be called your son" (Lk 15:21). And yet my Heavenly Father said, "Bring quickly the best robe, and put it on him; and put a ring on his hand, and shoes on his feet.... Let us eat and make merry; for this my son was dead, and is alive again; he was lost, and is found" (Lk 15:22–24). There is no more merry feast than the Supper of the Lamb. God, my loving and merciful Father, had forgiven me, cleansed me of my sin, and clothed me with a new robe—and fed me with the Body and Blood of his Son. All of my life had felt like Good Friday, but on Easter in my fortieth year, the resurrection came. I was reborn, a new man. My old, tattered robe had been discarded—my Father clothed me with a new robe, clothed me with the brightness of his Son.

And yet, as the years have passed since those domes first gleamed in the light of the sun, the copper has slowly faded. It is weathered and tarnished. It won't be long now before it becomes colored green again. There's a lesson there for me too.

The message is blindingly clear—Christ redeems us, Christ forgives us, Christ cleanses us. But we must not be content to stay in the comfort and warmth of our homecoming. No, we must go out into the world, proclaiming the Good News of the Gospel of Christ. After the resurrection, after our own rebirth, we have to help others find hope and joy too: "Go therefore and make disciples of all nations,... teaching them to observe all that I have commanded you; and behold, I am with you always, to the close of the age" (Mt 28:19–20). The new robe we've been given isn't there just to shine brightly—it's there to help us weather the storms of life while we shout from the mountaintops of the world the Good News of the Gospel of the Lord.

Trials and tribulations come—Christ promised us things wouldn't always be easy. "In the world you have tribulation; but be of good cheer, I have overcome the world" (Jn 16:33). The domes become weathered: Saint Paul was imprisoned; Saint Peter was crucified. But when you know joy—joy, not merely as a feeling, not merely as an idea, but real, lasting Joy in the Person of Christ—how can you be silent? The tribulation doesn't matter then, for, as Saint Paul said, "To live is Christ" (Phil 1:21). That means joyfully taking up our crosses and following him. It's not hard to do once you've tasted from the fountain where Living Water flows. You just can't help yourself then.

All I want to do for the rest of my life is to tell others where the Living Water is. And I hope, by the time my days are numbered, the robe that was given me is tattered and worn, so that, by the grace of God, at the end of my life, my Heavenly Father, to whom I owe everything, might say to me, "Well done, good and faithful servant."

But of course, any good that I might do is Christ within me. That's a relief, and the most important lesson I have ever learned.

Thanks be to God.